GENDER PLAY in Mark Twain

Mark Twain and His Circle Series

Tom Quirk, Editor

GENDER PLAY
in Mark Twain

Cross-Dressing and Transgression

Linda A. Morris

University of Missouri Press   Columbia and London

Library of Congress Cataloging-in-Publication Data

Morris, Linda.
  Gender play in Mark Twain : cross-dressing and transgression /
Linda A. Morris.
      p. cm.
  Summary: "Explores Mark Twain's use of cross-dressing across
his career by exposing the cast of his characters who masqueraded
as members of the opposite sex or who otherwise defied gender
expectations. Morris grounds her study in an understanding of the
era's theatrical cross-dressing and changing mores, and events in
Clemens's own household" — Provided by publisher.
  Includes bibliographical references (p.   ) and index.
  ISBN 978-0-8262-1963-3 (pbk.: alk. paper)
  1. Twain, Mark, 1835 – 1910 — Criticism and interpretation.
2. Sex role in literature.   3. Twain, Mark, 1835 – 1910 —
Characters.   4. American wit and humor — 19th century —
History and criticism.   I. Title.
  PS1338.M67 2007
  818'.409 — dc22
                                                      2007017493

∞™ This paper meets the requirements of the
American National Standard for Permanence of Paper
for Printed Library Materials, Z39.48, 1984.
Designer: Kristie Lee
Typesetter: The Composing Room of Michigan, Inc.
Printer and binder: Thomson-Shore, Inc.
Typefaces: Galliard and Myriad

Frontispiece: Mark Twain in 1899. *Courtesy of the Mark Twain
Project, Bancroft Library, University of California, Berkeley
(call no. 00222 - 1899)*

For Kay

Contents

Acknowledgments xi

1. Misplaced Sex 1

2. Sarah Mary Williams George Elexander Peters 27

3. Beneath the Veil: Gender Play in *Pudd'nhead Wilson* 59

4. Troubling Gender: *Personal Recollections of Joan of Arc* 89

5. Transvestite Tales 124

Works Cited 167

Index 177

Acknowledgments

I have many to thank for their assistance in the course of my writing this book. I benefited especially from the research conducted by a group of talented graduate assistants, most of whom now have thriving academic careers of their own: Joseph Mills, Roy Kamada, Paula Harrington, Michael Borgstrom, Tiffany Aldrich MacBain, and Steven Blevins. I thank also Melissa Strong, who aided me in the final stages of manuscript preparation. Three colleagues read and critiqued various versions of the manuscript, and I thank them for their many insights and helpful suggestions: Bishnu Ghosh, Elizabeth Freeman, and Jean Pfaelzer. This study benefited greatly from the critical readings it received from Tom Quirk and Susan K. Harris, on behalf of the University of Missouri Press. My editors at the press—Clair Willcox, Sara Davis, and Julianna Schroeder—have been patient, encouraging, and always helpful. I am especially grateful to my daughter, Kate Morris, who cheerfully took time out from her own writing to read and comment on the manuscript in all its iterations; she was my most rigorous and most enthusiastic critic. Her assistance has been invaluable.

I wish to thank the Regents of the University of California for supporting the initial research for this work through a President's Fellowship in the Humanities; the Academic Senate of the University of California, Davis, for supporting my research through their annual grants; the Office of the Provost, University of California, Davis, for appointing me as a UC Davis Washington Fellow; and the Elmira College Center for Mark Twain Studies, especially Gretchen Sharlow, for awarding me a Quarry Farm Fellowship. I thank archivists at the Library of Congress and the Hamilton College Library. I am particularly indebted to the editors and staff of the Mark Twain Papers in the Bancroft Library at the University of California, Berkeley, for their patience, generosity, and extraordinary knowledge: Robert Hirst, Lin Salamo, Victor Fischer, and Neda Salem were especially helpful and always encouraging. Thanks to Steven Blevins for preparing the index.

Finally, and most especially, I thank Kay Ellyard, for her patience, for her enthusiastic readings of the manuscript, and for her moral support from start to finish.

GENDER PLAY in Mark Twain

Misplaced Sex

Throughout his writing career, Mark Twain played with gender issues, gender roles, and sexual relationships. His approach to gender is much more playful and experimental than critics have generally credited. To borrow a phrase from Judith Butler, he "troubled gender" in much of his fiction (even while at other times remaining remarkably traditional). Twain's gender play took many forms, including an interest in domestic space, ordinarily the purview of female humorists; a fascination with descriptions of characters' clothing; and works filled with sexual innuendo and bawdiness. Preeminent, however, and persistent throughout his career, was his fascination with characters who cross-dress and with characters who otherwise resist, indeed disrupt, gendered expectations. Through such gender play he subverted Victorian notions of fixed gender roles and essentialist constructions. Twain's depictions of cross-dressing and gender disruptions are the focus of this study.

Perhaps the most cherished example of Twain's depiction of cross-dressing is the comic scene in *Adventures of Huckleberry Finn* when Huck dresses as a girl and is put through a series of tests by Judith Loftus designed to determine, in her eyes, if he is an "authentic" girl. Other examples abound in *Huckleberry Finn,* such as the king playing the role of Juliet in a Shakespearean parody, or Jim escaping from the Phelps farm at the end of the novel dressed as Aunt Sally. Such cross-dressing, as we shall see, has meaning that transcends the scenes themselves and the fun they engender. Cross-dressing figures prominently as well in *Pudd'nhead Wilson,* where multiple acts of gender impersonation take on more serious overtones. In a novel in which appearance and reality are regularly confounded, in which a "white" woman is represented as being *really* "black," and a "black" child is exchanged for a "white" child and no one notices, cross-dressing is intricately bound up with issues of race and racial crossing. Roxana's cross-dressing as a man, in blackface, and her son's dressing up in women's clothes to commit crimes in a small antebellum community have signification far beyond the characters' motivations. As Marjorie Garber has noted, the unexpected presence of a transvestite figure in a text is a sure indicator of "a category crisis *elsewhere.*"[1] The cross-dressing in *Pudd'nhead Wilson* and the gender confusion it generates, especially since it is practiced only by the two prominent mixed-race characters in the novel, underscores the novel's radical challenge to society's accepted and determinative racial binaries. A similar argument can be made for the role of cross-dressing in *Huckleberry Finn.* In both these novels, disrupting one major social paradigm inevitably disrupts another.

Cross-dressing, a historical "given" in Twain's *Personal Recollections of Joan of Arc,* ultimately offers the one and only justification the Catholic Church can summon for executing Joan of Arc. In appreciation of this fact, Twain faithfully recorded the details of Joan's dress, first the armor that she wore in battle, then the male clothing she wore during her imprisonment. But a surprising anomaly appears in the text, for Twain's ultimate representation of Joan of Arc is physically elusive. He celebrates her liminality and her gender and social transgressions, but, as we shall see, as a physical being, as a transvestite figure, she seems to elude him. However, he was not nearly so constrained in the representation of his wholly fictional characters. By the end of his career, Twain repeatedly explored cross-dressing and other gender transgression in both published and unpublished stories. There he also flirted at times with same-sex relationships, challenging conventionally held no-

---

1. Marjorie Garber, *Vested Interests: Cross-Dressing and Cultural Anxiety,* 17.

tions of proper gender roles for both men and women. He became especially interested in transgressive figures, some of whom cross-dressed, some of whom did not: girls raised as boys; "tomboys" (his term); a young woman passing as a man married to another woman; two men, one a male-to-female transvestite, married to each other; and a male French painter who impersonates his own sister and becomes engaged to another man. In every instance, expressed through a variety of tones, some form of cross-dressing or gender disruption (or both) takes center stage.

Complementing Twain's fascination with the phenomenon of gender crossings was his interest in the details of both men's and women's clothing. Susan Gillman was among the first to call attention to this interest, citing his delight with the "bright colors and silky fabrics" of native dress in *Following the Equator*, especially in Ceylon. His interest in bright-colored clothing of various native populations was associated in Twain's mind, according to Gillman, with a lack of "sexual differentiation," with men whose dress and beauty seemed feminine to Twain, and with male and female clothing blending into each other. He was titillated by such androgyny and by the apparent crossing of gender lines native clothing represented to his Western sensibility. Characteristically, he embedded that fascination in a joke: "January 14. Hotel Bristol. Servant Brompy. Alert, gentle, smiling, winning young brown creature as ever was. Beautiful shining black hair combed back like a woman's, and knotted at the back of his head—tortoise-shell comb in it, sign that he is a Singhalese; slender, shapely form; jacket; under it is a beltless and flowing white cotton gown—from neck straight to heel; he and his outfit quite unmasculine. It was an embarassment [*sic*] to undress before him."[2]

As this study will make clear, Twain had been interested in details regarding clothing long before he traveled around the world in 1895–1896. Such a concern is central, for instance, to understanding both *Pudd'nhead Wilson* and *Personal Recollections of Joan of Arc*, novels founded upon disruptive female figures who defied society's expectations. It is also key to the exchange that sets *The Prince and the Pauper*

2. Susan Gillman, *Dark Twins: Imposture and Identity in Mark Twain's America*, 97, 99; Mark Twain, *Following the Equator: A Journey around the World*, 336–39.

into motion. In that novel, however, it is social class, not gender, that is the major focus of Twain's attention.

Underlying Mark Twain's fascination with cross-dressing and gender transgression was first and foremost the element of play, even though in some central texts such as *Pudd'nhead Wilson* a grim sense of irony makes that play seem more dangerous and serious than not. Nonetheless, Twain took delight in representing characters who for a variety of motivations masquerade as members of the opposite sex. Purely at the level of play, Twain displayed an increasing awareness that traditional gender binaries, and their accompanying descriptors of what constituted appropriate gendered behaviors and mannerisms, were social constructions, not immutable laws. Further, he was well aware that not everyone easily inhabited the gender category to which he or she was born; or as his character Hellfire Hotchkiss expresses her dilemma, she is "hampered" by her "misplaced sex."

Before turning our attention to the multiple works by Mark Twain featuring cross-dressing and other gender transgressions, it is important to understand the historical and cultural contexts in which they were written and to identify the theoretical underpinnings for our discussion about the meaning of cross-dressing and gender play. Specifically, a nexus of the historical and cultural converged and influenced Twain's writing of his transgressive works. These influences include theatrical cross-dressing in the minstrel theater and vaudeville; changing ideas about sexuality in late Victorian society; and events unfolding in the Clemens household, especially when Twain's eldest daughter, Susy, developed a romantic attachment to a fellow college student, Louise Brownell. I conclude by considering contemporary theoretical perspectives on the meaning of cross-dressing, the performative nature of gender, and carnivalesque humor.

Cross-Dressing and the Minstrel Theater

Samuel Clemens is likely to have first encountered public cross-dressing in the blackface minstrel theater, which he loved from his boyhood onward. In addition to minstrelsy's hallmark music and dance and its banter among the interlocutor and the blackface "end men," as early as the 1840s minstrel shows frequently included "wench" acts that featured white men in blackface playing women's roles. Sometimes the women were depicted as mixed-race, flirtatious "yellow gals"; sometimes they were exaggeratedly black women. After the Civil War, the representation of cross-dressed actors in the minstrel theater continued to evolve, with some white male actors presenting themselves on stage as relatively elegant black women. The most famous postwar "serious" female impersonator in minstrelsy was Francis Leon, who played his female roles so convincingly that many audience members "refused to believe he was a man." In this era, the female impersonators were frequently the stars of the show and purported to command the highest salaries among the minstrel players.[3]

Cross-dressing had always played an important role in the legitimate theater as well, from the Shakespearean "boys" who played all women's parts during the English Renaissance, right through the nineteenth-century stage in England. In the United States there were both "serious" female impersonators and "glamorous dames" who moved beyond blackface minstrelsy into vaudeville and legitimate theater. By the 1880s one of the leading actors playing dame roles was Neil Burgess, who, according to Shelley Fisher Fishkin, was known to Twain. Burgess began playing women's parts in vaudeville, then played the roles of four different middle-aged female protagonists in plays entitled *The Widow and the Elder, Betsey Bobbet: A Drama,* (rewritten as *Vim*), and *The County Fair.* In all four productions, playing throughout the 1880s in New York, the rather burly Burgess impersonated middle-aged women. In spite of his clearly comic manner, and his obvious masculinity, some contemporary accounts of Burgess as the Widow Bedott praised his "realistic" representation of women. A number of years after the fact, George C. Odell wrote about the cross-dressed Burgess in these terms: "I still see him as Widow Bedott in the kitchen, making pies, straightening out the affairs of the neighborhood, and personifying, in spite of his sex, the attributes of a managing woman. He was not the least bit effeminate, not at all like the usual female impersonator of minstrelsy

---

3. On Clemens and minstrelsy, see, for example, Eric Lott, "Mr. Clemens and Jim Crow: Twain, Race, and Blackface"; and Gregg Camfield, *The Oxford Companion to Mark Twain,* 565–66; on Francis Leon, see Robert Toll, *Blacking Up: The Minstrel Show in Nineteenth-Century America,* 142; on female impersonators, see Vern L. Bullough and Bonnie Bullough, *Cross Dressing, Sex, and Gender,* 233.

or of variety, and yet he was Widow Bedott to the life, and with little suggestion of burlesque."[4]

Burgess was by no means the only such actor playing in "dame" roles in the late nineteenth century. As Fishkin notes, one of the most popular plays at the end of the century was Brandon Thomas's *Charley's Aunt,* which opened in New York in 1893 "after a London run of 1,469 consecutive performances." The lead actor in the play was Etienne Girardot, "whose cross-dressing impersonation of a widow dissolved the audience in laughter night after night at the Standard Theatre." After the lengthy popular success of *Charley's Aunt,* public tastes changed, and the "dame" role faded away on the stage. Shortly thereafter, male actors who cross-dressed in the theater began to appear as elegant, younger women. By the early twentieth century, Julian Eltinge, who began his cross-dressing career in minstrelsy, became "the most celebrated female impersonator of his time."[5]

By the end of the Civil War, women also began to cross-dress on the stage in men's roles. The actress Annie Hindle, according to one contemporary report, came to New York in 1867 "as the first out-and-out male impersonator New York's stage had ever seen." Women who played males on the American stage apparently had to retain "feminine attributes, and it was thus their sexual ambiguity that seemed most to please the audience. Indeed, such actresses came to be known as the 'principal boys,' a term that remained in the pantomime vocabulary into the twentieth century." Perhaps the best-known of the refined male impersonators was Sarah Bernhardt, who not only played dozens of female roles, including Ophelia and Lady Macbeth, but also ap-

---

4. Scholars have written extensively about male actors playing women's roles, especially in Elizabethan times, and about the controversies surrounding the practice. A helpful summary of this scholarship, as well as an interpretation of the meaning of these practices, is to be found in Vern L. Bullough and Bonnie Bullough, *Cross Dressing, Sex, and Gender.* See also *Crossing the Stage: Controversies on Cross-Dressing;* Stephen Greenblatt, *Renaissance Self-Fashioning: From Moore to Shakespeare;* Jean E. Howard, "Cross-dressing, the Theatre, and Gender Struggle in Early Modern England"; and Shelley Fisher Fishkin, afterword to *Is He Dead? A Comedy in Three Acts,* 192–93. Three of the plays starring Burgess were based on characters created by prominent women humorists of the day: Frances M. Whitcher, author of *The Widow Bedott Papers,* and Marietta Holley, author of an extended series of comic novels featuring Josiah Allen's Wife. See Linda A. Morris, *Women Vernacular Humorists in Nineteenth-Century America: Ann Stephens, Frances Whitcher, and Marietta Holley;* and George C. D. Odell, *Annals of the New York Stage,* 11:170.

5. Fishkin, afterword to *Is He Dead?* 194; on Eltinge, see Garber, *Vested Interests,* 276.

peared early in her career as Richelieu, and late in her career as Cyrano de Bergerac. In the United States, however, she was most famous for her role as Hamlet. As Twain scholars well know, her widely circulated image as Hamlet served as the illustrator Dan Beard's model for his mischievous representation of Clarence in the original publication of *A Connecticut Yankee in King Arthur's Court.*[6]

"New Sexuality" in the 1880s

To understand how Twain might have first become interested in playing with issues around gender and sexuality, beyond the obvious timelessness of such topics and their nearly unlimited humorous possibilities, it is useful to take note of some of the changes in cultural and social attitudes toward sexuality taking place in the late nineteenth century. Historians of American sexuality widely agree that the decade of the 1880s saw important changes in the way people understood and viewed both sex and gender. Lisa Duggan has observed that the years 1880–1920 "were a crucible of change in gender and sexual relations in the United States. This long transition was neither even nor easy; it was deeply marked by conflict and tragedy as well as by erotic excitements. As Victorian certainties faded and the possibilities of the modern slowly materialized, new sexualities took shape and the modern desiring subject emerged." Three dramatic public events in particular exemplify the changes that were taking place in Victorian society, and these in turn might well have shaped the ways people understood their own and others' sexuality. These were the sensational Alice Mitchell trial for the murder of her lover, Freda Ward, in Memphis, Tennessee, in 1892; the public trials of Oscar Wilde for sodomy in England in 1895; and the publication in 1897 of *Sexual Inversion,* the first of Havelock Ellis's six-volume *Studies in the Psychology of Sex.*[7]

The first trial was followed avidly in the press. According to Carroll

6. On Hindle, see Laurence Senelick, "Boys and Girls Together: Subcultural Origins of Glamour Drag and Male Impersonation in the Nineteenth-Century Stage," 90; on principal boys, see Bullough and Bullough, *Cross Dressing,* 227; see also Mark Twain, *A Connecticut Yankee in King Arthur's Court,* 18.

7. Lisa Duggan, "The Trials of Alice Mitchell: Sensationalism, Sexology, and the Lesbian Subject in Turn-of-the-Century America," 791; I am indebted to Siobhan Somerville, *Queering the Color Line: Race and the Invention of Homosexuality in American Culture,* 3, for her original juxtaposition of the Mitchell and Wilde trials in her work on late-nineteenth-century "scientific racism."

Smith-Rosenberg, the details revealed in the trial "electrified the country." The plaintiff was nineteen-year-old Alice Mitchell, who had murdered her lover, seventeen-year-old Freda Ward, with whom Mitchell had hoped to elope, cross-dressed as Alvin. The Mitchell trial was in fact a sanity hearing, not a murder trial, because the murder had been committed in full view of no fewer than five witnesses; a plea of insanity was deemed by Mitchell's family to be her best and only defense. After recounting how Alice pursued masculine activities as a child, the defense got to the core of the story of the relationship between Alice and Freda (referred to throughout as "Fred") in these terms:

> In Feb. 1891, Alice proposed marriage. She repeated the offer in three separate letters. To each Fred replied, agreeing to become her wife. Alice wrote her upon the third promise that she would hold her to the engagement, and that she would kill her if she broke the promise. . . .
>
> It was agreed that Alice should be known as Alvin J. Ward, so that Fred could still call her by [her] pet name Allie, and Fred was to be known as Mrs. A. J. Ward. The particulars of formal marriage and elopement were agreed upon. Alice was to put on man's apparel, and have her hair trimmed by a barber like a man; was to get the license to marry, and Fred was to procure the Rev. . . . [or] a justice of the peace to marry them. The ceremony performed, they intended to leave for St. Louis. Alice was to continue to wear man's apparel, and meant to try and have a mustache, if it would please Fred. She was going out to work for Fred in men's clothes.[8]

Before the marriage could take place, however, a young man, Ashley Roselle, began to court Freda, causing her to have second thoughts about her "engagement," and causing Alice no small degree of jealousy. Meanwhile, Freda's sister learned of Alice and Freda's planned elopement, seized the engagement ring, which she sent back to Alice, and forbade Freda to have any further communication with Alice. Some months later Freda traveled to Memphis, where Alice lived, but not to visit her. Alice learned she was in town, and as Freda walked to the ferryboat with her sister to return to her home town, Alice slowly drove be-

8. Carroll Smith-Rosenberg, *Disorderly Conduct: Visions of Gender in Victorian America,* 273; details of the murder are reported in Duggan, "Trials of Alice Mitchell," 796–97.

side her in a buggy. A few minutes later she leapt out of the buggy and slit her lover's throat with a razor.[9]

Not only was the case widely circulated in the popular press in 1892, as Duggan has determined it also "persisted as a topic of newspaper sensationalism and of scientific sexology well into the twentieth century. The case also served as the partial basis for at least three works of fiction, a folk ballad that survived in oral tradition into the 1960s, and a proposed play for Sarah Bernhardt to be written by famed librettist Victorien Sardou (Bernhardt visited Mitchell in jail and kept a scrapbook on the case)." If nothing else, the Mitchell trial brought to the public's attention what might have been until that point only privately imagined and discussed: sexual relationships between women. As Smith-Rosenberg expresses it, the "*cause célèbre* catapulted the discussions of lesbianism, until now quite a minor theme in the medical and asylum journals, into polite and influential circles."[10]

Three years later, in 1895, the Oscar Wilde trials in England explicitly featured same-sex relationships between men, also causing a sensation. The trials began when Wilde, already well known as a playwright, poet, wit, and aesthete, brought a libel suit against the Marquess of Queensberry, who had publicly accused Wilde of "posing" as a sodomite. Queensberry was the father of Lord Alfred Douglas, a young man with whom Wilde was indeed sexually involved. In the course of the ensuing libel trial, the Marquees was able to prove that his accusations against Wilde were in fact true, and hence there was no libel. Wilde was forced to withdraw his suit, but not before the evidence had accumulated against him. As Wilde's friends predicted, the evidence presented against Wilde in the libel suit led to further trials, which also took place in 1895, and in which Wilde and a friend, Alfred Taylor, were charged with twenty-five counts of gross indecency. Both were convicted and given maximum sentences of two years imprisonment and hard physical labor. When Wilde was released, he lived the remaining few years of his life in exile.[11] What is especially important about this

9. From the transcript of the counsel's case, reprinted in full in Lisa Duggan, *Sapphic Slashers: Sex, Violence, and American Modernity*, Appendix A, 209.

10. On Sarah Bernhardt, see Duggan, "Trials of Alice Mitchell," 795; Smith-Rosenberg, *Disorderly Conduct*, 273.

11. Jonathan Fryer, *Wilde*, 96–100.

trial is that it was the subject of sensational coverage in the press, both
in Europe and in the United States, and it was the first time a public
figure was tried for sodomy in modern England. Wilde was a startling
public figure, and his defense of "the crime that dare not speak its
name" was eloquent and passionate, if ultimately unsuccessful. Never
before in modern times had the subject of male homosexuality been so
widely publicized and discussed. Even though there was not yet, in cir-
culation, a standard term to denote homosexuality, the fact of its exis-
tence was laid before the public in ways that would have made it impossible for citizens to ignore.

It took a psychologist writing about the history of sexuality to offer
a broader context in which Victorians could begin to understand the
sexually deviant behavior featured in the Wilde and Mitchell trials. That
figure was the Englishman Havelock Ellis. Ellis, who was trained as a
physician, ultimately wrote a six-volume treatise entitled *Studies in Sexuality,* published between 1897 and 1910. The first in the series was
published under the title *Sexual Inversion* and was immediately censored in England. In contrast to his immediate predecessor, the Aus-
trian Richard von Krafft-Ebing, whose *Psychopathia Sexualis* (1886)
"details sex in all its varieties, as a 'nauseous disease,'" Ellis viewed myriad sexual acts and inclinations as "natural" biological drives. As historian Jeffrey Weeks observes, Ellis's most lasting achievement was as "a
pioneer in bringing together and categorizing information on the different types of sexual experience. Even this, to us apparently elementary, task shocked his contemporaries." Historians John D'Emilio and
Estelle Freedman represent Ellis's contributions in these terms:

> Described by historian Paul Robinson as the first of the sexual mod-
> ernists, Ellis assaulted almost every aspect of the nineteenth-century
> sexual heritage. For Ellis, sexual indulgence did not pose the threat to
> health or character that preoccupied many earlier writers. Rather, he
> described it as "the chief and central function of life . . . ever won-
> derful, ever lovely." . . . He asked his readers: "Why . . . should peo-
> ple be afraid of rousing passions which, after all, are the great driving
> forces of human life?" . . .
>   . . . Perhaps most daringly, Ellis wished to remove the stigma at-
> tached to homosexual behavior. "Sexual inversion," as he termed it,
> was a congenital condition, as natural for its practitioners as hetero-

sexual relations were for the majority. Because he viewed it as inborn, Ellis believed that the laws criminalizing homosexual behavior were archaic and unjust, and he supported efforts to repeal them.[12]

While Ellis's work was censored in England, it was welcomed in America, particularly in the medical community, and some say it was read more widely. As Jeffrey Weeks observes, Ellis was "the most influential of the late Victorian pioneers of sexual frankness."[13] The changed awareness of unconventional sexual behavior brought to public attention by the Mitchell and Wilde trials, and the light Ellis attempted to shed on sexual behavior, primarily through "case studies," marked the late 1880s and 1890s as a time of profound challenges to established notions of proper gendered and sexual behavior. While such cultural phenomena might have remained only distant abstractions to a family such as the Clemenses, events conspired to bring these issues much closer to home through an unlikely source, their eldest daughter, Susy (Olivia) Clemens.

Susy Clemens and Louise Brownell

Susy Clemens was the eldest of the three Clemens daughters, and she has frequently been represented by biographers as her father's favorite. There is little doubt that she was precocious; her sister Clara described her "as the genius among the children." When she was thirteen, she began writing a biography of her father, called "Papa," and she wrote plays that she and her sisters and the neighboring children performed for the adults. In the words of Peter Stoneley, "to a large extent she functioned as a muse for her father; indeed, her presence in the household seems to have substantially affected his ability to progress with his feminine work." In the summer of 1890, the summer before Susy left for college, the family spent time together in the Catskills at the Onteora Club. "It was a light-hearted retreat, on its surface: Sam and his daughters starred in the nightly rounds of Charades." One such

12. On Havelock Ellis, see Jeffrey Weeks, *Making Sexual History,* 23, 47; on Ellis's view of sex, see John D'Emilio and Estelle B. Freedman, *Intimate Matters: A History of Sexuality in America,* 224.

13. Weeks, *Making Sexual History,* 27, 17.

performance, starring Susy and her father, is preserved in a photograph. It was also captured in the words of Clara Clemens: "We were trying to enact the story of Hero and Leander. Mark Twain played the part of the impassioned lover obliged to swim across the Hellespont to snatch a kiss from his sweetheart on the other side of the foaming water. For this scene Father wore a bathing-suit, a straw hat tied under his chin with a big bow, and a hot-water bottle slung around his chest."[14] Characteristically, Mark Twain stole the show.

Three months later Susy entered Bryn Mawr, where she began to call herself "Olivia," her given name, and otherwise to establish an adult identity apart from her family. She was soon chosen to play the lead role in a college production of Gilbert and Sullivan's *Iolanthe*, and she began to make friends among her classmates, including a more senior student, Louise Brownell. A series of letters written over a three-year period (1891–1894) attest that Susy and Louise had established a passionate, romantic relationship. Although none of Louise's letters to Susy are extant, only those written by Susy to Louise,[15] the relationship was clearly reciprocal; furthermore, it followed a pattern familiar in women's colleges of the era, involving as it did a younger student (Susy), and a more senior, well-established student (Louise), and ardent expressions of longing, professions of love and desire, and references to physical intimacy.

Historians have shown that in late-nineteenth-century society, it was common for girls and young college women to develop "smashes," "mashes," or "crushes" on one another. In addition to the romantic friendships enjoyed by many late Victorian women, female students

---

14. Clara Clemens, *My Father, Mark Twain*, 57; Peter Stoneley, *Mark Twain and the Feminine Aesthetic*, 98; on the Onteora Club, see Ron Powers, *Mark Twain: A Life*, 532; Clemens, *My Father*, 57–58.

15. One must speculate about the fate of Louise's letters to Susy. It is entirely possible that they were destroyed by someone in the Clemens family after Susy's death. However, improbable though it may seem, it is more likely that Susy herself, at Louise's request, destroyed the letters after she read them. In a letter from one of Louise's lifelong friends, Elizabeth Winsor, Elizabeth reveals that Louise insisted that she destroy Louise's letters: "I will destroy your letter, dear, if you like—of course. But it is very precious." Two years later she tells Louise that she had just torn up a recently received letter, "but if you don't mind I do want to keep anything that I am sure you could not mind ever having other eyes than mine read. May I?" (June 9, 1891; June 1893, Saunders Family Papers, Hamilton College Library). In marked contrast, Louise seems to have kept every letter written to her.

Sam Clemens and Susy Clemens as Hero and Leander, 1890. *Courtesy of the Mark Twain Project, Bancroft Library, University of California, Berkeley (call no. 00130-1890)*

openly pursued "courtship" rituals that promoted same-sex partner-ships. An 1873 letter to the Yale *Courant,* written by a Vassar student, describes the custom known among the students as "smashing":

> There is a term in general use at Vassar, truly calculated to awaken within the *ima penetralia* of our souls all that love for the noble and the aesthetic of which our natures are capable. The term in question is "smashing." When a Vassar girl takes a shine to another, she straightway enters upon a regular course of bouquet sendings, inter-spersed with tinted notes, mysterious packages of "Ridley's Mixed Candies," locks of hair perhaps, and many other tender tokens, until at last the object of her attentions is captured, the two become in-

separable, and the aggressor is considered by her circle of acquaintances as—*smashed*.

According to historian Helen Horowitz,

> The shift from the word "smash" to "crush" at the end of the nineteenth century involved a change in focus from the dominant to the subordinate actor. As a Smith clipping clarified, this "distinctly woman's collegiate word" described the situation when "one girl, generally an underclassman, and usually a freshman, becomes much attached to another girl, ordinarily an upper-class girl. The young girl is "crushed" on the other, sends her flowers, and tries in various ways to give expression to her admiration.

Horowitz goes on to declare that whether "smashed" or "crushed," whether officially sanctioned or disparaged, "the experience of dominance and subordination remained at the heart of the college experience for women."[16]

Students who ventured into same-sex relationships at women's colleges also had significant role models on the faculty. According to Horowitz, "by their mature years, many of the women professors within the women's colleges had committed themselves to other women. They had made choices, and in the process had formed deep and meaningful attachments to other women, which opened up realms of self-knowledge, emotional growth, and a shared life. As women left the residence halls, they generally withdrew in pairs of friends to apartments or houses, to which the women of their families were usually invited." At Bryn Mawr, during Susy's year at the college, M. Carey Thomas lived on campus, in the "deanery," with a devoted female companion, Mamie Gwinn. Somewhat later, in 1894, Gwinn left the college and Mary Garrett, a wealthy philanthropist, moved in with Thomas, who became president of the college; the two of them lived together, on campus, in a committed romantic relationship until Garrett's death in 1915.[17]

16. On romantic friendships, see Carroll Smith-Rosenberg, "The Female World of Love and Ritual"; on "smashing," quoted in Nancy Sahli, "Smashing: Women's Relationships before the Fall," 21; Helen Horowitz, *Alma Mater: Design and Experience in the Women's Colleges from Their Nineteenth-Century Beginnings to the 1930s*, 166, 167.

17. Horowitz, *Alma Mater*, 190; on M. Carey Thomas, see Lillian Faderman, *Odd Girls and Twilight Lovers: A History of Lesbian Life in Twentieth-Century America*, 30.

Louise Brownell was a young woman who readily commanded Susy's attention and affection. After attending Miss Griffith's private school in New York City, she entered Bryn Mawr in 1889 as a member of the class of 1893. By the time Susy arrived at college in the fall of 1890, Louise had a well-established circle of friends, several of whom remained lifelong friends and correspondents. Louise was an honor student, well on her way to becoming a leader in the college; she was elected president of the self-government association, the first such organization in women's colleges, and editor of Bryn Mawr's literary magazine, the *Lantern*. In 1893 she graduated at the top of her class and was awarded a coveted Bryn Mawr fellowship to study for a year at Oxford. Louise retuned to Bryn Mawr to take her Ph.D. in English literature, which she completed in 1897. Ultimately she married Percy Saunders, a professor of chemistry at Hamilton College, bore four children, one of whom she named Olivia, after Susy, and became renowned for hosting lively literary salons. She lived to the age of ninety-one.[18]

The letters between Susy and Louise began in April 1891, with Susy writing from Bryn Mawr to Louise, who was home visiting her ill mother and then fell ill herself. At the time of the next letter, written only nine days later, Louise was back at college, but Susy was home with her family in Hartford, never to return to college. The assumption that has been advanced by Twain biographers—that Susy's midterm departure from Bryn Mawr was because she was homesick or in frail health—is not borne out in either letter she wrote to Louise in April 1891.[19] Nor is there any reference to the Clemens family's impending departure for Europe; yet in June the family closed down their Hartford house and moved to Europe, in part ostensibly to economize and in part for Livy's health. They remained living abroad until 1895, with much of the first year spent in German health spas, half a year in Florence, where Livy was ordered by her doctor to remain at rest and eschew all social engagements, and additional time in France.

It will perhaps never be known why the Clemenses removed Susy

18. "Guide to the Saunders Family Papers," Hamilton College Library.
19. The letter, dated April 20, was written from Hartford but postmarked from Bryn Mawr. The original Susy Clemens letters to Louise Brownell are located in the Saunders Family Papers, Hamilton College Library; copies are available in the Mark Twain Papers, University of California, Berkeley. Excerpts from Susy's letters may also be found in Charles Neider's introduction to *Papa: An Intimate Biography of Mark Twain, by His Daughter, Susy Clemens*.

from Bryn Mawr at precisely this time—she easily could have remained in college until the end of the term, then joined her family in Germany. She also could have remained in the States and pursued her studies while the family lived abroad; her younger sister, Clara, was allowed to live apart from the family to study music in Germany; thus it is clear that Sam and Livy Clemens were able to accept some degree of separation from their daughters. It is more likely that they insisted that Susy accompany them to Europe in order to put distance between their daughter and Louise, as Andrew Hoffman has asserted. A letter from Louise's friend Elizabeth Winsor, written to Louise in the fall of what would have been Susy's second year, alludes to the fact that Louise had invited Susy to live with her for the academic year 1892–1893 and that the Clemens family had insisted instead that Susy accompany them abroad. It further gives a glimpse of a fellow student's appraisal of Susy's "temperament":

> It is a thousand pities that she [Susy] could not have finished her college course; they must have felt very strongly about the good she was to get out of her two years abroad to refuse your offer for '92–'93. I should consider it such a chance for the child as she will never get again. I don't believe you realize however what a care she would be to you; such a temperament as hers I should think would be tremendously exciting to live with, and then besides that she would be so absolutely dependent—you would be so responsible for her all the time. I don't know, though, why I say you could not have realized—that was probably exactly what you did do.[20]

Over the nearly four years that the Clemens family remained in Europe, and Susy and Louise were consequently separated, Susy wrote more than thirty letters to Louise, all attesting in some way to her love for her. Remarkably, Susy rarely repeats her salutations, finding anew endearments to express her affection for Louise: "My dearest—," "Dear Sweetheart—," "My darling—," "Dearest Louise—," "My precious Louise—," "My dear *dear* Louise—," "Very Dear Louise—," "My darling darling—," "My dearest love—," "My beloved—." The same may be said of the letters' closings, when Susy stretches to find

20. Andrew Hoffman, *Inventing Mark Twain: The Lives of Samuel Langhorne Clemens*, 367–68; Elizabeth Winsor to Louise Brownell, September 11, 1891, Saunders Family Papers, Hamilton College Library.

language to carry the depth of her emotion, from her first restrained "Always lovingly yours—I do love you so—" to the closing words of her last plaintive letter, written some time after the two young women were reunited briefly in London:

> Please come to me and let me lie down in your arms and forget everything. . . . Write me *that you will let me see you once,* one little once before you go. Ah & write *soon* and say you love me. Forgive whatever there is wrong in this letter. It's my love that's so violent and demanding, my poor terrified love that *cannot* give you up.
>
> Goodnight, darling, darling my beloved. I take you in my arms & see you so clearly as you were in London. What a fated friendship ours is!—Oh I lo[ng] for you so[.] The loneliness, the *loneliness* of life is the hardest.
>
> Yours for ever and ever.
>
> Olivia[21]

Between these salutations and closing comments, Susy evokes memories of some of the physical passion that had passed between them: "My darling I do love you so and I feel so separated from you. If you were here I would kiss you hard on that little place that tastes so good just on the right hand side of your nose." The following month she writes: "I think of you these days, the first of college. If I could only look in on you! We would sleep together tonight and I would allow you opportunities for those refreshing little naps you always indulged in when we passed a night together."[22]

After they had been apart for two years, Susy's expressions of physical passion do not so much evoke Susy and Louise's past experiences as they tell of her current longing and desires:

> This time of silence has been hard to bear. I have thought of you and longed for you and loved you so much lately. Oh my beloved I cannot tell you how precious you are to me! Your letter is beautifully reassuring and makes me resolve never again to be afraid about our friendship. In fact I don't think I ever am deeply afraid and yet I wish that when I see you I could just slip into your room and take you in

---

21. July 29, 1894. This is the last of the extant letters. Shortly after this, the Clemenses returned to the United States, and Susy saw Louise at least twice more, once in Elmira and once in Hartford.

22. September 7, 1891; October 2, 1891.

my arms without any questionings between us, as if we have never been apart.

And now goodby darling, *my* darling and please write me very soon. I feel so near you today precious beautiful Louise! I take you in my arms I kiss your lips, your eyes, your throat.[23]

Beyond their references to the remarkable relationship between Susy and Louise, the letters offer occasional glimpses into the comings and goings of the Clemens family. They reveal, for instance, that while abroad Susy encountered two celebrated sexual nonconformists of the era: Oscar Wilde and Vernon Lee. The reference to Oscar Wilde comes in a letter of October 1891, written from Berlin, and is as casual a reference as imaginable at the end of a paragraph in which she describes their life as "eventless": "Oscar Wilde was over here the other day, in a suit of soft brown with a pale pink flowered vest, a blue necktie and some strange picturesque white flowers in his button hole." Her encounter with the novelist and noted lesbian Vernon Lee, however, was reported in unflattering detail:

The only event of the week has been the meeting of Vernon Lee. A most attractive Russian lady invited us to a small tea where she was to be present. Well, she was *not* as I had pictured her! Gauche, lowely [*sic*], atrociously dressed, she seemed entirely ill at ease and out of her element. She was in every particular decidedly unattractive almost repulsive; and yet altho' she dissappointed [*sic*] every one in the room and was neglected and ignored and seemed to have no magnetism, no presence at all, still after all, there was a pathetic approachable quality about her personality, a humanness, a kind of half deprecatory appeal for sympathy and I did want to get acquainted with her. She only spoke one word to me on introduction, and another where she went out. So I only watched her from across the room. Of course she's a brilliant woman, she carried that about with her *somewhere*, in some very subtle way. . . . Lina Duff Gordon told me yesterday that Vernon Lee is very much disliked by all Italians and not received anywhere. She has a strange almost hypnotic influence over girls younger than herself and there is one staying with her now who can't be induced to leave her tho her parents pray, and threaten, and command!
Perhaps you won't thank me for writing you these curious things

23. June 21, 1893.

about her. But they interest me so much and seem so surprising and unexpected, I thought you might like to hear them. Vernon Lee's family, every member of it, is just on the verge of insanity. She has no religious belief and "no more illusions left." How does she write from such an atmosphere as that of her home surroundings? I should judge she is profoundly sad.[24]

The interest Susy showed in Vernon Lee is remarkable, as is her assumption that Louise will be interested in hearing in detail her unexpected reaction to Lee. Few other people received as much attention in her letters. Clearly Susy was eager to meet Lee, had high expectations about her, but found her to be "decidedly unattractive almost repulsive." Yet Susy felt great sympathy toward her, and almost in spite of herself, was drawn to her. The telling detail, added at the end of her first paragraph—that Lee commanded an almost hypnotic effect over young girls who stayed with her against their parents' protestations—receives no negative judgments from Susy, although she knows she has just described an extraordinary circumstance. She has difficulties of her own, tearing herself away from her subject, as exemplified through the way she explains to Louise why she goes on in such detail, then proceeds to add even more detail.

One of the striking points about Susy's references to both Wilde and Lee is that she has no need to remind Louise who they are; she can assume that Louise knows as well as she does that they are both celebrated figures—one a flamboyant, effete male playwright soon to be notorious for his homosexual acts, and the other a noted lesbian novelist—who openly defied conventional expectations about proper gendered behavior. Each exemplified in his or her own unique and public way changes taking place in late Victorian understanding of traditional gendered binaries. Finally, these references firmly link Susy and the Clemens family to transgressive figures who challenged conventional notions about sexuality.

Susy's relationship to Louise made itself felt in her father's late writing. While there is no evidence that Sam Clemens ever challenged Susy about her relationship with Louise, or even that he knew much about the details of her affection, he had to have been aware of its contours

---

24. November 7, 1892; written from Florence.

and its effect upon his daughter. This level of awareness manifested itself in his increasing interest in his writings about transgressive young
women who test the limits of social acceptability and gender roles. His
intense study of the transvestite figure Joan of Arc occurred precisely
during the years when Susy was most deeply emotionally involved with
Louise Brownell. His portrait of Joan, he later claimed, was based on
Susy Clemens at seventeen, although it was the twenty-some-year-old
Susy he was living with every day in Europe; she was at once the to-
tally familiar daughter and the daughter who was in some sense un-
knowable. As we shall see, for all Twain's diligent historical research in
preparation for writing *Personal Recollections of Joan of Arc*, Joan, too,
remained a somewhat elusive figure. Finally, after the untimely and
wholly unexpected death of Susy in 1896, a blow from which Sam and
Livy Clemens never fully recovered, the transgressive daughter figure
appeared more frequently in his work. In these late works, he wrote
about men who married men, women who married women, and other
characters whose gendered behavior defied cultural norms. Such an interest was not entirely new to Twain, but it took on an urgency in his
late works. This is not to say that he lost his sense of humor about gendered performances, or indeed that he lost his sense of play with this
rich and multifaceted material. It is to say, however, that he became
even more interested in exploring through fiction various forms of gender transgression. It was as though he sought through his writing to
test the limits of gendered expectations, as well as the pleasures to be
had in thwarting them.

Theoretical Underpinnings

The cultural and literary critic who to my mind has written most cogently and imaginatively about the meaning of cross-dressing in literary texts and popular culture is Marjorie Garber in *Vested Interests:
Cross-Dressing and Cultural Anxiety*. Four principal elements in Garber's thesis about the phenomenon are particularly useful in understanding how cross-dressing works in Twain. The first of these is her
assertion that cross-dressing "offers a challenge to easy notions of bi-
narity, putting into question the categories of 'female' and 'male,'
whether they are considered essential or constructed, biological or cultural." As I will argue throughout this book, when Twain turns to

cross-dressing, he is ever and always calling into question restrictive gender norms. In the words of historian Leslie Ferris, cross-dressing "carries with it the possibility for exposing that liminal moment, that threshold of questioning, that slippery sense of a mutable self." Inherent within Twain and other writers' deconstruction of such categories, however, there is always the possibility in the end of reinscribing those very binaries. Thus critics often read Twain's representation of his characters' challenges to gender categories as only fleeting and momentary acts, and hence ultimately a conservative rather than radical rethinking of gender roles.[25] My own reading of his transgendered, transgressive work leads me to a different conclusion.

A second tenet of Garber's overall argument crucial to my reading of Twain is her insistence that one of the primary functions of the cross-dressed, or transvestite, figure is to indicate a "'category crisis,' disrupting and calling attention to cultural, social, or aesthetic dissonances." Garber elaborates:

> In a similar way, . . . the apparently spontaneous or unexpected or supplementary presence of a transvestite figure in a text (whether fiction or history, verbal or visual, imagistic or "real") that does not seem, thematically, to be primarily concerned with gender difference or blurred gender *indicates a category crisis elsewhere*, an irresolvable conflict or epistemological crux that destabilizes comfortable binarity, and displaces the resulting discomfort onto a figure that already inhabits, indeed incarnates, the margin.[26]

In other words, when we encounter characters cross-dressing in texts such as *Huckleberry Finn* or *Pudd'nhead Wilson*—texts that are not fundamentally about gender—we should be aware that we are in the presence of another sort of category crisis, in both instances the epistemological crisis of race. By attending to the cross-dressing we stand to gain valuable insight into that "other" category crisis. Especially in these two texts, issues of gender and race are intricately bound up with each oth-

25. Garber, *Vested Interests*, 10; Lesley Ferris, ed., *Crossing the Stage: Controversies on Cross-Dressing*, 9; on meaning of gender roles, see, for example, Susan Gillman's reading of "Hellfire Hotchkiss" as one of the tales that "momentarily confounds sexual categories, only in the end to give way to the clarification of gender and hence to proper, community-sanctioned identity" (*Dark Twins*, 111).
26. Garber, *Vested Interests*, 16, 17.

er; to read gender correctly and fully, we must also read race fully. When we do, we will see how cross-dressing destabilizes both categories.

Third, Garber further insists that we "read" the transvestite figure directly, rather than simply looking "through" such figures. In Garber's words, we must "confront the extraordinary power of transvestism to disrupt, expose, and challenge, putting in question the very notion of the 'original' and of stable identity." Finally, Garber makes a point that is especially pertinent to a study of Twain's transgressive gender work:

> No analysis of "cross-dressing" that wants to interrogate the phe-nomenon seriously from a cultural, political, or even aesthetic vantage point can fail to take into account the foundational role of gay iden-tity and gay style. . . . Just as to ignore the role played by homosexu-ality would be to risk a radical misunderstanding of the social and cul-tural implications of cross-dressing, so to restrict cross-dressing to the context of an emerging gay and lesbian identity is to risk ignoring, or setting aside, elements and incidents that seem to belong to quite dif-ferent lexicons of self-definition and political and cultural display.[27]

Thus one challenge in this study is to strike a balance between un-derstanding the "role played by homosexuality" while not restricting our consideration of cross-dressing to the "emerging gay and lesbian identity." If one overreads and overinterprets homosocial relations in Twain, if one imposes a twenty-first-century sensibility and gay and les-bian identity politics on the texts, then the full daring of Twain's play-ing with cross-dressing and gender transgressions will be lost; on the other hand, if we look clearly at the places where Twain entertains same-sex relations, we will find genuine disruptions and dissonances.

Another, more radical, critic whose theorizing about gender is crit-ical to an appreciation of gender play is Judith Butler. At least three principles of Butler's argument about gender are pertinent here. Fun-damentally, she insists that gender is not a stable "category of analysis." Butler observes, for instance, that when we think we see "a man dressed as a woman," we take the first part of the equation as the reality, and the second half as an illusion, as not real. But in the mere fact of ques-

27. Ibid., 16, 4–5.

tioning the categories of man and woman, "it becomes unclear how to distinguish the real from the unreal. And this is the occasion in which we come to understand that what we take to be 'real,' what we invoke as the naturalized knowledge of gender, is in fact, a changeable and revisable reality."[28]

In applying this notion to Twain, I do not mean to suggest that he consciously doubted "the reality of gender," but as his works make clear, he understood that gender norms could be called into question, and that they are to some extent an artifice. His work plays with the notion that gender is slippery and that it is mutable. Also foundational to Butler's theorizing is that gender is a performance, and it requires constant repetition. This is as true for heterosexuals as for homosexuals, who are sometimes regarded, according to Butler, as though they were imitations of "the real thing." From Butler's perspective, this latter point is illustrated most vividly through drag, a specific form of cross-dressing:

> The performance of drag plays upon the distinction between the anatomy of the performer and the gender that is being performed. But we are actually in the presence of three contingent dimensions of significant corporeality: anatomical sex, gender identity, and gender performance. If the anatomy of the performer is already distinct from the gender of the performer, and both of those are distinct from the gender of the performance, then the performance suggests a dissonance not only between sex and performance, but sex and gender, and gender and performance. . . . *In imitating gender, drag implicitly reveals the imitative structure of gender itself—as well as its contingency.*[29]

As we shall see, it is precisely the notion of dissonance between a character's sex and his or her gender that Twain capitalizes on, especially in some of his later works. But from the beginning, and throughout the works under consideration, he embraces the principle that gender is performative. His characters who cross-dress are particularly aware that they have to practice and perform their newly acquired gender.

28. Judith Butler, new preface to *Gender Trouble: Feminism and the Subversion of Identity*, xi, xxiii.
29. Ibid., 175; emphasis in the original.

Judith Butler returns repeatedly in her work to one other fundamental principle, which is that gender is constructed. In reflecting on
her own earlier work, Butler concludes, "It is important not only to understand how the terms of gender are instituted, naturalized, and established as presuppositional but to trace the moments where the binary system of gender is disputed and challenged, where the coherence
of the categories are put into question, and where the very social life of
gender turns out to be malleable and transformable."[30] In the chapters
that follow, I will be examining the many instances in Twain's work
when he challenged, toyed with, explored, and transformed "the binary system of gender."

Finally, at key moments in my analysis of cross-dressing and gender
transgression in Mark Twain's work, I also turn to Mikhail Bakhtin's
discussions of the carnivalesque. In particular, I am interested in the
way that Bakhtin's work sheds light on the humor that emerges from
the texts. I am mindful that no single theory of humor can satisfactori-
ly explain, or contain, Twain's work; nor do I imagine that all such the-
ories taken together are equal to the task. Nevertheless, Bahktin's writing about carnivalesque humor provides a useful point of departure. In
Bakhtin's terms, medieval and Renaissance festive carnivals (as opposed
to formal, sanctioned festivals) represented for ordinary people a temporary liberation from the restrictions of the established order; during
carnival the world was turned topsy-turvy and inside out: "As opposed
to the official feast, one might say that carnival celebrated temporary
liberation from the prevailing truth and from the established order; it
marked the suspension of all hierarchical rank, privileges, norms, and
prohibitions."[31] Whether one emphasizes the temporary nature of the
carnivalesque or the celebration associated with being free from conventional constraints, carnival blurred established boundaries and overturned "the official life." These notions seem especially relevant to

30. Judith Butler, *Undoing Gender*, 216.
31. Peter Messent has found "Bakhtin's notions of carnivalization . . . a useful model to apply to 'The Man That Corrupted Hadleyburg' and 'Stirring Times in Austria'"
(*The Short Works of Mark Twain: A Critical Study*, 171–72); and he has made a cogent
argument for Bakhtin's theory of heteroglossia illuminating critical moments in *Adventures of Huckleberry Finn* (*New Readings of the American Novel: Narrative Theory
and Its Application*, 204–42); Mikhail Bakhtin, *Rabelais and His World*, 9.

reading Twain, whose literary cross-dressing challenged the "prevailing truth" about gender norms and prohibitions, and did so primarily in a celebratory manner.

Bakhtin places great emphasis upon the fact that death is an integral part of carnival, even as it celebrates rebirth. The two are inseparable. Indeed, for Bakhtin, "all the images of carnival are dualistic; they unite within themselves both poles of change and crisis: birth and death (the image of pregnant death), blessing and curse (benedictory carnival curses which call simultaneously for death and rebirth), praise and abuse, youth and old age, top and bottom, face and backside, stupidity and wisdom."[32] Recalling that death is a vital part of the carnivalesque will help us understand why cross-dressing and gender transgressions are so often linked in Twain's work with death and morbidity. It helps us see that death almost always hovers at the margins of any of Twain's stories featuring cross-dressed figures, even as he celebrates their "misplaced sexes."

Above all else, the carnivalesque depends upon laughter, upon parody, upon the antics of clowns and jesters. The laughter it engenders is complex:

> It is first of all, a festive laughter. Therefore it is not an individual reaction to some isolated "comic" event. Carnival laughter is the laughter of all the people. Second, it is universal in scope; it is directed at all and everyone, including the carnival's participants. The entire world is seen in its droll aspect, in its gay relativity. Third, this laughter is ambivalent: it is gay, triumphant, and at the same time mocking, deriding. It asserts and denies, it buries and revives. Such is the laughter of carnival.

Laughter in carnival is also directed toward the high, the official, the "truth" as it is commonly understood. It frequently relies upon parody, which is itself a form of reversal and a challenge to that which is revered. Finally, "all forms of ritual laughter were linked with death and rebirth, with the reproductive act, with symbols of the reproductive force. Ritual laughter was a reaction to *crises* in the life of the sun (solstices), crises in the life of a deity, in the life of the world and of man

---

32. Mikhail Bakhtin, *Problems of Dostoevsky's Poetics*, 126.

(funeral laughter). In it, ridicule was fused with rejoicing." Thus, the carnivalesque is deeply ambiguous; the laughter, especially, contains within it its own opposite, and as such is "a profoundly universal laughter, a laughter that contains a whole outlook on the world."[33]

In the chapters that follow, I take up, in turn, both major and minor texts that feature cross-dressing and other forms of gender disruption. After an examination of two early works of cross-dressing, "An Awful— Terrible Medieval Romance" and "1002nd Arabian Night," Chapter 2 is concerned primarily with *Adventures of Huckleberry Finn,* with an emphasis on the effect of gender crossing, racial crossing, and the relationship between Huck and Jim. Chapter 3, devoted to *Pudd'nhead Wilson,* extends the consideration between gender crossing and racial crossing as it is played out in complex and disruptive ways through the mixed-race characters Roxana and her son, Tom. Chapter 4 focuses exclusively on *Personal Recollections of Joan of Arc,* a book that features the most famous cross-dresser in history, and a figure who, paradoxically, seems ultimately to elude Twain. The final chapter considers four short stories and a play written late in Twain's career; all feature transvestite figures or characters who otherwise transgress established gendered expectations.

33. On festive laughter, see Bakhtin, *Rabelais,* 11–12; on ritual laughter, see Bakhtin, *Problems of Dostoevsky's Poetics,* 127.

2

Sarah Mary Williams George Elexander Peters

Mark Twain began his exploration of cross-dressing relatively early in his career, specifically during the first year of his marriage when he was writing articles for the Buffalo *Express*. His first such piece was entitled "An Awful—Terrible Medieval Romance" (1870). In this initial foray, Twain sets the stage for many of the episodes of the more embellished scenes and stories of cross-dressing that would follow: he creates a female cross-dresser who is accused of fathering a child, he further blurs gender categories by playing with the pronouns he assigns his characters, and he links cross-dressing with the threat of death. Uncharacteristically, however, he writes himself into a corner from which he is unable (at this juncture in his career) to extricate himself and, as we shall see, simply stops his story abruptly after an apology of sorts.

He returned to the theme of cross-dressing in 1883, when he wrote "1002nd Arabian Night," a piece also set in the distant past, which, according to Susan K. Harris, Twain composed "with the intention of upsetting his contemporaries' gender assumptions."[1] As in "An Awful—Terrible Medieval Romance," cross-dressing in "1002nd Arabian

---

1. Susan K. Harris, "Mark Twain and Gender," 164.

Night" is not a choice made by the hero(ine) but instead has been conferred since birth—it is the "given" of the story. In this tale there is an additional plot twist of not one but two opposite-sex children assigned to the other's gender, a classic twinning evoked so powerfully throughout Twain's work, as in the *Prince and the Pauper, Pudd'nhead Wilson,* and *Those Extraordinary Twins.* Again he plays with pronouns, calling the child born a female and raised as a male "she," and the reverse for the child born a male and raised as a female. In contrast with the "Medieval Romance," the emphasis ultimately falls not on the issue of female paternity but, equally improbably, of male maternity. Whereas death by execution threatens the cross-dressed hero of the earlier story, here the tone of the story is lighthearted and entirely comic, reveling in the absurdity of the situation Twain has created. The only real threat of death hanging over the story applies to the classic storyteller herself—Scherezade.

The most extended and satisfying exploration of cross-dressing in the period before 1890 is in *Adventures of Huckleberry Finn.* The novel features multiple scenes of cross-dressing by both the major male characters, Huck and Jim, and one brief but important scene in which Tom Sawyer also puts on women's clothing. In this novel, cross-dressing is also firmly linked with racial crossings and racial transgressions. If, as Marjorie Garber insists, the transvestite figure is an indicator of a category crisis elsewhere, in *Huckleberry Finn* that crisis is unmistakably race. Thus, during the period 1870 to 1885, through a variety of tones and plots—some comic and some more serious—Twain explored gender instability. He tested assumptions about gender-defined behavior for both males and females, and he began to explore in earnest the limits of racialized categories and the dehumanizing effects of those categories. At the very time that the nation was tightening and patrolling the borders of legally imposed racial categories and enforcing racial segregation, Twain was slipping across racial boundaries through cross-dressing. His exploration of other simultaneous gender and racial crossings would reach its apotheosis in *Pudd'nhead Wilson,* but remarkably in the works that followed *Pudd'nhead Wilson,* that is, after 1894, his interest in racial crossing and racial categories seems to abate, while his challenges to fixed notions of gender categories only increased. Before we turn to the main text of this period, *Adventures of Huckleberry Finn,* let us look at Twain's initial fictional excursions into creating cross-dressed characters, specifically those assigned at birth to the "wrong" gender category—that is, characters whose gender did not line up with their biological sex.

"An Awful—Terrible Medieval Romance"

"An Awful—Terrible Medieval Romance" is set in the year 1222 in a Germanic castle, and immediately the plot is complicated. The main character is the twenty-eight-year-old Conrad, clad in full mail armor but addressed as "My Daughter" by his father, Klugenstein, brother of the reigning duke. Conrad is called into the presence of his father to learn for the first time the "mystery" of his life. His father explains to Conrad that as a male, rather than the female he "really" is, he stands to inherit his grandfather's kingdom. According to the line of succession set down by the grandfather, if Conrad's uncle, Ulrich, has a son, that son would inherit the kingdom; if Ulrich has a daughter, she would inherit, but only if Klugenstein has no son, and then only if that daughter is "stainless." As Klugenstein's *daughter,* Conrad is behind any cousin, male or female, in the line of succession; hence his father's decision to raise Conrad as a boy from birth. As far as anyone knows, then, Conrad is the heir apparent because Ulrich has only a daughter, Constance. Further, because Ulrich is growing old and feeble, he sends for Conrad to take up his responsibilities immediately, although he will not officially be crowned as duke until Ulrich dies. This is the news that makes Klugenstein reveal the mystery of Conrad's life. One further piece of information is given to Conrad before he sets off to assume his responsibilities: there is an ancient law that dictates that if a woman "sits for a single instant in the great ducal chair before she hath been absolutely crowned in the presence of the people, she shall die." Hence, Conrad is warned by his father never to sit in that chair.[2]

Conrad travels to his uncle's dukedom and begins to rule, wisely and

2. Mark Twain, "An Awful—Terrible Medieval Romance," 332 (hereinafter cited as AT). Such stories lead to their own gender confusions for the critic writing about them; in the interest of simplification, I will refer to Conrad as "he" because he publicly appears only as a male. Tom Quirk points out that "the death penalty for a woman sitting in the ducal chair before she has been crowned has no rational justification other than it thickens a plot that is doomed from the beginning" (*A Study in Short Fiction,* 36).

mercifully, as it turns out. Meanwhile, his scheming father has secretly sent a man named Count Detzin to seduce Conrad's cousin, Constance, which he does. He impregnates her, then disappears. In the ensuing months, Constance declares her love for Conrad, but he rebuffs her: "Conrad was appalled. He bitterly cursed himself for having yielded to the instinct that made him seek the companionship of one of his own sex when he was new and a stranger in the palace—when he was sorrowful and yearned for a sympathy such as only women can give or feel" (AT, 335). Constance gives birth to her child, the news gets out, and she is put on trial for having an illegitimate child. It falls to Conrad to sit in judgment of her, and in so doing he is thereby forced to sit in the forbidden ducal chair. The penalty for Constance's indiscretion is death—that is, unless she names the father of the child and "deliver him up to the executioner." To save herself, and to get revenge on Conrad for rebuffing her, she names Conrad. With wonderful unconscious irony, Constance "points her finger straight at Conrad," and pronounces "'Thou art the man!'" (AT, 338). Conrad is caught in a fatal double bind: "To disprove the charge, he must reveal that he was a woman; and for an uncrowned woman to sit in the ducal chair was death! At one and the same moment, he and his grim old father swooned and fell to the ground" (AT, 338–39). Here Twain breaks off the story, with nothing resolved: "The truth is, I have got my hero (or heroine) into such a particularly close place that I do not see how I am ever going to get him (or her) out of it again—and therefore I will wash my hands of the whole business and leave that person to get out the best way that offers—or else stay there. I thought it was going to be easy enough to straighten out that little difficulty, but it looks different, now" (AT, 339).

Tom Quirk characterizes the story as having a "self-devouring plot, and the burlesque follows the irrefutable logic of his premises to their inevitable and ridiculous irresolution." Susan Gillman suggests that Twain found that "coming to a formal conclusion is out of the question when the issues are sexual indeterminacy and boundary breakdown"; she adds, "the lack of closure is the most telling, if not the most titillating, aspect" of this tale.[3]

---

3. Quirk, *A Study in Short Fiction*, 35; Gillman, *Dark Twins*, 112. John Cooley, in his introduction to the story in his collection of Mark Twain's transvestite tales, briefly as-

A further reason might help explain why the story lacks closure: in this first transvestite story about a young woman raised from infancy as though a member of the opposite sex in order to satisfying her father's ambitions, Twain is caught not only by his own improbable plot but also by too early and too dramatically linking cross-dressing with death. This linkage, which will be an undercurrent in many of his tales involving cross-dressing, here is overdetermined. Having decided at Conrad's birth to raise his daughter as a transvestite, Conrad's father hanged eight serving women because they knew that the child was a girl—"I hanged them every one before an hour had sped" (AT, 332). Death threatens Conrad if his "true" gender is revealed and he has sat in the ducal chair, in effect rendering him stuck forever as a transvestite, and death faces him as the accused father of Constance's child unless he reveals that he is not a man. In later stories, Twain will work the connection between cross-dressing and morbidity much more subtlety, although especially in works such as *Adventures of Huckleberry Finn,* it will hover over the plot from start to finish. At this point in his writing, Twain is not yet especially interested in how his protagonist passes as a male, what he looks like in that role, what his inner thoughts might be. Partly because the story is set in medieval times and revolves around royal inheritance, there is a decidedly remote quality about the story. Still, Twain does exploit some of the linguistic possibilities in the gender confusion and he plays with the specter of female paternity that he will return to later.

"1002nd Arabian Night"

In this tale, written in the same summer he finished *Adventures of Huckleberry Finn,* Twain mischievously invents one more tale for Scherezade to tell King Shahriyar, thereby extending her own life one more night. The tale, told in what the king calls tedious detail, is filled with comic burlesque and absurdity.[4] After two chapters, featuring magicians, a gigantic mysterious egg, and a soothsayer, it is foretold that

---

serts that "marriage could have saved them both," but in fact it would only have saved Constance, for the text asserts that the father, so named, would be turned over to the executioner (*How Nancy Jackson Married Kate Wilson and Other Tales of Rebellious Girls & Daring Young Women,* 15).

4. "1002nd Arabian Night" (hereinafter cited as AN), in Franklin R. Rogers, ed., *Mark Twain's Satires and Burlesques,* 94.

the Sultan will soon have a beautiful son, and his friend, the Grand Vizier, will have an equally beautiful daughter. All are pleased. The two babies are eventually born, but a witch intervenes, and *"by parting the hair of the Sultan's boy-babe in the middle had made it seem to be a girl, and by parting the hair of the Grand Vizier's girl-babe on the side, had thus caused it to seem to be a boy"* (AN, 101). And so the boy baby was given a girl's name, Fatima, and raised as a girl, and the girl baby was named Selim and raised as a boy. No mention is ever made of the biological sex of each child, and no one ever seems to notice the discrepancy between sex and gender. Yet biology would seem to be destiny for Twain in this story. The biological boy raised as a girl is interested only in "masculine" things: he had no interest in dolls, singing birds, or cats, but wanted to hear only tales of "massacres and harems." Selim, the female-to-male cross-dressed child, is only interested in dolls—"how despicable is this, in a boy" (AN, 106). Further, Fatima, we are told, hated "his" female clothing and would steal away "and there rid himself of most of the hated garments; and then, being unencumbered, he would comfort himself with the forbidden exercises of the manly sex" (AN, 108). The ambiguity of this last statement is representative of the sense of play and absurdity underlying the entire improbable story.

After several chapters in which the children, now young adults, secretly enter into a romantic relationship, the two profess their love for one another and express their wish to marry. The Sultan, however, does not want his daughter to marry because of a curse that says that if she gives birth, both she and the child must die. The two young people eventually overcome his objections and at the age of nineteen are married. In time a child is born, and the curse would seem to be upon Fatima and the child's head, when suddenly Fatima announces that her husband was the one who had given birth to the infant:

> ". . . the miracle of miracles has come to pass, and thy daughter and thy dynasty are redeemed; for lo, *not I but my husband is the child's mother!*"
> And straightway unwinding a blanket, he showed him the babe, a wee little red-haired thing, and the transported Sultan kissed it and blessed it and named it Ethelred.
> And now at this instant flew *Selim* into the presence, crying:
> "Lo, it is twins, for I am mother to yet another, and our happiness is complete!" (AN, 131; emphasis in original)

Amidst all the telling of this tale, Twain plays with the gendered pronouns, insisting upon calling the ostensible male "she" and the ostensible female "he." Twain combined this pronoun confusion with his insistence, in this story, that no matter how the twinned children are raised, their biological sex seems to determine their gendered behaviors. Yet as Susan K. Harris has observed,

> Twain's playful reassignment of gendered pronouns indicates that on some level he perceived that the words themselves produce the gender; that femininity or masculinity are constituted by the language employed to evoke them. The story, written at the apex of his literary career and at the time when his own children were very young, suggests that Twain was questioning an entrenched cultural assumption that to be male or female meant to have a predetermined set of behaviors as well as a particular genital organization.[5]

It is unfortunate that the story was never published in Twain's lifetime, when, in spite of the tale's absurdity, it might have contributed to the debate about the difference between gender and sexuality, or the degree to which biology determines behavior. Further, he had obviously invested considerable time and energy in the story, creating 131 of his own illustrations to accompany the text. Those illustrations were lost early on and have never been recovered. Perhaps the discouragement he received from his good friend William Dean Howells also contributed to his decision not to publish the story. Howells declared to Twain that "on the whole it was not your best or your second-best; and all the way it skirts a certain kind of fun which you can't afford to indulge in."[6] What Howells no doubt imagined would be objectionable was the way Twain toyed with gender identity, and the specter of a male giving birth to twins. It was precisely the "kind of fun," however, that Twain returned to frequently during the rest of his career. And it was the kind of fun that he had just created in what was to become his magnum opus featuring a boy and an escaped slave on a raft floating down the Mississippi River.

5. Harris, "Mark Twain and Gender," 166.
6. On the illustrations, see Rogers, *Mark Twain's Satires*, 89; Howells is cited on the same page.

Adventures of Huckleberry Finn

One of the most endearing comic scenes in *Adventures of Huckle-berry Finn* is the one in which Huck dresses in girls' clothing, then fails a series of tests designed by Judith Loftus to determine if he is an au-thentic girl. The scene is notable for its good-natured humor and for its playfulness. It offers comic relief from the grim events that have brought Huck and Jim, separately, to Jackson's Island and that will send them out onto the Mississippi River and the perils that await them on their journey south. Unlike the events that surround this scene, no se-rious novelistic purpose seems to underlie this one, and no social insti-tution is singled out for critique; the comic visual images Twain evokes appear to contain no particular underlying anxiety. Huck's motivation for going ashore underscores his youth and innocence: life on Jackson's Island "was getting slow and dull, and I wanted to get a stirring up, some way." Yet as we shall see, beyond the good humor generated by Huck's cross-dressing and his subsequent encounter with Judith Lof-tus, this scene, too, has deeper, more serious significance for the novel as a whole. While it plays with gender in the most classic sense of the term, for the first time it also joins Huck's fate with Jim's. This move is made possible by, and is propelled by, their momentary mutual ex-change of subject-object positions brought about by Huck's dressing in girls' clothing.[7]

Once Huck decides to go ashore, Jim, not Huck, suggests that Huck should disguise himself as a girl, and Jim dresses him in a calico gown they have taken from a house floating down the river. As a final touch, Huck puts on a sunbonnet, "and then for a body to look in and see my face was like looking down a joint of stove-pipe" (*AHF*, 66–67). There is good humor in Jim's critical assessment of Huck: "Jim said nobody would know me, even in the daytime, hardly." His disguise complete,

---

7. Mark Twain, *Adventures of Huckleberry Finn*, 66 (unless otherwise noted, all ref-erences are to the 2001 University of California Press edition, hereinafter cited as *AHF*). James Cox, in "A Hard Book to Take," points to the system of "emotional exchange" that underlies our reading of any comic scene in the novel: the more seriously we inter-pret an individual episode in the novel, the more we diminish the humor; similarly, when one emphasizes the humor we seem to take the book less seriously. The challenge is to keep both the comic and the serious in sight, to offer up "serious" interpretation but not forget the comedy and irony that led us to that interpretation (174).

"A FAIR FIT."
Jim dressing Huck as Sarah Williams.

Huck has to practice being a girl, to perform his female gender, and Jim is his audience and instructor. Huck works "to get the hang of the things, and by and by I could do pretty well in them, only Jim said I didn't walk like a girl; and he said I must quit pulling up my gown to get at my britches pocket. I took notice, and done better" (*AHF*, 67).[8] E. W. Kemble's illustration in the first edition captures perfectly the inherent playfulness of the scene. Jim, who is on his knees so he can hook the back of Huck's dress, is laughing with obvious pleasure, while Huck looks over his shoulder at Jim with a bemused look on his face. He holds his hands out in front of him, his wrists limp in imitation of a girl, or more accurately, in a classic exaggerated imitation of a boy impersonating a girl.

Huck gets in his canoe and crosses over to the Missouri shore. He

8. As Judith Butler has established, one of the consequences of gender being a performance is that the performance requires constant repetition (*Gender Trouble*, xv).

immediately comes upon Judith Loftus, living in what had been an abandoned shack. Within minutes, Loftus spins out stories about her family, Huck's murder, Jim's running away and the accusations that he killed Huck, Pap's disappearance, and her surmise that Jim is hiding out on the island. Then she puts Huck through a series of tests involving him throwing a "lump of lead" at a rat and her dropping a hank of yarn in his lap. Based on Huck's performance on these tasks, Loftus presses Huck to tell her his real name: "Is it Bill, or Tom, or Bob?—or what is it?" (*AHF*, 72). Before he can come up with an answer, however, she informs him that he is a runaway apprentice who has been treated badly; she then picks up the strands of her imagined story about this apprentice and spins out a story of her own. Next she tests him with questions designed to find out if he is really from the country. Reassured this time by Huck's answers, she proceeds, like Jim, to teach Huck how to be a more convincing girl—how to thread a needle like a girl, throw like a girl, catch something on his lap like a girl. With that, and a comic stringing together of all Huck's assumed names, and one of her own devising—"Sarah Mary Williams George Elexander Peters"—she sends him off, so she imagines, to Goshen.

The scene, much of which is reported in direct quotation, is laced with good humor. Sometimes the laugh is on Loftus herself, who can construct spontaneously such clever tests for Huck and who can see through one of Huck's disguises, but who still cannot "see" the real Huck Finn, whom she presumes is dead; instead, she confers upon him a new identity, one that Huck readily adopts, as a runaway apprentice. There is considerable irony in the episode, too, arising from the fact that Huck's cross-dressing in itself calls into question culturally constructed notions of gender while, at the same time, Judith Loftus's tests and ensuing instructions reinscribe gendered behaviors as though they were absolute and universal.[9]

9. It has always been a source of delight to me that students frequently want to know if it is true that girls thread a needle one way and boys another, some expressing a bit of anxiety that they might not be doing it the "right" way. The same question has intrigued other Twain scholars. The editors of the University of California edition took the trouble to determine that in the nineteenth century how one threaded a needle was not necessarily a gendered trait; in fact, they point out, Twain "gave the opposite gender information in Chapter 13 of *The Prince and the Pauper*." See Twain, *Huckleberry Finn*, 401, nn. 74.14–75.1. They also offer at least six sources for the gendered notion of how

For all its comic moments, the serious work this episode performs in the novel reflects on the relationship between Huck and Jim. The episode takes place just after a minor crisis point in the relationship between them: because of a practical joke Huck plays on Jim, a rattlesnake bites Jim on the ankle and he spends four days and nights in torment. Jim has no idea that Huck is the likely cause of his being bitten, and Huck still thinks that Jim is someone to be toyed with. Their relationship is represented as inherently unequal. Before they set off on a raft together, some fundamental shift must take place in that relationship. Huck's dressing in girls' clothing, and Jim dressing Huck in those clothes, represents that shift. As Laura Skandera-Trombley suggests, Twain's purpose in having Huck cross-dress is "to assist him in gaining insight into Jim's dilemma," presumably the dilemma both of being a slave and of being a runaway. "Before Huck can understand Jim's plight, he must experience what it means to be powerless. Twain cannot make Huck African-American but he can make him a girl," according to Skandera-Trombley.[10] While the "powerlessness" Huck experiences is limited compared with Jim's obvious and deeply embedded powerlessness as a slave and as a fugitive, there is an exchange that takes place here that is crucial for the actions that will follow.

The cross-dressing scene sets up a symbolic exchange of subject-object positions between Huck and Jim, which in turn establishes a degree of reciprocity between them. In masquerading as a girl, Huck moves momentarily from the subject position to the object position. He becomes the object of Jim's gaze, thereby taking on a female stance with his female disguise. Jim, who until this point has been the "other" in the text, assumes momentarily the subject position. It is his idea to dress Huck in girl's clothing, he shortens the dress for him, he fastens it, he observes Huck practicing to be a girl, and he critiques Huck's performance. The black man, heretofore the object of the gaze, now fixes the white boy in his sight. Thus the crossing of traditional gender boundaries via cross-dressing leads almost instantaneously to a disruption of socially defined racialized boundaries. This extraordinary shift

---

girls catch things on their laps, but they remain silent on Loftus's description of how girls throw.

10. Laura Skandera-Trombley, "Mark Twain's Cross-Dressing Oeuvre," 86.

challenges outright the notion of fixed boundaries and culturally assigned roles, and in so doing signals the degree to which *Adventures of
Huckleberry Finn* will be a subversive text. More immediately, it sets the
relationship between Huck and Jim on a new, more equal, plane, as
Skandera-Trombley has suggested. Kembel's illustration reinforces this
notion, for with Jim kneeling and Huck standing, their heads are nearly at the same height; if anything, Jim's head is slightly higher than
Huck's, which was an unusual visual representation of a white and black
person together in the nineteenth century.[11] Huck and Jim's momentary exchange of subject/object positions, in turn, makes possible one
of the defining moments in the text, namely Huck's first words to Jim
after he has learned from Judith Loftus that a hunting party will try to
capture Jim that night: "Git up and hump yourself, Jim. There ain't a
moment to lose. They're after *us!*" (*AHF*, 75; emphasis added). Huck
has learned nothing on shore that suggests anyone is searching for him;
indeed, he is presumed to be dead. Nonetheless, he embraces Jim's per-
il as his own, and the die is cast.

The cross-dressing episode is the first of many times when Huck will
assume a different identity. It is one of the few times he puts on a disguise, and it is the only time when he literally wears one identity over
another, to say nothing of the fact that Judith Loftus confers upon him
multiple female and one male identity as well. In fact, his female identity is literally layered over his familiar male identity. His calico dress
does not replace his male clothing but instead is put on over his "britches." In composing *Huckleberry Finn,* Twain constructed this layering
carefully and deliberately. In the original manuscript, he contemplates
having Jim and Huck cut off Huck's trouser legs to keep them out of
sight, an action that was both permanent and vaguely threatening.[12] In
the published version, however, Huck merely rolls up his trouser legs
and thereby can readily return to an intact male self at the end of the

11. Patricia Turner demonstrates through her collection of nineteenth-century illustrations featuring Uncle Tom and Little Eva that the black man is never depicted as
standing above his white companion. Even though Tom is a grown man and Eva a child,
she inevitably stands while he sits, and she therefore assumes a visually superior position
(*Ceramic Uncles and Celluloid Mammies: Black Images and Their Influence on Culture,*
69–88).

12. Alteration to MS page 233.14, cited in Mark Twain, *Adventures of Huckleberry
Finn,* in *The Works of Mark Twain,* 8:1027.

episode. Later, Huck will assume a host of other identities, most of them adopted spontaneously and almost all of them assumed to get him out of a tight place. Here, however, Huck puts on one identity over another, and he spends a day performing that new identity.

Although Huck has practiced being a girl, he cannot remember *which* girl he is. First he says he is Mary Williams, then Sarah Williams, and in a quick-witted response to Judith Loftus's challenge, Sarah Mary Williams. For Twain, Huck's assuming of another gender is more powerful than purporting to be a particular person; what is important is not that he is Sarah or Mary, but that he is a girl who has to perform his assumed gender under the watchful eye of Judith Loftus. In keeping with her essentialist notions, she tells him he might be able to fool men by his disguise, but not women. Following her cue, he drops his female guise and readily takes up a new identity as George Peters, but he does not shed his female clothing to do so. Thus the episode plays out with Huck in at least a triple layer of identities: a boy, Huck Finn, dressed in his usual clothing, layered over with a girl's dress and three different girls' names, and a final (false) male identity layered over them all. As Myra Jehlen has observed, provocatively, this episode plunges Huck into "the deepest possible limbo of identity."[13]

The scene is a brilliant introduction for Huck into a world in which he will need to assume multiple identities, an art he will perfect in the course of his adventures. One of the ongoing pleasures of the novel is that we always believe we know who and what Huck is—without such a sense the multiple ironies of the narrative would not work. As a boy who stands on the margins of society, occupying a vernacular perspective, as Henry Nash Smith so cogently argued,[14] his relationship to the dominant culture is always problematic. In this episode, as simultaneously both a male and female figure, Huck by his very presence and performance challenges traditional boundaries and values; through Huck, Twain is putting his readers on notice that all social boundaries and constructs will be open to interrogation.

For all its good fun, Huck's donning of female clothing and a female identity also evokes the shadow side of the novel. As critics have shown,

---

13. Myra Jehlen, "Reading Gender in *Adventures of Huckleberry Finn*," 515.
14. Henry Nash Smith, *Mark Twain: The Development of a Writer*, 113–37.

there is a distinctly morbid side to Huck's imagination, and a preoccupation with death haunts the entire novel. Leslie Fiedler describes Huck as "a strangely melancholy child—not one possessed of a sense of alienation ('lonesome' is almost his favorite adjective), but obsessed by, more than half in love with death." Fiedler continues:

> From the first, the reader is made aware of Huck's dark preoccupations: "I felt so lonesome I most wished I was dead. . . . I heard an owl . . . who-whooing about somebody that was dead, and a whippoorwill and a dog crying about somebody who was going to die." And, indeed, he plays dead in order to survive, rigs a scene of murder to persuade his Pap (who has taken him for the angel of death!) and the world that he is beyond their reach: "They won't ever hunt the river for anything but my dead carcass. They'll soon get tired of that, and won't bother no more about me." Afterwards, he seems a ghost to everyone who knew him; and even at the moment just before what he calls his rebirth ("it was like being born again") at the Phelps farm, his original melancholia returns.

James Cox recounts an even longer, more persuasive list of death scenes in the novel, from "the house of death" to the exhumation of Peter Wilks, all linking, in Cox's terms, the "theme of rebirth" with the "central image of death."[15]

What has been missing from these analyses and subsequent critical studies is a consideration of the way Twain almost always links crossdressing with death and morbidity. Precisely why Twain makes this connection will always be open to interpretation and debate, but I propose two primary explanations. The first is that cross-dressing and other forms of gender transgression in Twain's work clearly challenge the socially constructed nature of gender boundaries; this in turn both creates and reveals deep-seated anxieties about the corporeal body, the site upon which and through which gender is performed. Such anxieties are expressed through feelings of morbidity as well as the very real threat of death. It can be read, too, as testimony to Twain's own anxieties about the dangerous waters he has entered in *Adventures of Huckleberry Finn*. The second is the explanation offered by Bakhtin's analysis

---

15. Leslie Fiedler, *Love and Death in the American Novel*, 462; James Cox, "Remarks on the Sad Initiation of Huckleberry Finn," 146–47.

of carnivalesque humor, in which death and renewal are all but inseparable, and in turn were historically linked to cross-dressing: "From the
wearing of clothes turned inside out and trousers slipped over the head
to the election of mock kings and popes the same topographical logic
is put to work: shifting from top to bottom, casting the high and the
old, the finished and completed into the material bodily lower stratum
for death and rebirth."[16]

But as Bakhtin also makes clear, carnival was but a moment in time,
a liminal moment, and at the conclusion of carnival the world would
be set "right" again. We should not, however, underestimate the im-
pact of that liminal moment. Lesley Ferris, in *Crossing the Stage,* underscores the potentially subversive side of the carnivalesque impulse as
it is played out on the stage: "Theatrical cross-dressing has provided
one way of playing with liminality and its multiple possibilities and extending that sense of the possible to the spectator/reader: a way of play,
that while often reinforcing the social mores and status quo, carries with
it the possibility for exposing that liminal moment, that threshold of
questioning, that slippery sense of a mutable self."[17] And so it was for
the cross-dressed Huck. Although he was a lowly member of society, a
boy on the margins of society, he was white and male, and hence privileged. He nonetheless donned female dress and linked his fate to that
of a fugitive slave.

In *Huckleberry Finn,* cross-dressing, then, is more than a signal of a
category crisis, and more than a sign of Huck's (and Jim's) vulnerabil-
ity; it is also firmly associated with death. Literally, for instance, the calico gown Huck wears as Sarah Mary Williams was taken by Jim and
Huck from a floating house that contained the naked body of a murdered man. Both Huck and Jim enter the house, with Jim admonish-
ing Huck not to look further at the dead man, and together they go
through the clothing hanging on the wall—two calico dresses, some
women's underclothes, a sunbonnet, and unspecified items of men's
clothing. They take all the clothes with them, plus a host of more practical household items, such as candles and a Bowie knife, leaving the
house (and the body) to float on to its destiny. The next day Huck wants

16. Bakhtin, *Rabelais,* 81–82.
17. Ferris, *Crossing the Stage,* 9.

to talk with Jim about the dead man, and "how he come to be killed, but Jim didn't want to. He said it would fetch bad luck; and besides, he said, he might come and ha'nt us; he said a man that warn't buried was more likely to go a-ha'nting around than one that was planted and comfortable" (*AHF*, 63). What Jim does not reveal is that he recognized that the murdered man was Pap, information he withholds from Huck until the final pages of the novel. Thus, behind the comic scene of Huck performing the female gender lies the likely death of strangers and the certainty of the death of his own father.

Behind this scene, in turn, lies yet another scene of death and cross-dressing. The first instance in the novel of a purported cross-dressed person also is associated with Pap. In the third chapter of the novel, when Huck is still living with the Widow Douglas, a drowned man, floating on his back, is pulled out of the Mississippi River. Because the body was in the water so long, his face was obliterated, but the towns-people speculate that it was the body of the missing Pap Finn, because of his size, his raggedy appearance, and his "uncommon long hair." Huck, however, knows better because, as he says, "I knowed mighty well that a drownded man don't float on his back, but on his face. So I knowed, then, that this warn't pap, but a woman dressed up in a man's clothes" (*AHF*, 14). Huck asserts this "fact" about how women float when dead with absolutely certainty, and of course he proves to be right that it was not his father's body. No narrative voice exists to contradict Huck's assertion, nor is there any speculation in the text about why a woman would have been dressed as a man—only the unchallenged gendered assertion. If Huck's folklore is true, it points to a sex-determined characteristic, and suggests that while gender can be "worn," biology will ultimately override masquerade. If, however, we accept Huck's "fact" as a superstition, an unsubstantiated folk belief, it casts further doubt on all the other pieces of gendered folklore offered up as fact by Judith Loftus.[18]

---

18. Laura Skandera-Trombley speculates that the drowned woman might have been a fugitive slave woman in disguise. She cites two slave narratives Twain might have known in which a light-skinned slave woman cross-dressed to escape from the South: *The Narrative of Ellen Craft*, and Harriet Jacob's *Incidents in the Life of a Slave Girl*. Skandera-Trombley rightly observes that such a possibility associates cross-dressing with the issue of race in *Huckleberry Finn* from the beginning of the novel ("Mark Twain's Cross-Dressing Oeuvre," 84); but is Huck's fact really a fact, or but one of his many su-

It will be many weeks before Huck cross-dresses once more during the elaborate "evasion" that concludes the novel, but before then he accidentally wraps himself in women's clothing. This event takes place when he is under the power of the duke and king as the latter two pose as Englishmen, bent on defrauding the nieces of the late Peter Wilks. Huck is assigned the identity of an English servant—a role he plays very poorly—and he seems nearly helpless to stop the two frauds from stealing the Wilks girls' inheritance. He does, however, try to find the bag of gold that the scoundrels essentially have already stolen from the girls. He begins by planning to search the duke's room, which is really Mary Jane Wilks's bedroom, but immediately he hears footsteps approach. His first thought is to dive under the bed to hide, but remarkably he cannot find the bed in the dark. His hand accidentally touches a curtain that covers Mary Jane's dresses, and he "jumped in behind that and *snuggled in amongst the gowns*" (*AHF*, 226; emphasis added). On the basic plot level, this action saves Huck from being discovered by the king and duke, for the first thing the duke does in entering the room is to look under the bed. Hidden among the dresses, Huck overhears an extended debate between the king and the duke about whether or not to slip away that night with the money or stay and sell the entire estate, slaves and all. Greed wins out, but before they leave the room to "go down there a whoopin'-up the mornin'" they hide the gold inside the straw tick beneath the feather bed. Before they are halfway down the stairs, Huck steals the gold back and hides it in his own "cubby," waiting for an opportunity to return it to the Wilks girls. Although on a literal level Huck is not cross-dressed in this vignette, he does stand the entire time enfolded in Mary Jane's gowns, where he is safe. Twain's choice of the word "snuggled" also suggests that on a sensual level, Huck is at home among the gowns. Huck's sympathies, which have already been aroused earlier by Mary Jane Wilks's femininity, are reinforced when he symbolically wraps himself in her clothing. They are confirmed when he hears her crying next to her uncle's coffin and when he comes upon her crying after the slave families are separated and sold

---

perstitions? The editors of *Adventures of Huckleberry Finn* cite a possible source for this bit of folklore in Lecky's *History of European Morals,* and they also cite a modern medical researcher who has determined that all bodies, no matter the age or gender, float face down (*AHF*, 388 n.14.24–25).

by the king and duke. That sympathy, aroused by Huck's snuggling into Mary Jane's dresses, almost immediately allows Huck to confide in her and set in motion events that he hopes will lead to the exposure of the two frauds. Once again, as in Huck's visit with Judith Loftus, his putting on women's clothing, even symbolically, gives him access to domestic situations in which confidences and sympathies are exchanged in a more feminized world than Huck would ordinarily enter.

The duke and king, who take over Huck and Jim's raft and drive the plot for nearly a quarter of the novel, are themselves responsible for two additional cross-dressing incidents, but to much different effects. The first of these occurs within days of their commandeering the raft, when they put on their "Shakespearean Revival!!!" and the king plays the part of Juliet in the balcony scene from *Romeo and Juliet*. Entirely comic in its effect, the scene evokes the American minstrel theater, which frequently staged burlesques of Shakespeare's plays. White actors in blackface played the roles of white characters, such as Hamlet, and white men in blackface also played the role of female characters, such as Desdemona. Thus, even in the minstrel prototype, gender and race were conflated. The duke's rendering of Hamlet's soliloquy, which he tries to teach to the king, would have struck a familiar chord in nineteenth-century readers accustomed to the mangled Shakespeare they encountered in minstrelsy, as the following excerpt from "Hamlet the Dainty: An Ethiopian Burlesque," illustrates. When first confronted with his father's ghost, the minstrel Hamlet declares:

> He's from the South! Oh grace defend us!
> Prythee! no more such frightful specters send us!
> Be thou blacked up, or goblin damned!
> Be thou with whiskey puffed, or old cheese cram'd!
> Be thy intents indifferent, good or bad,
> I'll speak to thee, though look'st so like my dad—
> In a trim box, so snugly was't thou lain,
> Say! what the deuce e'er brought you out again?
> I like a joke myself—but 'tis not right,
> To come and frighten us to death at night.
> Say, why is this, will you the reason tell us?
> Why come to frighten me, Horatio and Marcellus.[19]

19. Gary D. Engle, *This Grotesque Essence: Plays from the American Minstrel Stage*, 87. The play was first performed by Christy's Minstrels in 1866.

One is immediately struck by the superiority of Twain's burlesque, while his debt to the minstrel tradition is unmistakable:

> To be, or not to be: that is the bare bodkin
> That makes calamity of so long life;
> For who would fardels bear, till Birnam wood do come to Dunsinane,
> But that the fear of something after death
> Murders the innocent sleep,
> Great nature's second course,
> And makes us rather sling the arrows of outrageous fortune
> Than fly to others that we know not of. (*AHF*, 179)

In another minstrel Shakespeare production, "Desdemonum," (1874) Desdemona speaks in bowdlerized black vernacular English:

> 'Tel [Othello], my duck, I hear you; daddy's gone to bed.
> Fotch along your ladderum, I'm de gal to wed!
> Since burnt-cork am de fashion, I'll not be behind—
> I'll see Oteller's wisage in his highfalutin' mind.[20]

Desdemona, as a white man in blackface playing a white woman who speaks in a black vernacular, would have been a one-actor tour de force of race and gender impersonation, and a wholly comic character. No one would mistake her for a "serious" character or seriously believe she was a woman. The same holds true of the king playing Juliet, although he nonetheless attempts to perform "serious" Shakespeare in the guise of Edmund Kean the Elder, "a world-renowned Tragedian."

As with the minstrel Shakespeare, the king's cross-dressed performance as Juliet, apparently intended to be taken seriously, is entirely comic. Even the king himself is initially skeptical about his ability to impersonate the fair Juliet: "'But if Juliet's such a young gal, duke, my peeled head and my white whiskers is goin' to look oncommon odd on her, maybe'" (*AHF*, 169). The duke reassures him by saying that "'these country jakes won't ever think of that. Besides, you know, you'll be in costume, and that makes all the difference in the world.'" This is the mark of the true con man, whose success depends upon the success of his guile, and his disguise. To him, the essence is nothing and the dis-

20. Ibid., 63.

guise is all. The duke then hauls out "a long white cotton night-shirt and a ruffled night-cap to match" for the king to wear. Thus dressed as the fair Juliet, and performing before an audience of Arkansas rubes, he fools no one and evokes only laughter.

One further cross-dressed episode must be laid at the feet of the duke and king: their decision to dress Jim as a "sick Arab" when they are away from the raft. Earlier, troubled by the thought that they cannot leave Jim alone on the raft during the day for fear that he will be "stolen," the duke prints a poster describing Jim as a fugitive slave, with a reward offered for his capture; they pose as his captors. They tie him up every day when they go ashore and make him lie all day in the wigwam. When Jim complains, the duke comes up with the "sick Arab" scheme, designed to let Jim move about more freely on the raft.

> He dressed Jim up in King Lear's outfit—it was a long curtain-calico gown, and a white horse-hair wig and whiskers; and then he took his theatre-paint and painted Jim's face and hands and ears and neck all over a dead dull solid blue, like a man that's been drownded nine days. Blamed if he warn't the horriblest looking outrage I ever see. Then the duke took and wrote out a sign on a shingle, so—
>
> *Sick Arab—but harmless when not out of his head.*
>
> And he nailed that shingle to a lath, and stood the lath up four or five foot in front of the wigwam. Jim was satisfied. He said it was a sight better than laying tied a couple of years every day and trembling all over every time there was a sound. The duke told him to make himself free and easy, and if anybody ever come meddling around, he must hop out of the wigwam, and carry on a little, and fetch a howl or two like a wild beast, and he reckoned they would light out and leave him alone. Which was sound enough judgment; but you take the average man, and he wouldn't wait for him to howl. Why, he didn't only look like he was dead, he looked considerable more than that. (*AHF*, 203–4)

Because Jim is dressed in a calico frock, the scene might seem to echo Huck's dressing up as Sarah Mary Williams, but here almost all of the playfulness has gone out of Twain's gender play. Instead, dressed as a sick Arab, Jim represents the twice-exoticized "other," which puts Jim at a further remove from Huck.[21] This scene also recalls the minstrel

---

21. In Marjorie Garber's terms, Jim as the "sick Arab" would be placed under the rather mischievously named category "The Chic of Araby" (*Vested Interests*, 304–52).

tradition, widely understood to be degrading to black men. Jim, as a black man, is made to become even blacker—he "blues up." Surely at this moment Jim as transvestite is indicative of a category crisis of the first order. Most centrally, a crisis is emerging about Jim's status in the novel; he was fully marginalized when the duke and king took over the raft, and now he faces the ever-present danger of being dragged or sold back into slavery as the foursome travel deeper into slave territory. The king and duke clearly mean him harm, and their ostensibly humane act of dressing Jim up is deeply cynical and sinister. Unlike Huck, who dresses in calico on his own accord, Jim is forced into his costume and once again into bondage. Whereas Jim good-naturedly dressed Huck, the duke's dressing of Jim reinforces the duke and king's claims of ownership of Jim. And unlike Huck, who layers identities over one another in his guise as a girl, Jim's identity, and his humanity, is obliterated by his costume and blue face.

The association of death with cross-dressing is reinforced here, too, explicitly: Jim looked "like a man's that's been drowned nine days." And he "didn't only look like he was dead, he looked considerably more than that." Later, when Huck believes he has escaped from the duke and king, whom he assumes are being held captive by friends of the Wilks family, he races back to the raft and yells out to Jim to set the raft loose:

> Jim lit out, and was a coming for me with both arms spread, he was so full of joy, but when I glimpsed him in the lightning, my heart shot up in my mouth, and I went overboard backwards; for I forgot he was old King Lear and a drownded A-rab all in one, and it most scared the livers and lights out of me. But Jim fished me out, and was going to hug me and bless me, and so on, he was so glad I was back and we was shut of the king and the duke, but I says:
> "Not now—have it for breakfast, have it for breakfast! Cut loose and let her slide!" (*AHF*, 259)

Jim being held captive by the king and duke and being dressed like a cross between King Lear and a sick Arab represents his symbolic death as Huck's partner. Until his final capture and imprisonment on the Phelps farm, from this point on Jim is rendered nearly invisible. The particular humiliation and self-effacement he experiences in this brief episode is nearly as disturbing as the way he is treated at the end of the novel in the problematic "evasion" section. As the critic Harold Beaver has observed, in this scene Jim "is reduced by the duke to a neutered madman in a 'long curtain-calico gown.'"[22] A madman, a sick Arab, a "wild beast," a man "that's been drowned nine days," a cross-dressed black man in blackface—this is Jim's fate on the raft when the two con men are in charge. The comedy is thin here, and ominous signs proliferate. The Jim we have known is dead to the reader until the scoundrels are themselves captured and run out of town on a rail. When he does reenter, it is as a nameless captive slave being held on the Phelps farm until a fictitious owner from near New Orleans can reclaim him and pay the advertised two-hundred-dollar reward.

Crossing gender boundaries and racial boundaries as Twain has done in the text, and therein challenging social expectations and assumptions, seems to have given rise to other gender disruptions as well. Three times the novel threatens to move into more explicit sexuality, and three times pulls back, primarily by Twain editing out key passages and scenes. Two scenes involve the king or the duke, but one, potentially the most transgressive, belongs to Jim's "ghost" story.[23] The most ribald of the three edited scenes is "The Burning Shame," as Twain originally referred to "The King's Camelopard or The Royal Nonesuch!!!" In the published version, the king "come a-prancing out on all fours, naked; and he was painted, all over, ring-streaked-and-striped, all sorts of colors, as splendid as a rain-bow. And—but never mind the rest of his outfit, it was just wild, but it was awful funny" (*AHF*, 196).

The genesis for the scene was a story told to Twain by his old friend Jim Gillis. It is clear from comments Twain made many years later that he regretted that he had to modify the original tale, and that he did so

22. Harold Beaver, "Run, Nigger, Run."
23. I accept here Harris's succinct distinctions between gender and sexuality: "Sex is not gender, and sexuality is neither sex nor gender, but sexuality—the production and regulation of physical desire—is directly related to both. Most important, it is deeply disruptive on individual and group levels, and all cultures evolve systems to control it. The public policing of private sexuality has been a major concern in American life for at least one hundred and fifty years" ("Mark Twain and Gender," 167); the "Ghost" story appeared in the first half of the *Huckleberry Finn* manuscript, only recently recovered. It is reprinted, with extensive notation, in the University of California Press 2003 edition of *Adventures of Huckleberry Finn*.

as late as either the typescript or the book's proofs: "I had to modify it considerably to make it proper for print, and this was a great damage. As Jim told it ['The Tragedy of the Burning Shame'], inventing it as he went along, I think it was one of the most outrageously funny things I have ever listened to. How mild it is in the book, and how pale; how extravagant and how gorgeous in its unprintable form!" While Walter Blair in *Mark Twain and Huckleberry Finn* was unable to identify any "indecent connotations" to "The Burning Shame," James Ellis has teased out the histories of the original story, as well as the "Camelopard" and "The Royal Nonesuch." Ellis found a pastiche of references to naked men and women, giant phalluses, lighted candles stuck in a cavorting actor's anus or "into the private parts of a woman."[24]

Even in its highly modified form, the king's performance is staged to appeal to the crude tastes of the all-male Arkansas audience, and to get revenge on the people of Brickville for laughing at the king and duke's previous Shakespearean performance. The Brickville audience "most killed themselves laughing," and demanded that the king's cavorting be repeated twice more before they realize that there is nothing more to the show. Just as the two con men predicted, the audience will not admit publicly that they have been duped, and instead tell all their friends to come to the next night's performance, and the next. On the third night, they come prepared to seek revenge, with their pockets jammed with rotten vegetables, dead cats, and "sickly eggs by the barrel" (*AHF,* 198). Once again they are outmaneuvered by the duke and king, who skip out before the show begins and head off down river on the raft, and "laugh their bones loose over the way they'd served them people." The sinister laughter here proves to be ironic, for it was their "Royal Nonesuch" scam that caught up with them in the end. When they laugh "their bones loose" they have no way of knowing they will ultimately be brought to some kind of justice for the way they played the Arkansas rubes.

The second sexualized scene features the king at a camp meeting. The sexually suggestive scenes were again edited out before the book went to press. What is notable about the deleted material is that it is

24. Twain's comments in Walter Blair, *Mark Twain and Huckleberry Finn,* 317; James Ellis, "The Bawdy Humor of 'The King's Camelopard' or 'The Royal Nonesuch,'" 733.

both sexualized and racialized. We will recall that the king set out to "work" a camp meeting, or revival, in the backwoods of Pokeville where nearly a thousand people had gathered. In the first preacher's shed that Huck and the king happen upon, the preacher "was lining-out a hymn," and working the congregation into a greater and greater frenzy:

> He lined out two lines, everybody sung it, and it was kind of grand to hear it, there was so many of them and they done it in such a rousing way; then he lined out two more for them to sing—and so on. The people woke up more and more, and sung louder and louder; and towards the end, some begun to groan, and some begun to shout. Then the preacher begun to preach; and begun in earnest, too. . . .
>
> And so on. You couldn't make out what the preacher said, any more, on account of the shouting and crying. Folks got up, everywheres in the crowd, and worked their way, just by main strength, to the mourners' bench, with the tears running down their faces; and when all the mourners had got up there to the front benches in a crowd, they sung, and shouted, and flung themselves down on the straw, just crazy and wild. (*AHF*, 171–72)

The original draft of the scene was longer and more extravagant. There was more call-and-response between the preacher and the congregation; there was also more religious ecstasy expressed by the people as they "wallowed" and "whooped" and hugged each other:

> One fat nigger woman about forty, was the worst. The white mourners couldn't fend her off, no way—fast as one would get loose, she'd tackle the next one, & smother *him*. Next, down she went in the straw, along with the rest, & wallowed around, clawing dirt & shouting glory hallelujah same as they did.
>
> Well, the first I knowed, the king got a start. He begun to warm up, & by & by he laid over them all, for whooping & hugging & wallowing. And when everything was just at it boomingest, he went a-charging up on the platform & flung his arms around the preacher & went to hugging him & kissing him, & crying all over him, & thanking him for saving him.[25]

25. See Appendix C, "Three Passages from the Manuscript: Mark Twain's Revisions," in Twain, *Huckleberry Finn*, 488. The excised passage has been reintroduced into the text proper in the 1996 Random House edition of *Huckleberry Finn*.

The editors of the California Press *Adventures of Huckleberry Finn* suggest that Twain changed the scene by "toning down the racial and religious satire," but he also muted the sexual overtones, shifting the emphasis from the king as opportunistic lecher to the king as swindler (*AHF*, 481). In the draft, Twain had moved farther into the carnivalesque space of his imagination, but by the time the novel reached the public, the moral order had been restored. The lords of misrule had their day, but only a day.

The most sexually suggestive of the emendations is Jim's "ghost" story, which was fully excised before the novel's publication. The phallus, only implied in the "Royal Nonesuch," is ever present in Jim's unmistakably homoerotic and comic story. The tale, which Jim tells to Huck while the two of them are waiting out a storm in a cave on Jackson's Island, features no fewer than four naked cadavers. The story begins when Huck asks Jim if he had ever seen a ghost, and Jim replies he certainly has, when he was about sixteen years old. He then proceeds to tell, in his own words, about being sent out one stormy night by his master, a student in a "doctor college," to go to the dissecting room and warm up a particular cadaver "en git him soft so he can cut him up—" (*AHF*, 466). Jim recalls that four naked corpses, all covered with sheets, were lying on a long table, their knees drawn up. He has to pull the covers back from each body to find the "big man wid de black whiskers."

> He was naked—dey all was. He was a layin' on round sticks—rollers. just in his shroud—do' it was a pooty cold night[.] I took de sheet off'n him en rolled him along feet fust, to de en' er de table befo' de fire place. His laigs was apart en his knees was cocked up some; so when I up-ended him on de en' er de table, he sot up dah looking pretty natural, wid his feet out en his big toes stickin' up like he was warmin' hissef. (*AHF*, 467)

Jim puts the sheet over the corpse's head and back, to help warm him up. As Jim is doing this, the corpse's eyes come open, which Jim says made him "feel all-overish," so he pulls the sheet down over the man's face and ties it under his chin: "en den dah he sot, all naked in front, wid his head like a big snow-ball. . . . So dah he sot, wid his laigs spread

out, but blame if he didn't look no better'n what he did befo', his head
was so awful, somehow." (*AHF*, 468)

To this point, Jim's story is a macabre comedy, but it gets stranger
as he goes on. Jim decides to take the candle out of his lantern so he
can see better, and to do so he bends over between the man's naked
legs; the candle flickers and Jim thinks he sees the dead man's legs
move, or more accurately, Jim says that "the old man moved his laigs."
To reassure himself, Jim reaches out to touch first one leg, then the other, and since both are "cold as ice," he concludes that the man did not
move. He reiterates to Huck that all this time his head was between the
man's legs. Then it happens again—Jim sees the old man move his toes,
and he can "feel" his eyes,

> "en see dat old dumplin' head done up in de sheet, en—
>   "Well, sir, jis' at dat minute *down he comes,* right a-straddle er my
> neck wid his cold laigs, en kicked de candle out!"
>   "My! What did you do, Jim?"
>   "Do? Well I never done nuffin', only I jis' got up en heeled it in de
> dark. *I* warn't gwyne to wait to fine out what he wanted. No sir; I jis'
> split down stairs en linked it home a-yelpin' every jump." (*AHF*, 468,
> 470)

This is a remarkable story, beautifully and economically crafted, comic,
frightening, and filled with sexual and homoerotic imagery—the man's
legs apart and his knees "cocked up,"[26] the corpse's big toes "sticking
up," Jim's head between the naked body's legs, Jim fumbling for the
phallic candle between the dead man's legs—all brought to a climax by
the corpse straddling Jim's neck. Jim's comment that he was not going
to wait to see "what he wanted" resounds with comic overtones, for it
assumes that the dead man wanted something from Jim and that Jim
wanted no part of whatever it was. It also puts Jim in rhetorical control
(even as he flees), for the comment is in response to Huck's question,
"What did you do, Jim?" Jim makes it clear that he considers the question to be foolish. We are left in the end with the final image of Jim flee-

---

26. As early as 1618, *cock* was used as a synonym for *penis,* while the verb form of the
word meant "to stick or turn up," "to stick stiffly," as well as "to bend a joint at an angle" *(Oxford English Dictionary).*

ing the scene as fast as he can, and Twain may be said to be right behind him.

In creating a homoerotic, comic scene, one inextricably linked to
death, was Twain taking liberties with the fact that Jim was black? It is
difficult not to reach that conclusion. The medical student who sends
Jim on the errand was white, and he certainly took advantage of Jim's
status to have him perform a task as onerous as warming up a corpse
for dissection. Because Jim is black, a man on the far margins of American society in the era Twain depicts, Twain has more latitude to make
him the narrator of a shocking, transgressive tale. The scene may well
have been a transracial one as well, for while statistically it was likely that
the cadavers were black, I think we must reach a different conclusion
about Jim's corpse. As Toni Morrison has observed, the way we know
in American literature that a figure is white is because no one says so;
no one says so here. Instead, the medical student told Jim only to warm
up the corpse with the black whiskers. Further, the story of tending to
the corpse was in fact based not on a black man but on Twain's uncle,
Jim Lampton, the half-brother of Twain's mother, Jane Lampton. Jim
Lampton apparently had an "incident" with a corpse when he was a
young medical student at McDowell College. Twain made reference to
the incident four times in his notebooks, over a period of thirty years,
yet he never used the story anywhere but in the draft of *Huckleberry
Finn,* and then only in the voice and experience of a black man, Jim.[27]
The story as it appeared in the original manuscript finally draws to an
end when Jim, in retrospect, wishes that he, not the medical student,
had had the chance to chop up the corpse. Twain may well have wished
he did not have to chop out the story, but he no doubt realized that it
was too transgressive, both racially and sexually, to include. Remarkably, he never found another place to use it, either as a scene in a larger work or as a short tale—it simply disappeared from view until the re-
covery of the first half of the novel's manuscript.

In his working notes, Twain wrote, "Wouldn't give a cent for an ad-

27. Toni Morrison, *Playing in the Dark: Whiteness and the Literary Imagination,* 47.
On the corpse with the black whiskers, the editors of *Huckleberry Finn,* while suggesting that it is likely the corpse was a black man, helpfully go on to point out that when a
medical student encounters a cadaver in *The Gilded Age,* it is black, and it is explicitly
identified as black (464, 463).

venture that ain't done in disguise." But of all the disguises Huck, Tom, and Jim might have assumed in the final adventures at the Phelps farm, the only costumes they don are women's. All three of the main characters cross-dress at some point, and these are the last disguises each of them will assume in the novel after a long and complex layering of identities. At the Phelps farm, Huck has assumed the identity of Tom Sawyer, and Tom takes on the identity of his half-brother, Sid Sawyer. Jim, too, is saddled with a false identity created by the duke's "wanted" posters and capitalized upon when the duke sells Jim to Silas Phelps for forty dollars. So each hero begins the "evasion" scene masquerading as someone else. Scores of scholars have debated the merits and disappointments of Twain's elaborate ending for *Huckleberry Finn,* beginning with Lionel Trilling's introduction to the novel in 1948. Gary P. Henrickson, in 1993, stated that "there were no fewer than eighty publications—articles, chapters, monographs—defending the ending of *Adventures of Huckleberry Finn* and innumerable discussions in longer works."[28] What has escaped the notice of Mark Twain's critics, however, is the fact that in the final hours of the evasion, all three male heroes—Tom, Huck, and Jim—cross-dress in the process of "freeing" Jim. Furthermore, in keeping with earlier scenes in the novel, each time one of the heroes puts on female clothing he crosses a racial boundary as well, in increasingly complex ways.

Huck is the first to cross-dress at the end. Tom tells him that he has to pose as a servant girl and, under the cover of darkness, put a note under the Phelpses' door, warning that "trouble is brewing." Ever practical, Huck can see no sense in going in disguise, arguing that he is not going to be seen in any event, but Tom's rule prevails. Huck also protests against Tom's directions for him to steal "the yaller girl's frock," arguing that is likely to be the only one she has, but Tom assures him that he will only keep it for fifteen minutes, and she will nev-

28. Appendix A, "Mark Twain's Working Notes," in Twain, *Adventures of Huckleberry Finn* (2003), 756; Lionel Trilling, introduction to *Adventures of Huckleberry Finn,* v–xviii; Gary P. Henrickson, "Biographers' Twain, Critics' Twain: Which of the Twains Wrote the 'Evasion'?" 14. For an additional summary and reprinting of criticisms and defenses of the novel's ending, see also Gerald Graff and James Phelan, "The Controversy over the Ending: Did Mark Twain Sell Jim Down the River?" 279, 284.

"Trouble is brewing": Huck as a servant girl.

er be the wiser. So Huck dutifully "smouched" the frock and put it on, thus crossing for the occasion both gender and racial lines. This final scene of Huck cross-dressing occupies only three lines in the text and might escape our notice were it not for Kemble's illustration.[29] Because the scene takes place outside our ken, we have no way of knowing if Huck was able to put to good use any of the advice given him by Judith Loftus about how to be a more authentic girl. Instead, he delivers up the warning and, one assumes, returns the frock to its rightful owner.

For their final escape, Tom assigns himself the role of Jim's mother,

---

29. Twain, *Huckleberry Finn*, 333.

who, according to his rules, should trade both clothes and places with the prisoner. If Tom had done so, however, he would have been left behind when the escape takes place, so he changes the script. He proposes first to steal Aunt Sally's dress and put it on, thereby playing the role of Jim's mother; he then plans to have Jim take the dress off him and put it on himself. He embellishes: "I'll stuff Jim's clothes full of straw and lay it on his bed to represent his mother in disguise, and Jim'll take aunt Sally's gown off of me and wear it, and we'll all evade together. When a prisoner of style escapes, it's called an evasion." This crucial moment both defines the "evasion," per se, and it determines that Jim will escape dressed as Aunt Sally. This sustained act of cross-dressing creates a gendered and racialized exchange between Aunt Sally and Jim, which has significant consequences for how the white people in the Phelpses' world unconsciously come to view Jim. Tom does take his brief turn as Jim's mother, cross-dressed in Aunt Sally's dress, but he does so mostly offstage, so to speak. He puts the dress on in front of Huck, then sends Huck off to fetch more butter for their cornbread; because Huck is detained by Aunt Sally, he is not present to witness Jim taking Aunt Sally's dress off Tom. By the time Huck catches up with Tom and Jim again, it is too dark for him to see Jim's dress or the scarecrow version of "his mother in disguise" on the bed.

What is crucial here is that Jim's long-awaited escape takes place with him dressed in Aunt Sally's gown. It is in that disguise that Jim heroically presents himself to the doctor to help nurse Tom back to health, and it is also as a cross-dressed Aunt Sally that he is brought back into captivity. Except for the moment when Aunt Sally first sees him dressed "in *her* calico dress," there is no further mention of his female costume (*AHF,* 351; emphasis in original). Even the doctor, in praising Jim's skill as a nurse and his self-sacrifice, makes no mention of his being in a dress. It is as though by this point in the novel, crossing gender boundaries is so commonplace it is no cause for comment. But Jim is also crossing racial boundaries when he is dressed as Aunt Sally; he is a black man in a white woman's dress. As a consequence, characteristics belonging to both Jim and Aunt Sally are merged and magnified. It is not as though Jim puts on Aunt Sally–like characteristics with her clothes—his positive qualities have been evident to Huck and to the reader for most of the novel—but for the first time others can see them in Jim because of his disguise and its association with Aunt Sally. While others in the novel cannot see past race, they can see through gender; thus when Jim masquerades as Aunt Sally, others can see his good-heartedness and his faithfulness.

Aunt Sally is a more complex female character than has generally been credited.[30] Although it is absolutely true that Tom and Huck make her the butt of their practical jokes and befuddle her with their pranks, she responds to their antics with spunk and indignation. Her eyes "snap"; she has a temper, and expresses it freely; and she "dusts" off the boys with her hickory switch. The final scene between Tom and Aunt Sally establishes beyond any doubt that she is a worthy match for him:

> "Well, I never heard the likes of it in all my born days! So it was *you*, you little rapscallions, that's been making all this trouble, and turned everybody's wits clean inside out and scared us all most to death. I've as good a notion as ever I had in my life, to take it out o' you this very minute. To think, here I've been, night after night, a—*you* just get well, once, you young scamp, and I lay I'll tan the Old Harry out o' both o' ye!"
>
> But Tom, he *was* so proud and joyful, he just *couldn't* hold in, and his tongue just *went* it—she a'chipping in, and spitting fire all along, and both of them going it at once, like a cat-convention. (*AHF,* 356)

The doctor's favorable report on Jim, embedded though it is in painfully racist language, comes at the ultimate crisis point in the novel, the point when all three main characters still are masquerading in multiple identities, and most significantly, the moment when Jim is enfolded in multiple degrees of freedom and enslavement. In the space of only a few chapters, this legally free man has been sold, imprisoned,

---

30. Shelley Fisher Fishkin includes Aunt Sally among Twain's women characters who "tend to be severely limited, stereotypical, and flat" ("Mark Twain and Women," 58). Nancy Walker takes Aunt Sally seriously by including her in a trio of female reformers in the novel (along with the Widow Douglas and Miss Watson), but Walker concludes that she is not a very effective reformer ("Reformers and Young Maidens: Women and Virtue in *Adventures of Huckleberry Finn,*" 499).

freed, reimprisoned, and freed again. Eric Lott has made a very disturbing observation about the minstrel shows that seems to apply to this novel. The minstrel shows, he says, "imagine race to be mutable; very briefly they throw off the burden of its construction, blurring the line between self and other . . . canceling racial boundaries *only to (triumphantly) reinstitute them.*"[31] Were it not for the final acts of cross-dressing, *Adventures of Huckleberry Finn* would be doing the same thing to Jim. But the ways in which Twain has his key characters cross simultaneously both gender and racial boundaries blurs those lines so radically that they cannot be fully reinstated in the end.

---

31. Eric Lott, *Love and Theft: Blackface Minstrelsy and the American Working Class,* 77 (emphasis added).

3

Beneath the Veil
Gender Play in *Pudd'nhead Wilson*

Critics of Mark Twain's work have long seen *Pudd'nhead Wilson* as a companion piece to *Adventures of Huckleberry Finn*.[1] Like *Huckleberry Finn*, the novel is set in antebellum Missouri in a village that greatly resembles Hannibal. The issue of slavery resides at the core of each novel, with Twain's humor effectively exposing multiple absurdities and cruelties of that social institution. Comparing *Pudd'nhead Wilson* with *Huckleberry Finn* does prove useful, especially in order to consider how *Pudd'nhead Wilson* extends much further the intricate relationship of cross-dressing and racial crossing; indeed, toward the end of this chapter, I will turn precisely to this issue in my investigation of *Pudd'nhead Wilson*. Nevertheless, there are compelling reasons also to read this tale as a companion piece to *Personal Recollections of Joan of Arc*, the two-volume work that Clemens believed was his best work. These two texts, both of which Twain was writing in the early 1890s, have much

A variation of this chapter was originally published as "Beneath the Veil: Clothing, Race, and Gender in Mark Twain's *Pudd'nhead Wilson*" (*Studies in American Fiction*, 27, no. 1 [1999]: 37–52).

1. See, for example, Shelley Fisher Fishkin, "Race and Culture at the Century's End: A Social Context for *Pudd'nhead Wilson*."

in common. Both are texts in which cross-dressing plays a prominent role and in which Twain gives considerable attention to details of dress and clothing, and both texts feature strong-willed female characters who defy patriarchal law.

Twain began working on what he initially called *Those Extraordinary Twins* in the summer of 1892, while living in Europe. That summer he also began to write *Personal Recollections of Joan of Arc*, a book he had been researching and contemplating off and on for over two decades. Especially during the time he lived in Florence, he continued to work on both books, now writing one and setting the other aside.[2] Twain continued to work on both books until each was published serially approximately a year apart—*Pudd'nhead Wilson* from December 1893 to June 1894 in *Century Magazine*, and *Joan of Arc* in *Harper's*, beginning in April 1895.

Compositional proximity alone would not qualify the books as companion pieces; rather, it is the strong central female character of each that invites us to read the two books in dialogue with one other. Both central characters, Roxana and Joan of Arc, are strong women who reveal deep-seated social fissures in their respective societies. They are both cross-dressers, albeit for entirely different reasons: Joan cross-dresses to lead her troops in battle and, when in prison and surrounded only by men, in order to preserve her modesty; ultimately, she insists that she cross-dresses against the dictates of the church because her voices tell her to. Roxana cross-dresses to escape from slavery. In short, both heroines play with gender in deadly earnest. Finally, both defy the patriarchy, for which they pay heavy prices. In both books, the law of the fathers is reasserted in the end, and in both that law is shown to be profoundly unjust. Joan is burned at the stake for refusing to forswear wearing men's clothing while in prison—the only "sin" the church fathers can make stick—while the very fate that Roxana sought to escape is visited upon her by the law when her son is sold down the river as a slave. Even given their similarities, however, it is difficult to imagine characters who are farther apart, and not just in terms of the times and

2. The family chose to settle for a time in Florence because Livy's doctors thought it would be good for her health; she was under strict orders not to have any visitors and not to go out, so the family's time in Italy was an especially quiet one, comparatively, for Twain.

countries in which the books are set. The one heroine, Joan, is based on a historical figure who was on her way to literal sainthood in Twain's time, although she was not beatified until 1909, nor canonized until 1920. Nonetheless, when Twain was writing her story, Joan had already begun to achieve iconic status in Europe and America. She was a historic heroine, the savior of France, a virgin, and a martyr. Roxana, in stark contrast, was a fictional mixed-race antebellum slave mother who violently disrupted the social order of her small town by secretly exchanging her baby in the cradle with the son of one of the leading white families of Dawson's Landing. Her action threatens the fundamental social structure upon which slave society was built. If Joan heard God's voice, and obeyed God's order as it was spoken to her, Roxana heard only her own voice, urging her to save her son by switching him with a free, white heir to a prominent family. Her son, who becomes the villain of the piece, was the issue of a cross-racial sexual liaison with one of the "finest gentlemen" in town. In sharp contrast with Joan, who kept both her virginity and her female modesty while surrounded by legions of male soldiers and scrutinized by the gaze of her male captors, Roxana expresses no regret about her illicit sexual relationship with Colonel Essex. On the contrary, she is proud both of her own white heritage, which she traces to Captain John Smith, and the high social status of her son's father, a descendent from the First Families of Virginia.

These significant differences notwithstanding, we have biographical evidence that suggests that Twain's work on *Joan of Arc* influenced his creation of Roxana as a prominent character in *Pudd'nhead Wilson*. In Twain's preface to the published version of *Those Extraordinary Twins,* he reports, drolly, how his original conception for a tale about Siamese twins was transformed into the novel *Pudd'nhead Wilson:*

> But the tale kept spreading along and spreading along, and other people got to intruding themselves and taking up more and more room with their talk and their affairs. Among them came a stranger named Pudd'nhead Wilson, and a woman named Roxana; and presently the doings of these two pushed up into prominence a young fellow named Tom Driscoll, whose proper place was away in the obscure background. Before the book was half finished these three were taking things almost entirely into their own hands and working the whole

tale as a private venture of their own—a tale which they had nothing at all to do with, by rights.

What this description does not reveal is how he initially conceived of Roxana and the role he imagined for her, once he decided to interject her into his story. Remarkably, that information is to be found in Twain's handwriting on the reverse side of three typed manuscript pages of *Personal Recollections of Joan of Arc*.[3]

On one crucial page, Twain penned "Motive" in large block letters. He then imagines a quarrel between Roxana and her son, Tom, followed by a dialogue between mother and son in which Roxana tells Tom exactly what he must do:

> "If you don't slip down *'dis very night'* & steal the money & pay the debt dey'll go to yo' uncle, jes as dey says in de letter"
> "What happen *den?*"
> "Old Marse dissenhurrit you *again* en for *good* dis time.
> En he'll stop de *pension*.
> I can't stand *dat*, en I *won't*.
> Take yo' choice—hog de money dis night or I tells de Jedge in de mornin' who you *is*. You'll be on de oction block in 2 minutes."[4]

Twain's "Motive," written out as it is on pages of his *Joan of Arc* manuscript, bespeaks the symbiotic relationship between the figures of

---

3. Mark Twain, *Pudd'nhead Wilson and Those Extraordinary Twins*, 126 (hereinafter the 2005 Norton edition will be cited as *PW*); in the same introduction to *Those Extraordinary Twins*, Twain says he carried the manuscript for *Pudd'nhead Wilson* back and forth across the Atlantic Ocean three times. It is most likely that he was carrying his *Joan of Arc* typescript (unfinished) on a November crossing of the Atlantic, and used that manuscript for scratch paper to work out his new version of *Pudd'nhead Wilson*. See the *Microfilm Edition of Mark Twain's Literary Manuscripts Available in the Mark Twain Papers*.

4. What follows in the "Motive" is a working out of the plot in a form that never in fact makes its way into the final text—Twain has Chambers (the white child exchanged for Tom in the cradle) walk in on his murdered uncle, whereupon he is accused of the murder and rushed off to jail either to be hanged or burned by the townspeople, in spite of Roxana's attempts to save him. Twain also has the uncle reveal to Tom that he is Tom's father, whereupon Tom murders him for that fact alone. Finally, in the brief "Motive," Twain tries to work out the conundrum of whether it is the "white" blood or the "black" blood in Tom that causes his corruption; the conclusion he reaches here, that it is the "white" blood, is never expressed in the text. Instead, Roxana passionately articulates the notion that it is Tom's "black" blood that makes him a coward.

MOTIVE

A QUARREL—then:

If you don't slip down "dis very night" + ~~steal the~~ money + pay the debt dey'll go to yo' uncle, jes as dey says in de letter.

What happen den?

Old Morse dissenherrit you again ~~en once~~ en for good, dis time.

En he'll stop de pension.

I can't stand dat, en I won't.

Take yo' choice — hog de money dis night or I tells de pledge in de mawnin' who you is. You'll be on de action block in 2 minutes. ~~They are on their way home.~~

Chambers enters at one door + drops toddy-glass + stands transfixed at same moment that twins enter + rush to lift the moribund.

Enter Aunt Pratt + proclaims all three. Rushed off to jail. Town rises, snatch Chambers out + would hang or burn him. Roxy ~~interferes~~ + tries to save him — is heroic, but fails. "Well, 'twould a ben my son if I hadn't change' 'em."

"Motive": Original plan for Roxana, written on the reverse side of a page of the *Joan of Arc* manuscript. *Courtesy of the Mark Twain Project, Bancroft Library, University of California, Berkeley (ms box 36A)*

Joan and Roxana. For all his enthusiasm for the finished novel *Personal Recollections of Joan of Arc,* Twain must have found writing the story of the historical Joan highly constraining. She was pure, divinely inspired, and saintly, and the story of her life was already well known. By contrast, the fictional mixed-race Roxana offered him enormous creative freedom. It is as though Twain wondered what would happen if the religious and noble public figure, Joan, with all her force and energy, were refigured as a nineteenth-century American black woman motivated only by personal considerations. She would be, as Roxana is, a powerful, disruptive force, a trickster figure who threatens to rend asunder the foundation of the social order.[5] Thus the "given" of Joan's cross-dressing, a topic that Twain explores in great detail in his novel about Joan of Arc, inspired Twain to create also the cross-dressed Roxana. As we shall see, Twain's attention to clothing in both texts is extensive, and in both, clothing becomes an unreliable marker that is both difficult for others to interpret and crucial to the well-being of each heroine.

Against an admittedly thin field of contenders, *Pudd'nhead Wilson*'s Roxana has been widely regarded as one of Twain's most fully realized female characters. As early as 1895, critics recognized the unusual quality of Roxana; an anonymous reviewer for the *Athenaeum* declared that "the best thing in *Pudd'nhead Wilson* . . . is the picture of the negro slave Roxana, the cause of all the trouble which gives scope to Mr. Wilson's ingenious discovery about finger-marks. Her gusts of passion or of despair, her vanity, her motherly love, and the glimpses of nobler feeling that are occasionally seen in her elementary code of morals, make her very human, and create a sympathy for her in spite of her unscrupulous actions." Bernard DeVoto saw "intense artistic courage" in the creation of Roxana, while Henry Nash Smith saw a "haughty grandeur in her character." Kenneth Lynn has similar, but more elaborate, praise for Roxana: "For Roxy is truly one of Twain's volcanoes, at once a liberator and a destroyer, a cunning and ruthless idealist who does not hesitate to kill in order to save." With the exception of Huckleberry Finn, Lynn declares, she was "the finest character in all of Twain's fiction."[6]

---

5. See Susan K. Harris, "Mark Twain's Bad Women," 162.
6. *Athenaeum,* January 19, 1895, quoted in *Pudd'nhead Wilson and Those Extraor-*

Leslie Fiedler, characteristically, finds a spicy way to praise her characterization: "Roxy," he says, is "a creature of passion and despair rare among the wooden images of virtue or bitchery that pass for females in American literature." Arthur Pettit's 1974 view of her, also provocative, is more troublesome; he refers to her as "a good deal darker than her physical appearance would lead us to believe," as a "near-*white* hussy," and as an "off-white woman." More recently, and far more sympathetically, Susan K. Harris characterizes Roxana as one of Twain's two "wicked" women, an attribution that does Roxana more credit than shame. The most sustained attention to Roxana appears in Carolyn Porter's "Roxana's Plot," an essay that is critical to the argument I make in this chapter. Porter quite correctly identifies Roxana as the prime mover in the text: "What comes into and out of focus in Twain's portrayal of Roxana is a region where mothers are sexual, slaves are powerful, and women are temporarily out of (and thus in) control. Roxana's agenda as a protagonist is set by her status as a slave mother, but in pursuing that agenda, she exposes not only the falseness of the Mammy/Jezebel opposition but also the inadequacy of either 'Mammy' *or* 'Jezebel' to contain or represent the slave woman." In essence, Porter argues, "*Pudd'nhead Wilson* is the scene of conflict between a repressive paternal plot and a subversive maternal one," but, as Porter is quick to point out, the patriarchal order ultimately triumphs.[7] Before it does, however, Roxana upsets the social order of Dawson's Landing by exchanging in their cribs her legally black baby and the white heir to the most prominent family in town; the babies, born on the same day, are indistinguishable to anyone but Roxana.

Marjorie Garber uses the term "changeling boys" to refer to the kind of exchange Roxana makes between the two infants. In Garber's terms, the changeling boy is always something of a fantasy child, "an idea that can never be realized or possessed. Like the transvestite marking the space of representation itself, the changeling boy is that which, by def-

---

dinary Twins, 242; Bernard DeVoto, "Mark Twain's Presentation of Slavery," 247; Henry Nash Smith, "*Pudd'nhead Wilson* as Criticism of the Dominant Culture," 275; Kenneth Lynn, *Mark Twain and Southwestern Humor,* 264, 265.

7. Fiedler, quoted in *Pudd'nhead Wilson and Those Extraordinary Twins,* 249; Arthur Pettit, "The Black and White Curse: *Pudd'nhead Wilson* and Miscegenation," 329; Harris, "Mark Twain's Bad Women," 157–58; Carolyn Porter, "Roxana's Plot," 124.

inition, can never be present. For the minute he comes to be embodied, it is clear that he cannot be that which is so desperately sought."[8] Garber's observation proves to be true of both children Roxana exchanges, for she is never able to have the relationship she desires with her own son, Chambers/Tom, and Tom/Chambers disappears from the text shortly after the beginning. Once Roxana exchanges the babies, to save her son from the threat of being one day sold down the river as a slave, their lives are forever altered. It is a bold and spontaneous move, one motivated by a mother's love for her child, and one that upsets the social order not so much because of the social roles ascribed (wrongly) to each child, but more fundamentally because a race-based slave society depended upon people being able to tell who was "black" and who was "white," who was a slave and who a free man or woman.

Part of what makes Roxana such a powerful figure for many of Twain's readers transpires before the novel opens: namely, she is a sexual woman, and the proof of this fact is that she gives birth to Valet de Chambre. Certainly other female figures in Twain's work are mothers, and also presumably are sexually active, but somehow it is not the same. Roxana's sexuality does not take place within the bonds of marriage, and it is born out of desire, not marital duty. Historically, cross-racial sexuality during the time of slavery always carried the suspicion of coercion or rape, and indeed slave narratives, especially those written by women, almost all have rape or the threat of rape as one of the central oppressions faced by female slaves.[9] Had Twain followed his original "Motive" for *Pudd'nhead Wilson*, Chambers/Tom's father would have been Roxana's master/owner, thereby making Roxana the likely subject of sexual coercion or rape. Having Chambers's father be an equally powerful, but unrelated, white man, suggests instead the possibility of consensual sex across the color line, and powerfully suggests that

8. Garber, *Vested Interests*, 92. Although Garber devotes some critical attention to *Pudd'nhead Wilson*, she does not apply the term "changeling boys" directly to that text. It is a useful concept, however, in helping us understand Roxana's problematic relationship to her son, exchanged for the white heir to the Driscoll family.
9. The theme is not limited to narratives written during slavery; Toni Morrison's *Beloved* most famously and powerfully tells the story of white male sexual exploitations of slave women.

Roxana had agency in the affair. Roxana offers no apology for her illicit liaison with Colonel Cecil Burleigh Essex; to the contrary, she takes
great pride in his lineage and her son's heritage on both sides of his
parentage. Further, no one in Dawson's Landing comments on Roxana's sexual activity, nor does Twain's narrator. Instead, Roxana stands,
in the text, as a symbol for a subversive, barely suppressed, interracial
desire. Clearly the good citizens of Dawson's Landing have been crossing and recrossing the color line under the cover of darkness for generations.

Because Roxana is such an anomaly in Twain's work, or if Fiedler is
correct, in all of American literature, a few critics have become over-
invested in Roxana's sexuality. Kenneth Lynn, writing in the 1950s,
interprets Roxana in the following terms:

> Roxy . . . is a startling vital character with whom Mark Twain seems
> to have been emotionally involved. Portrayed alternately as *immense-
> ly desirable* and *luridly threatening*, as if Twain were not so much cre-
> ating a character as projecting an inner conflict, she has the daemon-
> ic magnetism of a figure of myth, or of dreams. In the fantastic scene
> where she looms up before Tom Driscoll in the haunted house and
> reclaims him as her son, we feel ourselves in contact not with the "re-
> ality" of the Negro slave, but with the guilt, the fears, and the illicit
> desires of the antebellum white South. From these emotions the adult
> Mark Twain had never shaken himself free. Whether Mark Twain ever
> fantasied, as so many Southern boys from time immemorial have
> done, that his real mother was a Negro mammy, we do not know; but
> a passage in Twain's notebook demonstrates that this son of the Old
> South had extremely ambivalent feelings about a black mistress, if not
> about a black mother. Long after he had left Missouri, the image of
> a sexually complaisant Negress continued to haunt Mark Twain's
> dreams.

Just as Lynn claims Twain projected the "illicit desires of the antebellum South" onto the figure of Roxana, here the critic also seems to project onto Roxana. How else do we account for the representation of
Roxana as "immensely desirable" and "luridly threatening"? How else
can we imagine Roxana's confrontation with her son as a moment when
we are "in contact with . . . illicit desires"? Others have suggested that
Roxana's blackness freed Twain from the usual constraints he exercised

in depicting female characters—his famous widows and spinsters—but few go as far as Lynn in confounding race, gender, and sexuality. Robert Wiggins says that Twain comes close to creating a "full-length female character in Roxana, probably because she was a Negro and therefore could be treated as a primitive like Huck, Tom, Jim, Pap, and a lesser gallery of such characters." Frederick Anderson, in his introduction to a 1968 edition of *Pudd'nhead Wilson*, says that Roxy is Twain's most successful female protagonist: "it appears that he required the distance provided by color to establish and sustain the vulgar quality of life in a female character."[10]

A whole complex of reasons, beyond her sexuality, entitles Roxana to be called one of Twain's most powerful female figures. She embodies, literally, the "fiction of law and custom" that identifies her as "black," although she is fifteen-sixteenths "white." Roxana looks white, and she is described as attractive—"even beautiful"—

> She was of majestic form and stature . . . and her gestures and movements distinguished by a noble and stately grace. . . . She had an easy, independent carriage—when she was among her own caste—and a high and "sassy" way, withal; but of course she was meek and humble enough where white people were.
>
> To all intents and purposes Roxy was as white as anybody, but the one-sixteenth of her which was black out-voted the other fifteen parts and made her a negro. She was a slave, and salable as such. (*PW*, 9)

Even as a slave, she exerts her independence by boldly exchanging the babies in their cribs. Once she is freed from slavery, upon the death of her master, she ventures off to a life of her own. She becomes a successful chambermaid on a Mississippi riverboat, and she saves money for her old age. Through no fault of her own, she is the unfortunate victim of a bank closure and must return to Dawson's Landing to seek money from her son, now the heir to the Driscoll fortune. He is unusually rude to her, still believing her to be his mammy, not his mother, and he pushes aside her requests. He has only himself to blame when

---

10. Lynn, *Mark Twain and Southwestern Humor*, 266, emphasis added; Robert Wiggins, "The Flawed Structure of *Pudd'nhead Wilson*," 255; Fredrick Anderson, introduction to *Pudd'nhead Wilson and Those Extraordinary Twins*, 285.

she ultimately reveals to him that she is his mother and makes him call her "Mother." When he subsequently sells her down the river once more into slavery in order to pay his gambling debts, she escapes and makes her way back to St. Louis, where she compels her son to beg her forgiveness on his knees. From that moment on, they conspire in robbing their neighbors to gain the money they lack, but Roxana keeps the upper hand over her son. Even when she turns criminal, as she does as an accomplice, we have to admire her spunk and boldness. In short, she has earned her reputation as one of Twain's most powerful female characters, but the true nature of her complexity has yet to be fully appreciated.

If Roxana's character confounds racial categories, she simultaneously problematizes gender categories as well. So far as I can discern, there are no prototypes for her character in male-authored literature. To find a "black" female character with her strength and subversive quality, we have to go back either to slave narratives, such as the story of Ellen Craft, who escaped from slavery by traveling north cross-dressed as a white man, accompanied by her male "slave"—her husband. The cross-dressing parallel is instructive, and both Roxana and Ellen Craft, although slaves, are light enough to pass for white—Ellen if she is not asked to write, because she is illiterate, and Roxana if she is not asked to speak, because she speaks in black dialect. The influence of slave narratives upon *Pudd'nhead Wilson,* and especially upon Roxana, is felt most forcefully in the long account she gives her son of her escape from slavery (*PW*, 90–94). The scene occupies two full pages of text—approximately one thousand words—none of them essential to the main plot or to subsequent events. Instead, it is a story within a story, echoing slave narratives' familiar stories of physical oppression, an insecure Yankee mistress, and a cruel overseer. Roxana's escape is also familiar, brought about in this instance both by the cruelty she endures and the cruelty she witnesses, perpetrated against a young slave girl; Roxana rises up against the overseer, beats him with a stick, escapes on horseback, receives assistance from other black folks, and disguises herself as a man. Unlike Ellen Craft, however, who passes as a white man, Roxana wears the disguise of a black man, a role for which she must "black up" to be convincing.

Perhaps the most compelling fictional black woman comparable to

Roxana in strength and daring is Harriet Beecher Stowe's Cassy, from *Uncle Tom's Cabin,* as Kenneth Lynn astutely noted in 1986; however, subsequent critics have not followed his lead in crediting Stowe as an influence on Twain. Lynn emphasizes the similarities between the key figures, Roxana and Cassy, and offers an extended comparison between the two fictional, mixed-race figures:

> But with the single exception of Huck Finn, the finest character in all of Twain's fiction is volcanic Roxy. She is not, it must be said, entirely an original creation—her personality comes too close to that of Cassy in *Uncle Tom's Cabin* to be mere coincidence. In appearance, Cassy and Roxy are nearly identical—strong, beautiful, and nearly white; in personality, they are both proud, imperious, and as ruthlessly capable of wielding a knife as any man; sexually promiscuous, they are also fiercely devoted mothers who are prepared to sacrifice everything for the well-being of their sons. Striking as these similarities are, however, there are also significant differences between the two characterizations. Adhering to the formulas of the sentimental novel, Mrs. Stowe transformed Cassy toward the close of *Uncle Tom's Cabin* into a devout Christian and a doting grandmother who sends her son off to a life of happiness in Africa. Twain disdained such dishonest compromises. Roxy is a greater character than her prototype, first of all because Twain was more faithful to the tragic limitations imposed on the Negro woman's mind and morals by the institution of slavery: Roxy never reforms. Roxy, too, has much more emotional depth than Cassy. Cassy is a somewhat flat character, a character who is illuminated from without, by the white spotlight of her creator's New England conscience. Mrs. Stowe's understanding of her is a detached understanding; she sees Cassy as an object lesson; she is sorry for her; and there she stops.[11]

In calling Cassy a prototype for Twain's Roxana, Lynn acknowledges Twain's literary debt to Harriet Beecher Stowe, although he makes the claim in the negative—that is, the comparison is too close to be a coincidence. The explicit comparison, however, is built upon a partial mis-

---

11. Lynn, *Mark Twain and Southwestern Humor,* 265–66; on Stowe as a direct influence on Twain, see Ellen Moers, "A Note on Mark Twain and Harriet Beecher Stowe"; see also Judie Newman, who argues that Stowe's *Dred* was a precursor for *Pudd'nhead Wilson,* noting a series of parallels in the plots of the two novels ("Was Tom White? Stowe's *Dred* and Twain's *Pudd'nhead Wilson*").

reading of both Cassy and Roxana; for many modern readers of *Uncle Tom's Cabin*, Cassy is one of the most arresting and subversive characters in the text, and Twain's achievement in his creation of Roxana would not be lessened by granting full credit to Stowe's earlier, daring creation of Cassy. Lynn also partially misreads Roxana, for while she may not repent, she does retreat to her church at the end of the story. Twain's last words about Roxana represent her as heartbroken that her son was sold down the river into slavery: "In her church and its affairs she found her only solace" (*PW*, 120). These caveats notwithstanding, Lynn's observations about Twain's debt to Stowe confirm my own sense of her important, if sometimes subtle, literary influence on his career.

More recently, Leland Krauth devoted a chapter to the relationship between Harriet Beecher Stowe and Mark Twain, noting that "whatever genre Twain turned to as a writer, Stowe had already written in." He acknowledges, however, that Twain always fell short of crediting Stowe as an influence upon him, and Krauth follows his example. One of the many characteristics they shared in common, Krauth points out, was "the Gothic, especially what has come to be known as the Gothic body." Its most striking appearance in Stowe's work was in her depiction of Simon Legree and the Gothic horror he engenders. Cassy, by contrast, is seen by Krauth as relatively disembodied, a ghostly figure who nonetheless "frees herself (and Emmeline) by manipulating the Gothic. . . . In short, she plays with Legree's fear and creates for him stock but terrifying Gothic horror."[12] Krauth's view of Cassy, like Lynn's, is sympathetic to her plight as a virtual captive of Legree, but he does not credit her with the same kind of agency exhibited by Roxana.

One of the major subtexts in *Pudd'nhead Wilson* is the story's fascination with and reliance upon detailed descriptions of clothing and dress. These become distinctive, but unreliable, markers of both race and gender. Indeed, at major points in the text, they become unreliable markers of both simultaneously. Twain's fictional interest in dress and clothing began in earnest in *The Prince and the Pauper*, another story in which two boys look enough alike to be twins, and who exchange

---

12. Leland Krauth, *Mark Twain and Company: Six Literary Relations*, 88, 93, 102.

places when they innocently swap clothing. In that text, Twain crosses a class divide that appeared to be as fixed as the racial divide in the antebellum South. He intensifies class differences by playing at the extremes, with one boy being the heir to the throne of England while the other boy was from the poorest of the poor paupers of sixteenth-century England. The exchange of clothing between the two boys that sets the plot into motion occurs in the opening chapters of the book, but once the story begins to unfold, Twain's attention to the boys' clothing falls away and he becomes more concerned about the prince's experiences among the poor as he struggles to regain his rightful place.

In *Pudd'nhead Wilson*, clothing is at once a subject in its own right, as when Roxana dresses herself in her finest clothing as she prepares to drown herself and her son, and a marker of race and gender as these subjects are played out in relation to the two mixed-race characters in the novel, Roxana and her son Chambers/Tom. Representations of their clothing confound the already problematic category of race and problematize the category of gender. As Susan Gillman expresses the connection, "if 'male' and 'female' are as readily interchanged as 'black' and 'white,' then gender difference may prove to be as culturally constituted, as much 'a fiction of law and custom' as racial difference."[13] The effect of such confounding, as we will see, is to further destabilize the precarious social order of Dawson's Landing and the post-Reconstruction South of Twain's own time.

In our first introduction to Roxana we do not see her, only hear her, as she exchanges witticisms with a slave named Jasper. We do not need to see her, however, to know by her dialect that she is "black": "'Oh, yes, *you* got me, hain't you. 'Clah to goodness if dat conceit o' yo'n strikes in, Jasper, it gwyne to kill you, sho'. If you b'longed to me I'd sell you down de river 'fo' you git too fur gone'" (*PW*, 9). The narrator immediately both confirms and contradicts our assumptions: "From Roxy's manner of speech, a stranger would have expected her to be black, but she was not: Only one-sixteenth of her was black, and that sixteenth did not show." In Mark Twain's South—whether the antebellum era in which the story is set or the post-Reconstruction era in which it was written—"by a fiction of law and custom," Roxana is

---

13. Gillman, *Dark Twins,* 79.

"black." Her race is confirmed in the text by the fact that her "heavy suit of fine soft [brown] hair" is concealed "with a checkered handkerchief" (*PW*, 9). Set against her "white" appearance, including her "soft hair," Twain chooses here one of the most powerful and persistent racial markers with which to identify Roxana—her head rag.[14] From this moment on, Roxana *is* "black"—her race does "show." The head rag as a marker of racial identity is reinforced later in the text when Roxana becomes a fugitive slave, hotly pursued by her "master"; following the practice of the day, the master has a "wanted" poster made for Roxana: "The handbill had the usual rude wood-cut of a turbaned negro woman running, with the customary bundle on a stick over her shoulder, and the heading, in bold type, '*$100 Reward*'" (*PW*, 94). In other words, the handbill evokes the stereotyped image of the escaped slave woman, and it pins that stereotype on Roxana.

The two infant boys, one "black" and one "white," who are born on the same day and entrusted wholly to Roxana's care, can only be distinguished from one another by their clothing. Tom's clothes are described briefly, but in detail, calling attention to their fabric and their ruffles, while Chambers is dressed in the unmistakable clothing of a slave child: a "miserably short little gray tow-linen shirt" (*PW*, 15). The transformative event of the novel—the exchange of the babies—begins when Roxana privately declares her intention to drown herself and her baby to save him from the fate of being sold down the river. However, her action is arrested as she catches "sight of her new Sunday gown," a chance event that sets the plot in motion in a different direction. She looks down at her own slave's clothing, her linsey-woolsey dress, and vows not to be "fished out" of the river looking so "misable." In the passage that follows, Twain displays his unmistakable fascination with the details of female clothing, for nothing in the plot requires him to give so much attention to Roxana making her "death-toilet." Central to the process of preparing her death attire, Roxana sheds one marker of race, her head rag, and lets her soft "white" hair hang loose.

> She put down the child and made the change [into the dress]. She looked in the glass and was astonished at her beauty. She resolved to

14. See Turner, *Ceramic Uncles*, especially the chapter "Back to the Kitchen," 41–61.

make her death-toilet perfect. She took off her handkerchief-turban and dressed her glossy wealth of hair "like white folks"; she added some odds and ends of rather lurid ribbon and a spray of atrocious artificial flowers; finally, she threw over her shoulders a fluffy thing called a "cloud" in that day, which was of a blazing red complexion. Then she was ready for the tomb. (*PW,* 14–15)

What Roxana sees when she looks in the mirror is her own beauty—that is, her constructed white self—in contrast to the equally constructed black image reflected back to her by Southern society. The faintly mocking tone of the narrator is not heard by Roxana, who is clearly pleased by the image of herself that she creates. This image empowers her, just as later dressing as a man will empower her.

Roxana may be "ready for the tomb," but her son is not. Having completed her toilette, she turns her gaze on her son and is appalled by his clothing. When she "noted the contrast between its pauper shabbiness and her own volcanic irruption of infernal splendors, her mother-heart was touched, and she was ashamed." She was ashamed, that is, not of her own dress, but of her son's racially marked clothing that she characterizes as "too indelicate" for the heaven where they are bound. Ever resourceful (and spontaneous), Roxana dresses Chambers in the only fine clothing available, which is Tom's, and echoing her surprise at her own image in the mirror, she is now astonished at how "lovely" Chambers appears dressed in "white" clothing. Only then does she conceive the plan to exchange her "black" son with her "white" charge. Chambers has to be stripped naked in order to assume his new identity as Tom; only then can he don his "dainty flummery of ruffles" (*PW,* 15).[15] Tom, too, is "stripped of everything" and dressed in tow-linen, which marks him in everyone's eyes as a slave. By this act, Tom is stripped of his name, his identity, his inheritance, his paternity (albeit

15. As with gendered pronouns in stories such as "1002nd Arabian Night," the names of the exchanged boys can become confusing; I follow Twain's lead in calling each boy by the name that goes with his new identity. From the perspective of the casual modern reader of *Pudd'nhead Wilson,* confronted with the original illustrations of the two babies, there would appear to be gender confusions as well as racial confusions taking place: the fancy dress that is exchanged would be suitable now only for a girl. In the nineteenth century, of course, and into the early twentieth century, young male children wore what we would now call dresses. Further, Marjorie Garber points out that as recently as World War II, male babies were dressed in pink and female babies in blue (*Vested Interests,* 1).

both children are fathered by two of the town's most distinguished citizens), and his freedom. Roxana stands back to view her handiwork and exclaims, "Now who would b'lieve clo'es could do de like o' dat?" (*PW*, 16).

Thus, in the early pages of the novel, Twain establishes that clothing and dress will carry the weight of race as it is performed (and deconstructed) in the novel. The expected, indeed purportedly "indelible" stamps of race, both black and white—facial features, hair, skin color—are unreliable from the beginning. Because the supposedly "natural" boundaries between the races were threatened by racial mixing, society demanded they be reinforced by new socially constructed boundaries and powerful markers. Yet Roxana's action demonstrates that these, too, are unreliable, even deceptive. Dawson's Landing, unbeknownst to its principal citizens, is in the midst of a cultural crisis: its socially constructed codes are unraveling before their very eyes.

As a young boy, the changeling "Tom," who knows nothing of his black identity, is now the master of "Chambers," the real heir to the Driscoll name and fortune. Tom is spoiled by both Roxana and the white families with whom he resides. Pampered, undisciplined, indulged, he tyrannizes Chambers and treats Roxana with contempt. Chambers, in contrast, is quickly taught his place as a slave. The relationship between the two boys is expressed in part through metaphors of clothing. Tom, who is a coward and a bully, makes Chambers do all his fighting for him; consequently, Chambers earns a reputation as an accomplished fighter, until "by and by . . . Tom could have changed clothes with him, and 'ridden in peace,' like Sir Kay in Lancelot's armor" (*PW*, 21). There is no hint of irony in this passage, no sense that Twain is making a conscious joke about the exchange of identities that has already taken place, although the passage evokes in its readers that ever-present knowledge. The literal "armor" that Chambers wears is Tom's old cast-off, worn-out clothes that are described ironically by Twain as "holy": "'holy' red mittens, and 'holy' shoes, and pants 'holy' at the knees and seat" (*PW*, 21).

Twain's exploration of the childhood relationship between Tom and Chambers comes to an end when Chambers saves Tom from drowning, which earns him only insults for his trouble. Their playmates tease Tom that Chambers is his "Nigger-pappy—to signify that he had had a second birth into his life, and that Chambers was the author of his new being." Infuriated by the taunting, Tom orders Chambers to attack the boys. When he fails to do so, Tom "drove his pocket knife into him two or three times before the boys could snatch him away and give the wounded lad a chance to escape" (*PW*, 23). And escape he does. After this scene, Twain has no more interest in Chambers until the end of the story; he slips out of sight while Tom takes center stage as the (wrongful) heir to the Driscoll name and fortune.

When he is nineteen, Tom is sent off to Yale, where he learns to "tipple," to gamble, and to affect "eastern fashion." Upon returning to Dawson's Landing, he particularly offended the young people of his social set by his dandyism, especially his wearing of gloves. He also "brought home with him a suit of clothes of such exquisite style and cut and fashion—eastern fashion, city fashion—that it filled everybody with anguish and was regarded as a particularly wanton affront" (*PW*, 26). In a scene rich with foreshadowing, the young people of Dawson's Landing set about to cure Tom of his affectations by mocking his style of dress. Specifically, they tailor a suit that burlesques Tom's, and they put it on the town's "old deformed negro bellringer." He follows Tom through the streets, "tricked out in a flamboyant curtain-calico exaggeration of his finery, and imitating his fancy eastern graces as well as he could." The mockery works. "Tom surrendered, and after that clothed himself in the local fashion" (*PW*, 26).

In commenting on this scene, Myra Jehlen rather enigmatically asserts that "it is unclear just what is being satirized: is it simply foppish pretensions, or rather some absurdity of black foppery? Because the characters are unaware that their parody of Tom possesses this additional dimension, it becomes a joke shared by the narrator and the reader, a joke with a new target." Eric Lott reads the incident as "a sort of minstrel gag in reverse; the black man burlesques Tom's acquired graces, and does so at the behest of an audience of village white boys. . . . [I]t also suggests that Tom's whiteness is itself an act, a suggestion that is truer than either the bellringer or Tom can know since Tom's identity is precisely a black man's whiteface performance." More fundamentally, we might wonder why this scene has such a haunting quality about it. We are left with the image of the black bell ringer shadowing Tom through the streets of Dawson's Landing, mirroring Tom in a distorted mirror that reflects both his costume and his manners. Tom has been perceived by his contemporaries as feminized, which is suggested by reference to his "fancy eastern graces." Later, as we shall see, when Tom cross-dresses as a young girl and, like Huck Finn, practices *being* a girl, this same language is echoed in the text. By then he will know that, by society's definitions, he is "black" not "white," and he will assume a series of masquerades to deceive the townspeople. The bell ringer, by contrast, is a figure used to reestablish, at least temporarily, Dawson's Landing's social order, which its young male citizens believe has been disrupted by Tom's putting on airs. The scene is carnivalesque, with the lowliest member of the community, the deformed Negro bell ringer, dressed in clothing intended to mock a member of the town's most privileged class. While the black bell ringer is not protected by the customs of a festival as he would be in Bahktin's ceremonial world, he is protected by the cover of the white youths on whose behalf he performs. Nothing in the text suggests that the black bell ringer is himself foolish or absurd, and to assume the joke is somehow on Tom because he is "really" black but does not know it misses the point. Lott's notion that Tom's whiteness is itself a performance comes much closer to the mark, for race and gender converge here, as elsewhere in the story, and both require repeated performances. As a consequence, they are open to exaggeration and further imitation. In this text, it is often difficult to know what is the "real" and what is the imitation.[16]

Cured of his worst pretensions, Tom nonetheless continues to commit offenses against the social order. He accrues a sizable gambling debt that, if revealed, will cause him to be disinherited, so he resorts to theft and deceit to pay off his creditors. In order to steal from the villagers of Dawson's Landing, he assumes a series of disguises to mask his identity. Most powerfully (and most successfully), he cross-dresses both as a young girl and as an old woman. The first time we see him cross-

16. Myra Jehlen, "The Ties That Bind: Race and Sex in *Pudd'nhead Wilson*," 416; Lott, "Mr. Clemens and Jim Crow," 145. From Butler's perspective, this is precisely the point about gender performativity, particularly the relationship between homosexuality and heterosexuality, in which the latter is assumed to be the "real," and the former an imitation. Neither assumption is correct, according to Butler; each requires repeated performances (Judith Butler, "Imitation and Gender Insubordination").

dressed as a girl, we watch him through Pudd'nhead Wilson's eyes, although neither the reader nor Wilson know at that moment that the "girl" we are watching is Tom. The scene is represented twice in the text, first from David Wilson's perspective and the second time from Tom's; thus the text itself reinforces structurally that performing a gender requires repetition.

In the first instance, Wilson chances to look out of his window across a vacant lot into Tom's bedroom window in Judge Driscoll's house. There he sees a girl in a pink and white striped dress "practicing steps, gaits and attitudes, apparently; she was doing the thing gracefully, and was very much absorbed in her work" (*PW*, 36). Wilson wonders what a girl is doing in Tom's bedroom and for some time tries, unsuccessfully, to discover her identity. Three chapters later, Twain repeats the same scene but this time from Tom's point of view, not Wilson's. This second time, the scene is dramatized much more fully and more elaborately, so much so that we do not know at first we are witnessing the same dramatization we have seen before. Until close to the end of the scene, there is no mention at all of David Wilson.

> He [Tom] arrived at the haunted house in disguise on the Wednesday before the advent of the Twins,—after writing his aunt Pratt that he would not arrive until two days later—and lay in hiding there with his mother until toward daylight Friday morning, when he went to his uncle's house and entered by the back way with his own key and slipped up to his room, where he could have the use of mirror and toilet articles. He had a suit of girl's clothes with him in a bundle as a disguise for his raid, and was wearing a suit of his mother's clothing, with black gloves and veil. By dawn he was tricked out for his raid. (*PW*, 50–51)

While Wilson had seen only a girl in a striped summer dress in Tom's room, we now see Tom cross-dressed not once, not twice, but eventually three times—first in his mother's clothing, then as the young girl Wilson sees, than again as an old woman. The added detail of the second female identity assumed by Tom is further intensified by the new information that he had slipped into his own room at his uncle's house so "he could have the use of [a] mirror." While David Wilson is watching Tom, not knowing who he is, Tom is gazing at one of his female selves in the mirror. He is in the act of performing a gender as surely as his life has become an act of performing a race. Further, the scene and imagery recall his mother's act of looking at herself in the mirror just before she chances upon the scheme to exchange the babies, turning the "black" Chambers into the "white" Tom.

The scene is filled with images of performing, posturing, mirroring. Just after the scene cited above, Tom notices that Wilson is watching him from his house. The two men, to use Twain's words, "caught a glimpse" of each other peering through their respective windows. Far from being upset by his discovery that Wilson is watching him, Tom "entertained Wilson with some airs and graces and attitudes for a while" (*PW*, 51). Tom deliberately performs for Wilson as a girl, and as a girl he is apparently wholly convincing. Only after Wilson is confronted with other, overwhelming evidence that Tom is an impostor does he "see" beyond the female masquerade: "Idiot that I was! Nothing but a *girl* would do me—a man in girl's clothes never occurred to me" (*PW*, 109). This is the admission of one of the two founders of the Society of Free Thinkers in the town; if he is unable to see beyond Tom's cross-gendered disguise, who can?[17]

After his performance, however, Tom is not entirely confident that he has thrown Wilson off track and so changes back into his mother's clothes before leaving the house.

> Then [Tom] stepped out of sight and resumed the other disguise, and by and by went down and out the back way and started downtown to reconnoitre the scene of his intended labors.
>
> But he was ill at ease. He had changed back to Roxy's dress, with the stoop of age added to the disguise, so that Wilson would not bother himself about a humble old woman leaving a neighbor's house by the back way in the early morning, in case he was still spying. (*PW*, 51)

Tom's cross-dressing in order to commit burglaries sets the scene for the even more complex gendered and racial crossing that follows. It is

17. Carolyn Porter is less patient with Wilson, saying that he "is remarkably dull-witted when it comes to reading his evidence. Most noteworthy is his persistent and blundering confusion over the identity of the 'young woman' in Tom's room, 'where properly no young woman belonged'" ("Roxana's Plot," 132).

both a symptom and a cause of the category crisis that is at the heart of the novel. As Marjorie Garber has observed, "*Pudd'nhead Wilson* is in fact an exemplary instance of the category crisis, the slippage from one borderline to another, in this case race to gender, or gender to race, marked by the appearance of the transvestite. Or of two transvestites, mother and son."[18]

As the story progresses, Tom's debts mount; he is disinherited by his uncle, written back into the will, then threatened with being disinherited again. In as ugly an action as the story holds, in order to pay his creditors, Tom sells his own mother into slavery (remarkably, with her consent), but then, in a grave deception, down the river. Some months pass before Roxana shows up again in the story, now as a fugitive. To escape detection in St. Louis, where she has fled from the deep South, Roxana cross-dresses as a man. She puts on men's clothing and "an old slouch hat," and she *blackens her face.* That is to say, she alters all the visible markers of her former identity. The planter/slave owner from whom she escaped is looking for a "white" black woman, so she disguises herself as a "black" black man. Her disguise is so effective that it fools even Tom, whom she tracks down in St. Louis. When Tom first sees her, he notices only "the back of a man"; when the man turns around, he sees only "a wreck of shabby old clothes sodden with rain and all a-drip." Then the man says, "in a low voice—'Keep still—I's yo' mother!'" (*PW*, 90).

It is an arresting moment. While Tom "gasped" out a few feeble "incoherently babbling self-accusations" about why he has done such a terrible thing to his mother, Roxana takes off her hat, and her hair "tumbled down about her shoulders." Now she stands before Tom, and before Twain's reader, as a "white" woman in blackface, dressed in men's clothes. Her hair—a marker of her whiteness—now confounds the rest of her costume, and even the blackface can no longer disguise her "whiteness." Roxanna is "every man" and "every woman"; she is black *and* white, male *and* female. For this woman who has already been a forceful actor in her own life, this moment represents the most powerful embodiment of her strength. Roxana then proceeds to tell her story of enslavement, one that, as we have noted before, invokes and

18. Garber, *Vested Interests,* 289.

"Keep still—I's yo' mother": Roxana cross-dressed as a black man.
Century Magazine, May 1894, 16.

reenacts the genre of slave narratives—stories of brutal physical treatment, of ultimately striking back at the overseer (Roxana "snatch[ed]
de stick outen his han' en laid him flat"), and of escape (*PW,* 92). Roxana's story, seemingly a long and moving digression from the main plot
of the novel, propels the novel inexorably toward the tragedy that it
becomes.

With Roxana back on the scene (and in near total command of her
son), Tom becomes more desperate in his efforts to steal money both
to pay off his debts, and thus ensure his inheritance, and to buy his
mother's freedom, as she demands. Desperate, he ultimately plots to
steal from his uncle. Taking his cue from his mother (and evoking the
tradition of minstrel theater with its complex socially constructed images and enactment of blackness), Tom "blacks up" to commit the robbery. Surprised by his uncle in the act of stealing from his safe, Tom
thrusts a knife into him, killing him instantly, then flees upstairs to his
own room. There, still in blackface, Tom once again disguises himself
as a girl to escape from the house. The scene is represented in only one
sentence, but it is crucial:

> Tom put on his coat, buttoned his hat under it, threw on his suit
> of girl's clothes, dropped the veil, blew out his light, locked the room-
> door by which he had just entered, taking the key, passed through his
> other door into the back hall, locked that door and kept the key, then
> worked his way along in the dark and descended the back stairs. (*PW,*
> 100)

That is to say, Tom committed the murder in his own clothes (minus
his coat), and in blackface. Then he put on his "girl" clothes *over his
male clothes,* dropped a veil over his blackened face, and fled from the
house.

What is the meaning of the layering here? Is it, perhaps, a mistake, a
glitch in the manuscript such as those remnants of the Siamese twins
carelessly left in the *Pudd'nhead Wilson* story? All the evidence suggests
that it is not. Twain had hinted at just such layering before the murder.
In preparing to commit the robbery, Tom "laid off his coat and hat . . .
unlocked his trunk and got his suit of girl's clothes out from under the
male attire in it, and laid it by. Then he blacked his face" (*PW,* 99). The
male clothes in the trunk have concealed the female clothes, while af-

ter the murder, his female clothes hide his male clothes (and identity). In a move that mirrors his mother's triumphant moment of embracing white and black, male and female, Tom puts on layers of identities over the layers he already "wears." The whiteness of his skin hides his blackness; passing for white hides his true relationship to Roxana; blackface hides his whiteness; female clothing covers up his maleness; a veil covers his blackface. Tom, also known as Chambers, not only collapses all categories of socially constructed identities, but also, in murdering his purported uncle, transgresses against the social order itself. While death does not hover over this text in the way it does in *Adventures of Huckleberry Finn*, the connection between cross-dressing and death, when it does occur, is remarkably forceful. Death does not threaten the main cross-dresser, Tom, once his mother resolves not to drown him as an infant. Instead, he is the instrument of death. He is a cold-blooded killer who, immediately after murdering his uncle, clothes himself in women's dress and drops a veil over his face.

Marjorie Garber, in discussing briefly the transvestite theme in *Pudd'n-head Wilson*, draws a connection between Twain's use of the veil and W. E. B. Du Bois's image of the veil; Du Bois used the metaphor of existing "within the veil" to characterize the experience of being "under the burden of blackness." According to Garber,

> When Tom dresses as a woman, he disguises his *gender* because he is ashamed of his *race*. To "drop the veil" is to pull it over his face, to voluntarily veil himself. Inadvertently, then, read backwards through Du Bois's compelling image, Tom's disguise, the woman's veil, becomes a signifier of that very blackness he is so anxious to conceal. The irony of Tom's desperate ploy—to pass as a woman because he has been passing as white, and then to obliterate the damning evidence, burning both male *and* female clothes—is that it marks him unmistakably, if only for a moment, as a black transvestite, the true son of the mother he despises and sells down the river.[19]

This is a provocative observation, but it misses one critical point, for Garber fails to notice that Tom "drops the veil" over his blackface; thus the blackness he is so anxious to conceal is twice represented here, while

19. Ibid., 291.

the literal veil he wears is a socially encoded, unambiguous, if unreliable, marker of gender.

Thus, in order to escape detection, and literally to escape from the scene of the murder, Tom goes forth, as his mother did in St. Louis, as both man and woman, as both black person *and* white. Similar to his mother's blackface cross-dressing, this moment is a very powerful one in Tom's life—he has acted, and he has acted decisively, but with two crucial differences. While Roxana wears layered gender and racial identities, she pulls off her slouch hat and lets down her long, flowing hair; she strips off part of one layer to reveal herself to her son. Tom, by contrast, piles on his layers only to deceive, to cover up the shame of his deed. His act, unlike his mother's, is an act of cowardice that puts him beyond the pale of human redemption.[20]

It has been clear to generations of readers that for all its vexing statements about the role of race in determining Tom's character (and by extension, that of Chambers), *Pudd'nhead Wilson* exposes the absurdity and arbitrariness of the very racial categories upon which the slave society depended. As both Eric Sundquist and Shelley Fisher Fishkin have demonstrated, the novel also critiques racial divisions of the 1890s, the era of the enactment of Jim Crow laws and the bolstering of racial boundaries where they were clearly threatened.[21] This chapter has argued that the text is even more radical than these critics have suggested, for it also calls into question the socially constructed definitions and meanings of gender markers. In other words, in *Pudd'nhead Wilson*, the gender disguise is as hard to read as the racial disguise, and both reinforce the deconstructing of the other.

Pudd'nhead Wilson culminates with the trial of Luigi, one of the Italian twins, for the murder of Judge Driscoll. In the course of formally defending Luigi, David Wilson accidentally discovers the "true" identities of Tom and Chambers, and simultaneously reveals Tom to be the murderer of his uncle. The social, patriarchal order has been thus only temporarily subverted by Roxana, and her worst fears are realized in the

---

20. Eric Lott characterizes Tom's going forth in female dress as "an element of black female revenge for the master's rape of slave women, one of whose issue is Tom himself" ("Mr. Clemens and Jim Crow," 149).

21. Eric J. Sundquist, "Mark Twain and Homer Plessy"; Fishkin, "Race and Culture."

end as her son is deemed too valuable a piece of property to shut up in prison for life. He is sold down the river into slavery. The ending, read from Roxana's perspective, is like a Greek drama in which the very fate she had sought to escape is visited upon her son. Nonetheless, the social order has clearly been dealt a blow from which it is unlikely to recover fully. In a novel glutted with ironies, the ultimate irony may be that the one utterly reliable marker of identity that *cannot* be altered— finger prints—reveals nothing whatsoever about either the gender or the race of the individual. The community's carefully drawn and constructed racial and gender lines have been challenged and exploded. This is signified subtly, but forcefully, in the reintroduction in the final moments of the text of the man called Chambers, the "white" man who had been condemned to a lifetime of slavery by the treachery of his "mammy" but who is ostensibly set free by Wilson's discovery of his "true" identity:

> The real heir suddenly found himself rich and free, but in a most embarrassing situation. He could neither read nor write, and his speech was the basest dialect of the negro quarter. His gait, his attitudes, his gestures, his bearing, his laugh—all were vulgar and uncouth; his manners were the manners of a slave. Money and fine clothes could not mend these defects or cover them up, they only made them the more glaring and the more pathetic. (*PW*, 120–21)

As for the issue of gender, which seems not to play any role at all in Chambers's transformation back to being the white Tom, it is hinted at after all in the language describing his "vulgarity": "His gait, his attitudes, his gestures." This is the language, we will recall, used to describe Tom when he performs his female gender for David Wilson. The fact that Chambers is at home only in the kitchen evokes not only race but also the female gender, or a feminized male identity.[22]

22. Siobhan Somerville points out that the "scientific racists" of the nineteenth century, despite all their attempts to identify an objective anatomical criterion upon which to affix racial categories, were unable to discover such a category: "to their chagrin, every criterion they tried varied more within so-called races than between them" ("Scientific Racism and the Invention of the Homosexual Body," 40, quoting Barbara Fields); Jehlen argues problematically that "the subversion in Tom's usurpation of white identity turns Chambers into a woman, for femininization is the lasting result of that

Thus, a novel propelled into motion by the exchange of two babies, *Pudd'nhead Wilson* makes no effort, dramatically, to make the exchange reciprocal. Twain shows almost no interest in the white baby who is raised as a slave; most of his attention is focused on the black baby raised as white. In the terms of the novel, "really" being white does not mean much at all, or, in Lott's terms, "to be imitation black is to *be* black . . . to be imitation white is to be mere mimics." Nevertheless, Chambers, who has been absent from the novel for much of its duration, is left, in the end, on center stage. His clothes, taken from him at six months, are symbolically returned to him, but the power they had to undo him at the outset is not matched by a corresponding ability to restore him in the end. Even the whitest of black men can be sold into slavery, but a white man, once "crossed by the shadow of the Veil," cannot ever be fully white again. Or as Andrea Newlyn expresses it, "certain identities can be put on and taken off, but other identities—that of the slave, for example—once 'put on,' *even if inauthentically,* cannot be removed or altered."[23] While the old categories seem to be reinstated, they are now confounded to such a degree that the old order is shaken to its core.

In comparison with *Adventures of Huckleberry Finn, Pudd'nhead Wilson* picks up and greatly expands Twain's interest in cross-dressing and the performative nature of gender and gender crossing. Even with the former's association with death and morbidity, there is a significant element of play associated with cross-dressing in *Huckleberry Finn.* Through the putting on and taking off of clothing, characters in the novel enter, albeit briefly, into liminal states that are essentially benign because they are well contained. Nonetheless, even carefully delimited gender crossings begin to implicate socially constructed racial boundaries. Huck's experience of trying to "pass" as a girl brings Jim into the subject position as he fixes Huck in his gaze and critiques Huck's performance as a girl. This fact, plus Huck's encounter with Judith Loftus

---

unfortunate man's slave upbringing." But Jehlen never makes clear precisely how Chambers is feminized, except to suggest that the black man, in white men's stereotypes, is either an oversexualized, threatening being or "contemptibly effeminate" ("Ties That Bind," 418).

23. Lott, "Mr. Clemens and Jim Crow," 147; Andrea K. Newlyn, "Form and Ideology in Transracial Narratives: *Pudd'nhead Wilson* and *A Romance of the Republic,*" 52.

in which he proves to be a "failed" girl, results in his return to Jackson's Island fully identified with Jim's plight as a runaway slave: "Hump it, Jim, they're after us." The interconnections between gender and racial crossings in *Huckleberry Finn* are confirmed at the end of the novel when Jim and Aunt Sally unconsciously take on qualities of each other—that is, they engage in a gendered and racialized exchange—when Jim is brought back into captivity dressed in Aunt Sally's clothing.

The subtle racial and gender crossings explored in *Huckleberry Finn* and expressed through cross-dressing emerge full-blown in *Pudd'nhead Wilson*. With its much greater interest and investment in details of dress and clothing, with its layering of races and genders onto already racially ambiguous bodies, *Pudd'nhead Wilson* ultimately insists that race and gender are interconnected performances that are multivocal and highly unstable. Through racial and gender crossings, all meaningful social categories collapse. Thus the entire story partakes of what Victor Turner identifies as a liminoid experience. In contrast to liminal experiences, which take place within a highly structured society with clearly understood and accepted boundaries and limits, according to Turner, the liminoid experience is more open, unbounded, and individualistic.[24] Traditional boundaries are crossed and recrossed, but they are not readily reinstated in the end. The world is not inverted then righted; it is left in a state of disequilibrium. Thus any effort at closure, as in the trial and subsequent actions of *Pudd'nhead Wilson*, may prove to be ultimately unsatisfactory. The collapse of the intertwining categories of race and gender is at once the frustration and the brilliance of Mark Twain's *Pudd'nhead Wilson*.

Ironically, the subversiveness of *Personal Recollections of Joan of Arc* has inevitably appeared diminished when viewed in the context of its companion piece, *Pudd'nhead Wilson*. As James Cox observed in 1966, Joan and Roxana "stand like contrasting sculptures on the landscape":

> Against the background of *Pudd'nhead Wilson*, the figure of Joan of Arc assumes a strikingly meaningful identity. *Pudd'nhead* ironically chronicled the secret history of miscegenation; *Joan of Arc* rev-

---

24. Victor Turner, *From Ritual to Theatre: The Human Seriousness of Play.*

erently recounted a life of purity and inviolate maidenhood. In view-
ing these two books which literally accompanied each other in emerging from Mark Twain's imagination, the two women, Roxana and
Joan, stand like contrasting sculptures on the landscape. The one—
dark, voluble, and comical—who, though her sexuality is not dramatized, is nonetheless the sexual object at the mercy of a society of gentlemen; the other—pale, chaste, and serious—whose martial power
and childlike purity bring her into power over a society of rude and
barbarous soldiers.[25]

Twain's Joan, like Roxana, is a transgressive female. In taking up arms,
in donning armor, in leading the French army to victory over the English occupying forces, Joan went far beyond the boundaries of acceptable female behavior. Even five hundred years later, there is no historic female figure who so far exceeded public expectations for the role
women can play in Western society. Joan's transgressive behavior went
even further: she openly and repeatedly defied the all-powerful church
fathers in the self-defense she mounted in her public trials for heresy
and in her refusal to renounce her cross-dressing off the battlefield. Yet
in contrast with Roxana, Joan, in her religiosity and in her protection
of her sexual purity, is a more conventional female heroine. Especially
given Twain's decision to represent Joan of Arc through the perspective of her now-aged childhood male friend, the Sieur Louis de Conte,
Twain's Joan is a deeply ambiguous figure, at once boldly defiant and
a model of purity. The first-person perspective of the narrative partially masks the extremes she represents and the unexpressed ambivalence
Twain apparently felt about her. As we will see in the next chapter, that
ambivalence accounts in part for the degree to which Joan remains an
illusive figure in *Personal Recollections of Joan of Arc*.

25. James Cox, *Mark Twain: The Fate of Humor*, 260.

4

Troubling Gender
Personal Recollections of Joan of Arc

Linking Joan of Arc with Roxana enhances the stature of each, but only once we grant the profound differences between the two figures and the fictionalized worlds they inhabit. These two powerful, transgressive, highly disruptive females occupied Twain's imagination at the height of his creativity. They were truly liminal figures, standing on the margins of their societies, and although for profoundly different reasons, each revealed deep disturbances in the fabrics of their respective societies. Whereas Roxana cross-dresses only once—to escape from slavery—Joan cross-dresses for nearly two-thirds of the novel centered on her life; it becomes a way of life for her, requiring that we view her as a transvestite figure who seriously confounds gender categories and expectations.[1] But whatever their reasons, both heroines take up cross-dressing in deadly earnest; none of the playfulness of cross-dressing in *Huckleberry Finn* is attendant upon these two transvestite figures. Just as Roxana's cross-dressing points to a crisis of racial categories in her

---

1. Although Roxana cross-dresses only once in *Pudd'nhead Wilson,* her son, Tom, cross-dresses surprisingly frequently, always for nefarious reasons.

era (and subsequent eras), Joan's cross-dressing reveals crises with the patriarchy, as represented in Twain's story by the king and the church, and ultimately a growing crisis within the Clemens household. First and foremost, however, a crisis of gender categories underlies both major works of fiction by Twain.

Personal Recollections of Joan of Arc does pick up one of the threads of cross-dressing introduced in *Huckleberry Finn* and continued in *Pudd'nhead Wilson:* the association of cross-dressing with death and morbidity. Indeed, the relationship between death and cross-dressing is overdetermined in *Personal Recollections.* Even if Twain had ended his story after the French army's triumph at Orléans under Joan's leadership, as he had originally intended, the only way the longer story can end is with Joan being burned at the stake for refusing to give up wearing men's clothing.[2] This is the historical given of the story, known to everyone who knows anything about her life. Her dramatic death by fire, her martyrdom, is a shadow that hangs over the entire novel and over every historical or fictional re-creation of her life; it cannot be escaped.

This fact alone might account for Twain's fascination with Joan's dress and for his extended descriptions of the dress of two other figures in the novel, one historical and the other purely the work of his imagination: Charles VII and the Paladin, respectively. Against the foppish, extravagant dress of these two men, Joan's dress stands in stark contrast, especially the dark and foreboding clothing she wears in prison and throughout her trials for heresy. Indeed, the only "sin" she can be convicted of in the end is her refusal to renounce her "funereal" black masculine clothing. Her gender disruptions are writ large, and they are insisted upon by Twain. Joan's appropriation of male clothing, whether on the battlefield or subsequently in prison, is symbolic of her appropriation of male authority as the head of the French army; it exemplifies her confounding of traditional definitions of male and female, of masculine and feminine. A careful perusal of the many historical sources

---

2. Everett Emerson indicates that Twain originally had not planned to go past the siege but was persuaded by Henry Alden, editor of *Harper's Magazine,* to extend the story to the end of Joan's life (*The Authentic Mark Twain: A Literary Biography of Samuel L. Clemens,* 196).

Twain researched in preparing to write Joan of Arc reveals that he made numerous marginal notes in the texts related specifically to how Joan dressed. For example, his marginalia in Chabannes's *La Vierge Lorraine Jeanne d'Arc* reveal that he was interested in physical descriptions of Joan and, in six different locations, concerned with Joan's clothing in particular. Likewise, in his notes for Marius Sepet's *Jeanne d'Arc*, which contains illustrations of Joan that blend male and female clothing, Twain translated into English a passage in which Sepet reports that Joan wore female clothing over her male clothing.[3] Thus from the beginning Twain was vitally interested in how Joan dressed, both in civilian and in military garb, how she gained permission from the authorities to put on men's clothing in the first place, and how valiantly she resisted giving it up in the end in prison.

It has never been entirely clear what critics have wanted from *Personal Recollections of Joan of Arc*, but whatever it has been, they have not found it. Harsh criticisms of the novel began in the early months of its serial publication and have extended to this day, when indeed critics and scholars have taken the trouble to respond publicly to the novel at all. Especially in contrast with *Pudd'nhead Wilson*, which John Bird reminds us recently is the novel now regarded by Twain scholars as "second only to *Huckleberry Finn*," *Personal Recollections* continues to disappoint.[4] Critics have long lamented that *Joan of Arc* as a novel fails to satisfy its readers and has done so from the time of its creation to the present day. Over time, scholars have sought to understand precisely where they think the novel went wrong, collectively positing a variety of factors and judgments. Twain, they argue, was too bound by his historical sources; he made the mistake of filtering the entire story, and our subsequent view of Joan, through the sentimental narrative perspective of a fictional male friend of Joan's, Le Sieur de Conte, writing retrospectively in his dotage; Twain was unable to overcome his own excessive reverence for the young maid; Twain wrote the novel to try

---

3. Twain's copy of Armand de Chabannes, *La Vierge Lorraine Jeanne d'Arc*, 50–51, and Marius Sepet, *Jeanne d'Arc*, 324, with his marginal notations, are located in the Mark Twain Papers, Bancroft Library, University of California, Berkeley.

4. John Bird, "Killing Half a Dog, Half a Novel: The Trouble with *The Tragedy of Pudd'nhead Wilson* and *The Comedy of Those Extraordinary Twins*," 442.

to satisfy the tastes of his hypercritical daughter, Susy Clemens; Twain allowed sentimentality to overpower his otherwise irreverent and irrepressible sense of humor. Unfortunately, there is some truth to each of these explanations, and any attempt to rehabilitate the novel must come to terms with readers' disappointments.

Written in three parts, and initially published serially and anonymously, the two-volume book version appeared in 1896. Although not the first American book published about Joan of Arc, it anticipated by several years the growing popular interest in this iconic figure. Two other lives of Joan were published in the same year as Twain's, one by Francis C. Lowell and the other by a Mrs. Oliphant. All three were reviewed together in the *Nation*. While the reviewer preferred Lowell's biography, finding Oliphant's work by comparison too "slight," and Twain's too "modern" and anachronistic, he noted that Twain's biography "seizes the undying charm of Joan's character, and presents her in living flesh and blood to thousands for whom she would otherwise be a mere name." The same reviewer regretted that there was not enough humor in the book. In sharp contrast, another contemporary reviewer, writing for the *Literary Digest,* lamented that the portrait of Joan was "spoiled by the humor." Other contemporary criticism was mixed: The *Anthenaeum* thought there were too many Americanisms in the narrative, Laurence Hutton of *Literary Notes* found Twain's Joan to be the "most earthy, alive Joan since Hollynshed," while Twain's friend William Dean Howells was especially disparaging of the book in his review in *Harper's Weekly:*

> It would be impossible for anyone who was not a prig to keep to the archaic attitude and parlance which the author attempts here and there; and I wish he had frankly refused to attempt it at all. I wish his personal recollections of Joan could have been written by some Southwestern American, translated to Domrémy by some mighty magic of imagination. . . . My suffering begins when he does the supposed medieval thing. Then I suspect that his armor is of tin, that the castles and rocks are pasteboard, that the mob of citizens and soldiers who fill the air with their two-up-and-two-down combats, and the well-known muffled roar of their voices, has been hired in at so much a night, and that Joan is sometimes in an awful temper behind the scenes.

According to Kaplan, George Bernard Shaw dismissed Twain's Joan of Arc as "an unimpeachable American school teacher in armor."[5]

Twentieth-century criticisms of the work are legion. For instance, James Cox says the work embodies all the "reverence" Twain had spent his career debunking: "The whole performance is so dismal as to make one wish it were a parody, yet clearly it is no parody. Mark Twain is obviously serious—so serious that he cannot be Mark Twain." Everett Emerson simply declared that Joan was "an unsuitable subject for Mark Twain's talents." Justin Kaplan says that Twain's characterization of the nonsexual Joan is "so single-mindedly devout and so unabashedly sentimental that for once even Susy . . . was thoroughly proud and pleased." More recently, in the introduction to the Oxford edition of *Personal Recollections of Joan of Arc,* Kaplan once again took up his expressions of dismay about what he saw as the unfortunate influence of Susy on her father, and upon *Joan of Arc;* he again lays at Susy's feet the problem with the novel: "*Joan of Arc* was an act of piety, a surrender to the historical given of a virgin-martyr whom Mark Twain infused with the intolerant idealism of his own favorite daughter, Susy Clemens." Kaplan continues, "More even than her mother, whom Van Wyck Brooks blamed for Mark Twain's surrender to conventional values, Susy Clemens demanded purity, gentility, high sentiment—the criteria of the late-nineteenth-century female reading audience characterized by one of Mark Twain's contemporaries as 'the iron Madonna who strangles in her fond embrace the American novelist.'" Thus for Kaplan, Susy's influence was unmistakable and regrettable. We will return to this particular subject later. Peter Stoneley, while making positive claims for the novel, nonetheless characterizes Twain's Joan in these terms: "the heroine's insuperable goodness makes her responses very predictable, and has the effect of making the reader indifferent to her fate. Her absolute, depersonalized nature aligns her with a traditional

---

5. Anonymous, *Nation* 63 (July 16, 1896): 51–53; Anonymous, *Literary Digest* 13 (September 5, 1896): 603–4, located in the Mark Twain Papers Chronological file for 1896; Howells, quoted in Justin Kaplan, introduction to *Personal Recollections of Joan of Arc,* xxxii, with Shaw quoted on p. xxxvii. Earlier American publications on Joan of Arc included a play in five acts (John Burk, 1798), biographies of Joan (David W. Bartlett, 1853; John Fentonhill, 1864), and a poem in four books (George Calvert, 1860).

notion of womanhood, in that women were frequently represented as spontaneous prodigies of goodness, self-generating, independent of social circumstances."[6]

Against these negative assessments (and there are many more), one must place Twain's own regard for his longest, and last, major work of fiction. In 1908 Twain wrote, "I like the Joan of Arc best of all my books & it *is* the best, I know it perfectly well." Twain's biographer, Albert Bigelow Paine, went even further in his praise for the novel: "Considered from every point of view, *Joan of Arc* is Mark Twain's supreme literary expression, the loftiest, the most delicate, the most luminous example of his work. It is so from the first word of its beginning . . . to the last word of the last chapter."[7]

Even though we are unlikely to ever share Twain's or Paine's full enthusiasm for the work, there is too much of interest inherent in the novel to dismiss it out of hand, and there is too much of Twain's growing preoccupation with gendered transgression, and his ongoing exploration of cross-dressing, to turn aside from the novel. It is Twain's longest and most complete exploration of a transgressive heroine, and his most sustained engagement with a transvestite figure, albeit one from the distant past. Further, he invested long periods of time, over a period of many years, to researching his study, reading carefully a number of historical sources, in both French and English, which he drew upon to write his own fictionalized version of the life of Joan of Arc. By his own account, Twain used no fewer than a dozen historical sources to guide him in his writing: "The first two-thirds of the book were easy; for I only needed to keep my historical road straight; therefore I used for reference only one French history and one English one—and shoveled in as much fancy-work and invention on both sides of the historical road as I pleased. But on this last third I have constantly used five French sources and five English ones, and I think no telling historical nugget in any of them has escaped me."[8]

6. Cox, *Mark Twain: The Fate of Humor,* 263; Emerson, *Authentic Mark Twain,* 199; Justin Kaplan, *Mr. Clemens and Mark Twain,* 315; Kaplan, introduction to *Personal Recollections,* xxxiii, xl; Stoneley, *Mark Twain and the Feminine Aesthetic,* 92.

7. Quoted in Albert Bigelow Paine, *Mark Twain, a Biography: The Personal and Literary Life of Samuel Langhorne Clemens,* 1034; Paine's assessment in ibid., 1029.

8. Letter from Samuel Clemens to Henry H. Rogers, January 29, 1895, quoted in Camfield, *Oxford Companion to Mark Twain,* 428.

The primary French source was Jules Michelet's *Jeanne d'Arc,* and the English source was Janet Tuckey's *Joan of Arc;* Twain heavily annotated both books. For instance, in an effort to construct accurately the chronology for the period when Joan was seeking an audience with Charles VII, Twain, writing at a right angle to Tuckey's text, summarizes the dates of Joan's travel as follows:

> May 28–16—1st visit to Baudricourt & Laxart. Vision May 20, '28. May '28 goes to Laxart and Bau; returns to Dom., followed by the talk which has been sent flying everywhere by her strange interview; June 15, her father's remark; June 18, cited to Toul, to appear there Dec. 29. Frets away the months, appears at Toul, wins her case; has Laxart & come for her to nurse his wife, & leaves with him Jan. 6 '29 (birthday), Louis following, Jan. 10.—she stops with Cath. Royer, wheelwright's wife—"some weeks," going to mass & talking freely of her mission. Jan. 11 (Louis present, for he is a gentleman), 2nd visit to Baudri. No result. Jan. 12, Novelonpont visits her. Jan. 12, *he* takes her to B (3rd visit), & this time he listens. Jan. 20 Duke of Lorraine sent a safe . . . & she went to Nancy. No result. Feb. 14, on the day of—Rouvray. 4th visit to Baudri.[9]

Twain said he consulted ten other sources in preparing to write about Joan's trial; in addition, the trial transcripts themselves, in translation, were readily available for his perusal, presenting a vast wealth of detail to be digested and reformulated in Twain's fictional representation of Joan's life. He was determined to get "right" the string of charges brought against Joan, the examination and cross-examinations she had to endure, the constantly changing tactics of her accusers, and Joan's responses to the barrage of accusations and interrogations. His task, as he saw it, was to write the life's story of the person he regarded as "the wonder of the ages."

Who was the historical Joan of Arc who so captured Twain's imagination? Also known as Jeanne d'Arc, die Jungfrau von Orléans, la Pucelle, the Maid of Orléans, and Jeahanne d'Arc, Joan was born in the village of Gries, France, in 1412, and raised in the village of Domrémy in the midst of the Hundred Years' War. Joan's family were peasants, and she was illiterate. When she was about twelve years old, she began to have visions of three different saints, St. Catherine, St. Margaret, and

---

9. Written on pages 29–30 of Twain's copy of Janet Tuckey, *Joan of Arc: "The Maid."*

St. Michael, who ultimately instructed her to present herself to the French Dauphin, Charles, and to lead the French army against the Burgundians and the English then occupying France. Remarkably, at the age of seventeen, she succeeded in persuading the reluctant Charles to put her in command of the demoralized French forces, and with no previous military training or experience, she revitalized the army and raised the siege at Orléans, her most decisive and crucial battle. She won the hearts of the French common people and the respect of seasoned generals; she was heralded as the savior of France, and she stood with Charles in 1429 at his coronation as king of France.

In 1430, at the age of eighteen, Joan was captured and imprisoned by the Burgundians at Compiègne; four months later she was turned over to the English and charged with heresy. They transferred her to the prison at Rouen, where she was closely guarded day and night by English soldiers. She was put on trial with no one to defend her, counsel her, or bear witness on her behalf; day after day she had to respond to charges leveled against her by a tribunal of Inquisition clerics. She was accused of a vast array of sins against the Church: witchcraft, heresy, obeying her "voices" rather than the dictates of the Church, wearing men's dress and armor, libeling her sex, boasting that she knew the future, attempting to kill herself by throwing herself off a tower, seducing the people of France into adoring her like a saint, taking command over men, and preferring the company of men to women.[10] She was examined and cross-examined about these points, in public trials and in private. In the end, the only "sin" for which she was condemned was wearing men's clothing. She was forced to renounce men's clothing (upon penalty of death) and to promise henceforth only to wear women's clothing. When she finally agreed to do so, her captors stole her women's clothing from her prison cell while she slept, and she had no choice but to resume dressing in her male clothing. She was promptly sentenced to die and was burned at the stake in the courtyard at Rouen, in 1431.

Throughout Joan's trial and captivity, Charles VII, whom Joan had helped legitimate as the rightful king of France, apparently made no at-

10. *The Trials of Jeanne d'Arc: A Complete Translation of the Text of the Original Documents,* 140–226.

tempt to ransom her or to rescue her. In the 1450s, however, more than twenty years after her death, he initiated a rehabilitation trial, which resulted in Joan's name being cleared of the charges of heresy. Throughout the Early Modern period, she continued to be a legendary hero in France, but it was not until the end of the eighteenth century when the Latin transcripts of her trial were rediscovered and translated into French that she attained iconic status. Until this time, the English, in fact, had widely regarded her as a witch and a whore. In 1796 the English poet Robert Southey published an epic poem about her. Four years later the German writer Friedrich Schiller wrote a highly influential drama entitled *Die Jungfrau von Orleans,* which established Joan of Arc as a romantic hero and a tragic martyr. In the mid-nineteenth century, Jules Quicherat published a five-volume history of Joan of Arc, based on the court records from the trial and rehabilitation, as well as other historical documents. His work became "the supreme primary source for the rediscovery of Joan for the modern era, the complete edition of her trial record." Meanwhile, Quicherat's mentor, Jules Michelet, wrote a more condensed biography of Joan, which was widely read: "Michelet's lectures, related writings, and 'Jeanne d'Arc' so galvanized his public that his Joan would be reborn among many writers and artists. Michelet's *La Pucelle* spawned new approaches to the heroine in all manner of ways during the ensuing century, from the extreme rational to the sublimely mystical."[11] Both Quicherat and Michelet were direct sources for Twain's *Personal Recollections.*

Partially in response to the writings about Joan in midcentury France, citizens and clergymen began to recommend that Joan be nominated for sainthood. In 1894, the Church declared her "venerable," which was the first degree of canonization. In 1909 she was beatified, but she was not officially canonized until May 16, 1920, twenty-four years after Twain published his life of Joan of Arc. As Twain irreverently

---

11. See the chapter "Harlot of the Armagnacs," in Marina Warner, *Joan of Arc: The Image of Female Heroism,* 96–116; Ellen Ecker Dolgin, "So Well-Suited: The Evolution of Joan of Arc as a Dramatic Image," 149–50; according to Albert Stone, citing Olivia Clemens's journals, one of the pleasures the Clemens family enjoyed in the summer of 1885 was reading aloud Schiller's *Jungfrau von Orleans* (introduction to *Personal Recollections of Joan of Arc,* 4); on Michelet, see Nadia Margolis, "Trial by Passion: Philology, Film, and Ideology in the Portrayal of Joan of Arc," 448.

imagined it, Joan herself would have had little interest in the trappings of sainthood:

> She has been one—& the Chiefest—[in] the countless & limitless realms, & principalities & dominations of Heaven for four hundred & sixty-two years; & possibly—who knows?—she who never cared so much as a farthing for rewards & honors, might be pleased to have a poor little pasteboard, jimcrack, pinchbeck earthly saintship sent up to her on a tin plate from this potato-planet with the trade-mark of a little papal shop on it. Let us not object. The priests of the Church got fat things out of the enemies of France by stealing her & burning her, perhaps they can turn a neat political penny with France, now, by insulting and soiling her sacred memory with the tardy gift of a brass halo.

By the early twentieth century, Joan became an icon for the suffrage movement in both England and the United States.[12] She has continued into the twenty-first century to be regarded as a heroic figure, a symbol of nationhood and patriotism, of resistance and iconoclasm, a saint to be adored and worshiped, and heralded as a transgressive, transvestite figure.

Twain's own professed interest in the historical Joan was expressed in his own voice, not filtered by a nostalgic narrator, in an essay he published in *Harper's* in 1904, nine years after the publication of *Personal Recollections*. He seemed most impressed by the fact that she accomplished everything without benefit of any form of prior training or education, however informal:

> In the world's history she stands alone—quite alone. Others have been great in their first public exhibitions of generalship, valor, legal talent, diplomacy, fortitude; but always their previous years and associations had been in a larger or smaller degree a preparation for these things. There have been no exceptions to the rule. But Joan was com-

---

12. Twain's comment on sainthood is in Notebook 32; the entry is not dated but was written between December 20, 1892, and January 24, 1893; according to Laura Skandera-Trombley, citing a letter to Twain from W. R. Mitchell of the Jeanne d'Arc Suffrage League, dated January 6, 1910, Twain was enrolled as an honorary member in the league, "which thanked him for his 'splendid history of our patron saint'" (*Mark Twain in the Company of Women*, 161).

petent in a law case at sixteen without ever having seen a law-book or
a court-house before; she had no training in soldiership and no asso-
ciations with it, yet she was a competent general in her first campaign;
she was brave in her first battle, yet her courage had had no education—not even the education which a boy's courage gets from never-
ceasing reminders that it is not permissible in a boy to be a coward,
but only in a girl; friendless, alone, ignorant, in the blossom of her
youth, she sat week after week, a prisoner in chains, before her as-
semblage of judges, enemies hunting her to her death, the ablest
minds in France, and answered them out of an untaught wisdom
which overmatched their learning, baffled their tricks and treacheries
with a native sagacity which compelled their wonder, and scored every
day a victory against these incredible odds and camped unchallenged
on the field. In the history of the human intellect, untrained, inexpe-
rienced, and using only its birthright equipment of untried capacities,
there is nothing which approaches this.

Twain was not particularly drawn to Joan's piety or to her religious con-
victions, although he did portray them in his novel, but he was drawn
by what he saw as the pathos of her situation in having to defend herself against the cruel bishop of Beauvais, Chaucon:

> The spectacle of that solitary girl, forlorn and friendless, without ad-
> vocate or adviser, and without the help and guidance of any copy of
> the charges brought against her or rescript of the complex and volu-
> minous daily proceedings of the court to modify the crushing strain
> upon her astonishing memory, fighting that long battle serene and
> undismayed against these colossal odds, stands alone in its pathos and
> its sublimity; it has nowhere its mate, either in the annals of fact or in
> the inventions of fiction.[13]

Twain admired what he saw as Joan's Eve-like innocence. At the same
time, he delighted in how she defied and outwitted the church authorities, with all their power and learning.

Twain's overarching fascination with Joan of Arc, however, as it is
revealed in his text, was that she was an archetypal liminal figure. She
moved between earthliness and saintliness, between the centuries, between childhood and adulthood, between masculine and feminine—

---

13. Mark Twain, "Saint Joan of Arc," 593, 588.

and she partook of all. Randall Knoper identifies Joan's transvestitism as "a metaphor for the difficulties Twain raises, serving at once to define and distinguish the feminine and the masculine and to combine them." Her transvestitism, however, far from signaling a category crisis, from Knoper's perspective is seen as an "obedient transvestism" that "affirms" Joan's "subordination and femininity."[14] A closer look at how Twain depicts Joan's literal cross-dressing will, I believe, lead us to a different conclusion.

Joan of Arc is the most famous cross-dresser in history. By donning armor and leading the French army to victory over the English, she challenged gender conventions in the most profound way, and she paid the ultimate price for her troubles. Her initial choice to wear men's clothing in leading the French troops was so controversial that church officials felt compelled to rule on the efficacy of such an affront to custom. Remarkably, at the time they sanctioned her cross-dressing during war, but it was the very crime for which the Church later condemned her to death. In Twain's Joan, as Christina Zwarg argues, "clothing constitutes the single most important form by which Joan's behavior is judged. . . . Her adoption of masculine and feminine clothing reveals her extreme versatility of character, her ability to transgress traditional forms by subtle manipulation."[15] For Twain, Joan's cross-dressing, her transvestisim, came to symbolize her larger social transgression. Her whole public life was an affront to conventional expectations about how a young woman should behave. Assuming command of the French army, indeed demanding the right to do so, was an unthinkable act for a woman, as surely in the fifteenth century as it would be now. She donned men's clothes and assumed one of the most masculine of public roles. Also, from the time she left her home in Domrémy at the age of sixteen, Joan traveled almost exclusively in the company of men. Fi-

14. Randall Knoper expressed a similar idea in a longer series of binaries: "The realistic and the theatrical, the private and the public, the spiritual and the fleshly, the divine and the human, and the feminine and the masculine all converge in *Joan of Arc*. And if melodrama involves display of the private, or the spectacular recognition of feminine virtue, then ultimately Twain takes melodrama in this novel as an oxymoronic ideal, as a problem of contradiction" (*Acting Naturally: Mark Twain in the Culture of Performance*, 176); on Joan's transvestism, see Knoper, *Acting Naturally*, 176.

15. Christina Zwarg, "Women as Force in Mark Twain's *Joan of Arc*: The Unworkable Fascination," 67.

nally, she stood up, alone, against the full force of the authority of the Church, defending herself for months on end against the relentless charges and accusations that the Church and the English brought against her. In writing the story of Joan of Arc, Twain immersed himself in the life of a young woman who overturned every gendered expectation but two—she remained devoutly religious to the end, convinced of the efficacy of the voices she heard, and obedient to those voices, which she believed came from God. She also retained her sexual purity. The skeptical Mark Twain never directly challenged those assumptions; his interest, instead, lay in Joan's transgressive powers and in the physical manifestations of her liminality.

In tracing Twain's representations of the cross-dressed Joan, it is striking that he gives relatively little attention to the details of her armor, of her battle dress. In this, he was following the lead of his primary sources, Michelet and Tuckey. Twain's narrator, Joan's contemporary and childhood friend, describes her armor in the most succinct terms: "Meantime the King was having a complete suit of armor made for her at Tours. It was of the finest steel, heavily plated with silver, richly ornamented with engraved designs, and polished like a mirror."[16] Later the narrator, de Conte, says that the armor was "white," and that over it Joan wore a "silver-gilt cape" that the narrator recalls he could see "flap and flare and rise and fall like a little patch of white flame" (*PR*, 225, 313). While the wording is brief, the visual image is of the greatest importance. This is the dress that came to symbolize Joan of Arc's defiance of convention, her bold role as head of the French army, and her subsequent role as a national savior. It was the armor-clad Joan of Arc who became an icon for the woman's suffrage movement, for the changing and contested role of women in British and American society in the early twentieth century. As the undisputed mark of her transgression, it is the image that inspired the frontispiece for the first edition of *Personal Recollections*. The detailed depiction of Joan in the illustration, however, far exceeds any physical description of her offered by Twain in the text.

The illustrator, F. V. Du Mond, depicts a shapely Joan in full body armor, her hair cropped short, her arms raised over her head, her trans-

16. Mark Twain, *Personal Recollections of Joan of Arc*, 133 (hereinafter cited as *PR*).

Frontispiece for the first edition of *Personal Recollections of Joan of Arc.*

gressive body surrounded by Christian symbols; in short, even the illustration insists upon her liminal quality. In her left hand she holds a sword by its blade, and in her right hand a crown. All the lines of her figure are rounded and soft, with her raised arms making more prominent her curved figure and form-fitting armor; at the same time, she is depicted as a Christ figure. Her head is framed by a white circular orb, or aureole. There is a traditional Christian symbol—*a manus dei*—over her head. The hand, with palms facing forward and the thumb and first two fingers pointing upward, symbolizes the Trinity. Traditional and familiar marginalia—some religious, some secular—surround Joan: a plumed helmet, a mailed hand, two Jerusalem crosses set inside heart shapes, a lamb's head, teasels, and a heraldic shield. Joan's feet rest on a portrait of a secular figure who represents both England and France (as indicated by the writing that frames the figure and by a lion, rampart, and a fleur-de-lis).

There are two curiosities in the illustration, however, that are difficult to explain. At the bottom of the illustration, two prominent male heads face away from the secular ruler, one on each side, but they seem to be closely allied with him. Both figures have long hair and pointed ears. The one on the right has horns, and is clearly intended to be some sort of diabolical figure. Both seem to be blowing wind out of their mouths. Taken together, they imply that the secular ruler was propped up by Satanic forces, notable, perhaps, for their power of speech (as in Joan's trial). In any event, everything about the illustration makes it clear than Joan triumphs over these sinister forces.

The second curiosity is situated in a prominent place, on our right, in the decorative border near Joan's head. It appears to be a long, full, skein of human hair, surely meant to represent Joan's shorn hair. The hair is tied by two cords, one at the top and the other halfway down its length. What meaning is it intended to convey? Was it intended to remind the reader of Joan's femininity, which she sacrificed for France? Taken together with her soft, female figure, is it meant to soften the image of Joan, with her bobbed hair? To balance the plumed helmet opposite it? Has Joan's hair become a sacred object, a relic? Or does the image serve to remind us that Joan, for all her Christ-like representation, was human after all? It is a conundrum that will have to remain unresolved, for nothing in the text suggests that Joan's shorn hair had become iconic.[17]

17. Critics have speculated that Twain came to dislike Du Mond's representation of his Joan, citing Twain's denunciation of artists who remembered only one detail about Joan—that she was a peasant, "and so he paints her as a strapping middle-aged fishwoman, with costume to match, and in her face the spirituality of a ham. He is a slave to his one idea, and forgets to observe that the supremely great souls are never lodged in gross bodies" (Twain, "Saint Joan of Arc," 595).

Midway through the book another illustration shows Joan at the battle at Orléans. The armor is similar, but this time Joan is holding high her own standard—her legs apart, her feet firmly planted on the ground. She is surrounded by soldiers in the midst of battle—shooting arrows, carrying ladders—laying siege to the battlements. Compared to the frontispiece, this armored Joan is a much more active figure caught at the moment of one of her greatest achievements. This particular image is taken "from the painting by J. E. Lenepveu in the Pantheon at Paris" (*PR*, opposite p. 260). Given the similarity of the armor here with the armor in the frontispiece, it is likely that Lenepveu's painting served as the model for Du Mond's representation of Joan's armor.[18] It certainly offered Du Mond more detail to draw upon than Twain's text itself.

Twain makes it clear that Joan of Arc's intentions to dress like a soldier upset the priests and caused the church authorities to have to rule on the matter:

> There had been grave doubts among the priests as to whether the Church ought to permit a female soldier to dress like a man. But now came a verdict on that head. Two of the greatest scholars and theologians of the time—one of whom had been Chancellor of the University of Paris—rendered it. They decided that since Joan "must do the work of a man and a soldier, it is just and legitimate that her apparel should conform to the situation."
>
> It was a great point gained, the Church's authority to dress as a man. (*PR*, 130–31)

What is particularly interesting about this "point" is that the Church seems to confer upon Joan the right not only to dress in armor but also to otherwise dress in male attire in her role as general-in-chief of the armies of France. Even before she went into battle and even before the king had her armor made, Joan dressed in men's clothing. However, Twain does not describe this male clothing or explain Joan's motivation in dressing in this manner.[19] While Twain slid over how Joan ap-

18. About a decade ago, armor that some believe was Joan's actual armor turned up in a Paris antique shop. While experts are skeptical that it truly was Joan's armor, they agree it dated from the fifteenth century and was designed for a woman (W. Kole, "Joan of Arc's Armor").

19. All Tuckey says on the matter is that Joan "prayed them to pardon her for the

peared in her initial cross-dressed state, the Church was not so reticent. In its formal "Act of Accusation," which consisted of seventy articles, the Inquisition made much of her male clothing as a warrior:

> In order the more openly and better to attain her end, Jeanne asked of Robert de Baudricourt to have made for her a man's dress and armor appropriate. This captain, with great repugnance, ended by acquiescing in her request. These garments and armor made and furnished, Jeanne, rejecting and abandoning women's clothing, her hair cut en-round like a young coxcomb, took shirt, breeches, doublets, with hose joined together and fastened to the said doublet by twenty points, long leggings laced on the outside, a short mantle [surcoat] to the knees, or thereabouts, close-cut cap, tight-fitting boots or buskins, long spurs, sword, dagger, breastplate, lance and other arms in fashion of a man of war, affirming that in this she was executing the order of God, as had been prescribed to her by revelation.[20]

Furthermore, in the next article prepared for her trial, the church fathers are critical even of the style of her transvestite clothing, accusing Joan of dressing extravagantly and ostentatiously:

> Jeanne attributes to God, to His angels and to His Saints instructions that are contrary to the honesty of womankind, forbidden by divine law, abominable to God and man, and prohibited under penalty of anathema by ecclesiastical decrees, such as the wearing of short, tight, and dissolute male habits, those underneath the tunic and breeches as well as the rest; and, according to their bidding, she often dressed in rich and sumptuous habits, precious stuffs and cloth of gold and furs; and not only did she wear short tunics, but she dressed herself in tabards and garments open at the sides, whilst it is notorious that when she was captured she was wearing a loose cloak of cloth of gold, a cap on her head and her hair cropped round in man's style. And in general, having cast aside all womanly decency, not only to the scorn of feminine modesty, but also of well-instructed men, she had worn the apparel and garments of most dissolute men, and in addition, had borne weapons of offence.[21]

---

man's attire she wore; but in that lawless day the most modest women must have well understood that such a dress was fittest and safest for her who had to live among men" (*Joan of Arc*, 40).

20. Article 12, www.stjoan-center.com/Trials/sec.14.html.

21. *The Trial of Jeanne d'Arc*, Article 13, 154.

Here Twain missed a chance; had he relied more upon the historical record, the Act of Accusation, instead of his secondary sources, Twain could have presented a richly detailed picture of the cross-dressed Joan of Arc off the battlefield. Instead, his longest description of Joan's dress in the early chapters of the book is de Conte's attempt to describe Joan clothed in woman's dress as she is presented to the court of the still-uncrowned Charles VII:

> Queen Yolande wanted Joan to make the best possible impression upon the King and the Court, so she was strenuous to have her clothed in the richest stuffs, wrought upon the princeliest pattern, and set off with jewels; but in that she had to be disappointed, of course, Joan not being persuadable to it, but begging to be simply and sincerely dressed, as became a servant of God. . . . So then the gracious Queen imagined and contrived that simple and witching costume which I have described to you so many times, and which I cannot think of even now in my dull age without being moved just as rhythmical and exquisite music moves one; for *that* was music, that dress— that is what it was—music that one saw with the eyes and felt in the heart. Yes, she was a poem, she was a dream, she was a spirit when she was clothed in that. (*PR*, 108)

This description is notable for several reasons. One is the narrator's ironic choice of the word "witching," given that one of the long-standing charges against Joan, at the Inquisition and in England at least through the time of Shakespeare, was that Joan was a sorcerer, a witch. Further, de Conte says he will not describe Joan's "simple and witching costume" because he had described it to us so many times before; *yet that description never occurs.* We do not see that costume, here or at any other time. Instead, de Conte describes the effect of the dress upon himself, in the most striking terms. He confuses all the senses—the dress *is* music, but music that is "*seen* with the eyes and *felt* in the heart." Unable to focus even for a moment on the physical, concrete dress and the body it clothes, de Conte moves from the absent physical body to music, from music to Joan as a poem, to Joan as a dream, and finally to Joan as a spirit "when she was clothed in that." From the manuscript for *Joan of Arc,* we can discern that Twain took special care in writing this passage. He crossed out lines and passages so heavily that they can no longer be deciphered, and the passage as it finally appears in the text is inserted in handwriting into the typescript. Over all, this brief section of the manuscript is edited much more heavily than is characteristic of the manuscript as a whole.[22] Here is de Conte (and Twain's) opportunity to describe the feminine Joan, and it is as though there is no feminine physical self to portray. The transvestite Joan is a much less ephemeral and illusive being than Joan the supplicant in the court of the man to whom she would pledge her fealty.

Joan's desire to be "simply and sincerely dressed" contrasts sharply with de Conte's description of then-king Charles after Joan's triumphant raising of the siege of Orléans. The king is described in the most foppish terms:

> When we entered the presence he sat throned, with his tinselled snobs and dandies around him. He looked like a forked carrot, so tightly did his clothing fit him from his waist down; he wore shoes with a rope-like pliant toe a foot long that had to be hitched up to the knee to keep it out of the way; he had on a crimson velvet cape that came no lower than his elbows; on his head he had a tall felt thing like a thimble, with a feather in its jewelled band that stuck up like a pen from an inkhorn, and from under that thimble his bush of stiff hair stuck down to his shoulders, curving outwards at the bottom, so that the cap and the hair together made the head like a shuttlecock. All the materials of his dress were rich, and all the colors brilliant. In his lap he cuddled a miniature greyhound that snarled, lifting its lip and showing its white teeth whenever any slight movement disturbed it. The King's dandies were dressed in about the same fashion as himself, and when I remembered that Joan had called the war-council of Orleans "disguised ladies' maids," it reminded me of people who squander all their money on a trifle and then haven't anything to invest when they come across a better chance; that name ought to have been saved for these creatures. (*PR*, 211–12)

This comic description is built on absurd similes, and it is full of de Conte's disdain. The irreverent image of the king as looking "like a

---

22. Remarkably, the language that de Conte uses here echoes language Samuel Clemens uses in a letter to his wife's parents, describing the joy he took in the house they had presented to Sam and Livy on their honeymoon. Their house, he said, "is a poem, it is music—& it speaks & it sings, to us, all the day long" (letter dated Feb. 20, 1870, quoted in Susan K. Harris, "The Dream of Domesticity," 171); see also the Joan of Arc manuscript, *Microfilm Edition of Mark Twain's Literary Manuscripts Available in the Mark Twain Papers*.

forked carrot" is one Twain has evoked before. It is the same image Hank Morgan used to describe Clarence the first time he encountered him in *A Connecticut Yankee in King Arthur's Court:* "This was an airy slim boy in shrimp-colored tights that made him look like a forked carrot; the rest of the gear was blue silk and dainty laces and ruffles; and he had long yellow curls, and wore a plumed pink satin cap tilted complacently over his ear." Clarence, represented as a sexually ambiguous character, is nearly as ridiculous as the king in his orange tights.[23] The other similes de Conte uses to describe Charles's appearance are equally comic: long toes on his shoes like a rope, a hat like a thimble, a feather that stuck up like a pen, and a head like a shuttlecock. Twain's purpose in describing Charles in these terms is to convey through his clothing, as Twain does through Joan's, the nature of his character. In de Conte's eyes, at least, he is not worthy of Joan's unwavering personal loyalty and devotion. As the representative of the nation, he is a failed patriarch.

One of Twain's most original contributions to the Joan of Arc story was his creation of the character of the Paladin, Joan's childhood playmate; he becomes her standard bearer in battle, and ultimately he fights to his death to try to prevent Joan's being captured by the English at Compiègne. Until the final scene at the end of book 2, when he is killed, he is at once a comic and heroic figure, a tower of strength, a giant of a man, yet a bit of a fop himself. De Conte's descriptions of his fanciful costume, however, convey not contempt but affection and pleasure. When others are bogged down by endlessly waiting for the king to give them permission to proceed,

> The Paladin was the only exception—that is to say, he was the only one who was happy and had no heavy times. This was partly owing to the satisfaction he got out of his clothes. He bought them when he first arrived. He bought them at second hand—a Spanish cavalier's

23. Twain, *Connecticut Yankee,* 61; Dan Beard's illustration that accompanies Twain's description of Clarence shows him dressed in clothing modeled upon the costume worn by Sarah Bernhardt in her famous role as Hamlet. Thus in *Connecticut Yankee* we have a cross-dressed female serving as the model for the androgynous young boy on whom "the boss" will rely in trying to reform an entire nation—indeed history itself. It is worth noting that in 1890 Sarah Bernhardt played the role of Joan of Arc in Gounod's musical version of Jules Barbier's play *Jeanne d'Arc* (Warner, *Joan of Arc,* 242).

complete suit, wide-brimmed hat with flowing plumes, lace collar and cuffs, faded velvet doublet and trunks, short cloak hung from the shoulder, funnel-topped buskins, long rapier, and all that—a graceful and picturesque costume, and the Paladin's great frame was the right place to hang it for effect. He wore it when off duty; and when he swaggered by with one hand resting on the hilt of his rapier, and twirling his new mustache with the other, everybody stopped to look and admire; and well they might, for he was a fine and stately contrast to the small French gentleman of the day squeezed into the trivial French costume of the time. (*PR*, 115)

This is the image of someone both classically masculine and feminine—both "stately" and comic. The description does not rely upon metaphor or simile, as did de Conte's descriptions of the king's dress, though his dress could readily be mocked, had de Conte so desired. Instead, what we witness here is the lead-in to an extended chapter devoted to the Paladin's brilliant ability to entertain the simple villagers with his wild exaggerations.

The Paladin is in much demand as an entertainer and as a yarn-spinner, and he is a popular favorite with the ordinary people in the story. Like Twain himself, the Paladin uses comic exaggeration to amuse his audience. De Conte describes him as having "the narrative gift":

Most people who have the narrative gift—that great and rare endowment—have with it the defect of telling their choice things over the same way every time, and this injures them and causes them to sound stale and wearisome after several repetitions; but it was not so with the Paladin, whose art was of a finer sort; it was more stirring and interesting to hear him tell about a battle the tenth time than it was the first time, because he did not tell it twice the same way, but always made a new battle of it and a better one, with more casualties on the enemy's side each time, and more general wreck and disaster all around, and more widows and orphans and suffering in the neighborhood where it happened. (*PR*, 116)

Twain's own interest in "the narrative gift" was piqued during the time he was writing *Joan of Arc*. His descriptions of the Paladin's comic genius may have stimulated his own thinking about the craft of storytelling, or his reflections upon his own art may have influenced his representation of the Paladin; in February 1894, on one of his frequent trips between Europe and New York, Twain wrote "How to Tell a Story," one of the most acclaimed essays by a humorist about the nature of his craft.[24] Focusing primarily on oral humor, or platform humor, the essay describes the "innocent" narrator who appears to be unaware he has said anything funny. Here is de Conte's begrudging praise for the Paladin's narrative technique:

> He could not tell his battles apart himself, except by their names; and by the time he had told one of them ten times he had to lay it aside and start a new one in its place, because it had grown so that there wasn't room enough in France for it any more, but was lapping over the edges. But up to that point the audience would not allow him to substitute a new battle, knowing that the old ones were the best, and sure to improve as long as France could hold them; and so, instead of saying to him as they would have said to another, "Give us something fresh, we are fatigued with that old thing," they would say, with one voice and with a strong interest, "Tell about the surprise at Beaulieu again—tell it three or four times!" That is a compliment which few narrative experts have heard in their lifetime.
>
> At first when the Paladin heard us tell about the glories of the Royal Audience he was broken-hearted because he was not taken with us to it; next, his talk was full of what he would have done if he had been there; and within two days he was telling what he *did* do when he *was* there. His mill was fairly started, now, and could be trusted to take care of its affair. Within three nights afterwards all his battles were taking a rest, for already his worshippers in the tap-room were so infatuated with the great tale of the Royal Audience that they would have nothing else, and so besotted with it were they that they would have cried if they could not have gotten it. (*PR*, 116–17)

A very human level of jealousy creeps into de Conte's representation of the Paladin, for the latter is a crowd favorite, a decisive man of action, and a favorite of Joan's. Along with their childhood friend Noël, the three men also are rivals in their affection for Catherine Boucher, the eighteen-year-old "daughter of the house" where Joan and her staff await the return of their army so they could mount their first attack. As de Conte observes, "none of us had ever been in love before, and now we had the misfortune to all fall in love with the same person at the same time—which was the first moment we saw her" (*PR*, 161). The

24. Camfield, *Oxford Companion to Mark Twain*, 273.

Paladin gains most of the crowd's attention, including Catherine's, much to de Conte and Noël's dismay: "and to hear this windy giant lay out his imaginary campaigns and fairly swim in blood and spatter it all around, entertained them to the verge of the grave. Catherine was like to die, for pure enjoyment. She didn't laugh loud—we, of course, wished she would—but kept in the shelter of a fan, and shook until there was danger that she would unhitch her ribs from her spine" (*PR*, 161). In contrast with the physicality Twain bestows upon Catherine, Joan remains physically illusive throughout.

De Conte wrote a love poem for Catherine and, in order to gain the stage for even a few minutes, conspired with Noël to play a trick on the Paladin by calling him away in the middle of his telling one of his tales. Too shy to read the poem himself, de Conte persuades Noël to recite it for him. But first Noël, who is an exceptional mimic, takes up the Paladin's tale where he left off, and "turned himself into the Paladin—a dwarfed Paladin, of course—with manner, tones, gestures, attitudes, everything exact, and went right on with the battle, and it would be impossible to imagine a more perfectly and minutely ridiculous imitation than he furnished to those shrieking people" (*PR*, 165). Once again the laughter is physical—literally played out in the body:

> They went into spasms, convulsions, frenzies of laughter, and the tears flowed down their cheeks in rivulets. The more they laughed, the more inspired Noël grew with his theme and the greater the marvels he worked, till really the laughter was not properly laughing any more, but screaming. Blessedest feature of all, Catherine Boucher was dying with ecstasies, and presently there was little left of her but gasps and suffocations. Victory? It was a perfect Agincourt. (*PR*, 165)

Then, as planned, Noël begins to recite de Conte's love poem, "The Rose of Orleans." But de Conte's moment of glory is short-lived. The Paladin returns, but not to center stage; feigning great interest in the poem, he begins to wipe tears away from his face with the back of his hands. Then he begins to snuffle, to half sob, then to "cry like a calf":

> Then he went on from bad to worse, until I never saw such a spectacle; for he fetched out a towel from under his doublet and began to

swab his eyes with it and let go the most infernal bellowings mixed up
with sobbings and groanings and retchings and barkings and cough-
ings and snortings and screamings and howlings—and he twisted
himself about on his heels and squirmed this way and that, still pour-
ing out that brutal clamor and flourishing his towel in the air and
swabbing again and wringing it out. Hear? You couldn't hear yourself think. Noël was wholly drowned out and silenced, and those people were laughing the very lungs out of themselves. (*PR,* 166)

Joan's famous general, La Hire, joined in with an explosion of laughter, "and his jaws spread to that degree to let out his hurricanes and his
thunders that it amounted to indecent exposure, for you could see
everything that was in him" (*PR,* 167). The only thing that could possibly be worse, from de Conte's point of view, immediately comes to
pass—Joan of Arc enters the room and bursts into laughter, and an
"earthquake" of laughter follows. De Conte was bitterly defeated, and
in his characteristically humorless way concludes that "the effect of the
poem was spoiled" (*PR,* 167).

Two chapters are thus given over to the art of storytelling and exaggeration, to comic relief in which comedy and laughter are themselves the subject of the narration. Even the constrained de Conte,
whose love poem becomes the object of the Paladin's ridicule, breaks
out of some of his narrative restraints and seems to find pleasure in using colloquial rhythms and images—people laughing their lungs out,
and laughter so unrestrained that "it amounted to indecent exposure."
The scene is the major comic relief in the entire narrative, welcomed
not only by the immediate audience in Orléans, but also by modern
readers of *Personal Recollections.* The scene is also a classic example of
carnivalesque, festive laughter. It combines parody, the "high" and the
"low" mingling together, grotesque images of the body—people
laughing their lungs out, visceral "retchings" and "howlings"—and for
one brief moment, "the laughter of all the people." This major comic
interlude is the last time in the text when laughter will reign, but as
Bakhtin noted, "every act of world history was accompanied by a laughing chorus."[25]

Shortly after the scenes recounted above, Joan and her followers

25. Bakhtin, *Rabelais,* 474.

have their first real battle, including her major military accomplishment—raising the siege of Orléans. A series of other decisive victories followed—at Tours and Patay—and the Hundred Years' War was reaching an end. At Rheims, with Joan at his side, Charles was crowned king of France. Considering her work done, Joan begged to be relieved of her duties and to return to her hometown. Charles would not release her, nor give her permission to capitalize on the momentum she and her armies had gained, which would have allowed them to recapture Paris. Instead, they "drifted about" for eight months until Joan was captured at a battle at Compiègne. She became a prisoner of the English under the duke of Burgundy, who, in turn, delivered her "into the hands of the Church to be tried as an idolater" (*PR*, 319).

Joan's cross-dressing, which has been taken as a given in her role as commander of the French army, takes on new life and importance during her imprisonment and trial—the final third of Twain's work. Whereas battle conditions could be said to have dictated Joan's dress while in war, the fact that Joan clothed herself entirely in men's clothing while in prison became the centerpiece of her trial. Unable to make any headway on charges of witchcraft, on charges that she was in league with the Devil, on charges that her "voices" were satanic, Joan's inquisitors returned again and again to the fact that Joan cross-dressed. They were deeply offended by her transvestitism, which they saw as a sin against Nature and the Church, and as proof that her voices were not divine. In Twain's version of the "life," the matter of Joan's "male attire" is the subject of interrogation more than twenty times—more than in his sources, and more than in the official court record. Because her prison dress takes on such importance in the story, Twain describes that clothing with some care. The first time Joan is escorted into the chapel where the trial initially takes place, de Conte observes that "she had on men's attire—all black; a soft woolen stuff, intensely black, funereally black, not a speck of relieving color in it from her throat to the floor. A wide collar of this same black stuff lay in radiating folds upon her shoulders and breast; the sleeves of her doublet were full, down to the elbows, and tight thence to her manacled wrists; below the doublet, tight black hose down to the chains on her ankles" (*PR*, 337). The predominant impression de Conte conveys is of the intense blackness of Joan's clothing, repeating as he does the word "black" five times in just two sentences. His choice of the adverb "funereally" to modify "black" is especially important, for it overtly introduces a direct association between Joan's cross-dressing and the fate that awaits her. It joins Joan's transgressive dress, symbolic of a deeper, more profound rebellion, and her impending death. The details furnished by de Conte, even with the rather vague "black 'stuff'" of the woolen material, was sufficient to guide the text's illustrator to depict Joan in her "male attire," defending herself before her accusers. The illustration, in turn, underscores Joan's sexual ambiguity, for it is a very masculine woman who is shown on trial here.

Joan's interrogators understood perfectly well that Joan's cross-dressing was key to who she was. She was a woman who defied social convention, who transformed herself into an androgynous figure who could not be defeated on the battlefield and who would not conform to the patriarchal rule of the Church. She answered only to the highest authority, which infuriated her enemies. In Twain's *Personal Recollections,* and in other versions of her life, the inquisitors are interested in knowing why she has chosen to don men's clothing. They want to know who told her to wear men's clothing in the first place. They want to know if she has attended mass dressed in men's clothing (Joan admits she did, but never in her armor). Would she like to put on women's clothes in prison? Would she put on women's clothing in prison if they let her attend mass? Did her voices tell her to cross-dress? When St. Michael appeared to her, was he clothed or naked? When all other charges and lines of questions seem to fail, the Church increases its pressures on Joan to cast off her male attire and dress in women's clothing.

The only explanation offered in Twain's text for Joan's cross-dressing is modesty, yet behind the words lay a highly charged scenario with harassing guards and a sexually threatened young woman at the mercy of her captors. Tuckey had stressed, and Twain implies, that modesty is Joan's primary motivator throughout, but Tuckey argues more forcefully: "The perpetual presence of such watchers would have been a horror and an insult to the vilest of women: let us remember what Joan was—how jealously she guarded her purity—how among men-at-arms she had kept the delicacy of her womanhood—and we shall understand a little of the hourly misery she had to suffer." A number of times in Tuckey, Joan also says that she wears men's clothing because she prefers

Joan of Arc on trial, wearing her "male attire."

it, that "it pleases God that I shall wear it," or that the whole issue is "a trifling thing." At times Twain echoes Tuckey's language directly; Joan says at one point that her cross-dressing is "a trifling thing and of no consequence" (*PR*, 357). Unlike Twain, Tuckey also suggests that Joan's inquisitors insisted she revert to a peasant's dress, whereas Joan demanded they give her a long gown, "like that of a citizen's daughter."[26] In other words, Tuckey introduces the issue of class, with Joan refusing to dress like a peasant. Twain does not pick up on this, nor on the suggestion that when Joan did wear women's clothing it was "of such wanton fashion and costliness as to offend all honest men" (*PR*, 13).

For Michelet, crude male sexual behavior is the main threat to Joan's virtue. In his *Jeanne d'Arc*, a "gentleman, a lord" who visited her in her

26. On Joan's purity, see Tuckey, *Joan of Arc*, 124; she writes elsewhere: "The man's dress that had been her [Joan's] protection in the camp was her defense in the dungeon, and her unwillingness to lay it by *reveals what dangers that dungeon held for her.* Her judges, with amazing dullness, *or more amazing wickedness,* could not or would not understand her motives" (Twain's emphasis), 160–61; for "trifling thing" and "wanton fashion," see 138, 159.

prison cell attempted to rape her. He "patriotically devoted himself to this execution, bravely undertook to violate a girl laden with fetters, and being unable to effect his wishes, rained blows upon her." According to Michelet, the court brought in a group of matrons to examine Joan; they proclaimed her still a virgin.[27] Twain, by contrast, is extremely reluctant to sexualize Joan even by suggesting that she is in danger of physical assault in her cell. Instead, he keeps his focus firmly on the fact that Joan wore "men's attire." For Twain, it appears to be the defining point of her life in prison. "Of course the matter of the male attire was gone over again; and as usual at wearisome length; also, as usual, the customary bribe was offered: if she would discard that dress voluntarily they would let her hear mass. But she answered as she had often answered before—'I will go in a woman's robe to all services of the church if I may be permitted, but I will resume the other dress when I return to my cell'" (*PR*, 407–8). The phrase "male attire" becomes an incantation evoking the "crime" that Joan continues to commit; expressed as an abstraction, the phrase nonetheless comes to represent her highly disruptive affront to the church patriarchy and to gendered conventions. It underscores, moreover, the fact that Joan cross-dresses by choice.

That choice is a fatal one. Unable to make any of their many charges stick against Joan, the Church, headed by Cauchon, finally resorts to trickery to condemn Joan. After a full year in prison, exhausted by the cross-examinations and weak from being constantly in chains, Joan is brought out into a public square, where the executioner's stake, wood, and red-hot coals are prominent, and she is forced to foreswear cross-dressing. They threaten her with the only thing she fears, death by fire, and demand that she "abjure" wearing men's clothing. In a brief Twainesque moment, she replies "Abjure? What is abjure?" de Conte continues: "She did not know the word" (*PR*, 432). Joan finally submits and puts her "mark" to the papers, because she is illiterate, and a clerk guides her hand to write "Jehanne." Already the final deceit had begun, for the Church had substituted a much longer written confession for the oral one Joan had reluctantly made. Then more promises were broken—she was condemned to perpetual imprisonment, and

27. J. Michelet, *Jeanne d'Arc, 1412–1432*, 133.

rather than being sent to a prison run by the Church itself, where she would have female attendants, she is returned to the repressive English prison. There, the final trickery and deceit took place—while she slept, her female clothing was taken from her and replaced by only male clothing.

> Here is what had happened. While Joan slept, in the early morning of Sunday, one of the guards stole her female apparel and put her male attire in its place. When she woke she asked for the other dress, but the guards refused to give it back. She protested, and said she was forbidden to wear the male dress. But they continued to refuse. She had to have clothing, for modesty's sake; moreover, she saw that she could not save her life if she must fight for it against treacheries like this; so she put on the forbidden garments, knowing what the end would be. She was weary of the struggle, poor thing. (*PR*, 441)

This is a crucial scene in the story of Joan of Arc. According to Twain's biographer, Albert Bigelow Paine, Twain's first "acquaintance" with the historical Joan of Arc centered on this scene of treachery. One day when he was a boy, walking down a street in Hannibal, so the story goes, a piece of paper blew across the street and into his hands. He discovered that it was a page out of a book about Joan's life: "It was from her life in prison, in the cage at Rouen. Two ruffian English soldiers had stolen her clothes, and she was reproaching them and enduring their ribald replies. *It roused all my indignation.*"[28] By the time Twain came to write this scene for *Personal Recollections*, however, the indignation has abated. Instead, the dramatic denouement, Joan's relapse, is rendered in surprisingly flat prose.

Immediately, Joan is condemned to death. Ironically, Joan is led to her execution clothed in a long white gown, obviously chosen by the church fathers. "She looked girlishly fair and sweet and saintly in her long white robe," according to de Conte, and as she was brought to the marketplace at the center of Rouen, "thousands upon thousands" fell to their knees. Joan said a public prayer for her king and asked all present to pray for her. Then she was put to death. Twain, and therefore de Conte, apparently had no stomach for representing in vivid de-

---

28. Quoted in Paine, introduction to *Personal Recollections*, xv (emphasis added).

tail her actual death, unlike the way he had described dying at the stake in both *Prince and the Pauper* and *A Connecticut Yankee*. De Conte makes a point of telling us that he himself could not bear to watch her execution:

> All these things I saw, albeit dimly and blurred with tears; but I could bear no more. I continued in my place, but what I shall deliver to you now I got by others' eyes and others' mouths. Tragic sounds there were that pierced my ears and wounded my heart as I sat there, but it is as I tell you: the latest image recorded by my eyes in that desolating hour was Joan of Arc with the grace of her comely youth still unmarred; and that image, untouched by time or decay, has remained with me all my days. Now I will go on. (*PR*, 456)

For all those present, the smoke and the flames hid Joan from sight, and she died as a martyr.

In a final chapter, entitled "Conclusion," de Conte tells what happened to Joan's friends as time passed, and to her family, with the "rehabilitation" of Joan sponsored by King Charles. De Conte concludes by insisting that above all Joan stood for patriotism:

> She was the Genius of Patriotism—she was Patriotism embodied, concreted, made flesh, and palpable to the touch and visible to the eye.
>
> Love, Mercy, Charity, Fortitude, War, Peace, Poetry, Music—these may be symbolized as any shall prefer: by figures of either sex and of any age; but a slender girl in her first young bloom, with the martyr's crown upon her head, and in her hand the sword that severed her country's bonds—shall not this, and no other, stand for PATRI-OTISM through all the ages until time shall end? (*PR*, 461)

Joan's love for France and the French people, for its king, was never for a moment in doubt, but the final notion that Joan stood above all else for patriotism simply does not ring true. Her king had abandoned and betrayed Joan, and her death was the ultimate indictment of both the sovereign patriarch and the church patriarchy. De Conte's words, no matter how soaring, cannot smooth over the rupture that Joan's transvestitism exposes.

A final, more personal, patriarchal crisis that lies just behind the writing of *Joan of Arc* was being played out in the Clemens household in 1893 and 1894 when Twain was writing his tome. The two eldest Clemens daughters, Susy and Clara, were on the threshold of adulthood and sexual maturity, much to the consternation of their father. Everything was unsettled in the family. We will recall that the family moved to Europe in 1892 for a variety of reasons, the most immediate being to try to head off personal bankruptcy; the expectation was that the family could dramatically cut their expenses by living abroad. They also went abroad because Twain's wife, Livy, was experiencing poor health, and her doctors believed she would be helped by seeking treatment in German spas; their first European destination, therefore, was Germany. Sam and Livy also seemed determined to put literal distance between Susy and Louise Brownell, the woman with whom Susy had fallen in love at Bryn Mawr, so Suzy was abruptly withdrawn from college before the spring term ended. Livy's health continued to be compromised, and she was ordered to have complete rest and isolation, which the family found in a villa they rented on the outskirts of Florence. Clara, meanwhile, was determined to remain in Germany, where she could continue to study music, and in spite of her father's extreme reluctance to allow her to do so, she stayed on when her family moved to Florence.

For a family that had been as social and as public as the Clemens family had been in Hartford, life in Florence must have seemed like being in exile. Livy was not allowed to go out or receive visitors in Villa Viviana, Clara was in Germany, and Susy was restless. She had had a taste of freedom and independence at Bryn Mawr, and now she was back in the family household with few suitable social outlets or connections. Sam Clemens, meanwhile, made numerous trips to the United States, most of them to try to rescue the family's financial situation and to meet with his publishers. Otherwise, they relied upon one other for company, and while it is unlikely they got in each other's way in their eighteen-room villa, there clearly were family tensions, especially between Susy and her father. Susy was often bored, and her attention continued to be fixed on Louise, as her correspondence attests. At the same time, there is no doubt that Susy did figure large in Twain's representation of Joan. In retrospect, Twain admitted that he based his physical representation of Joan on Susy at the age of seventeen:

Susy at 17—Joan of Arc at 17. Secretly I drew Joan's physical portrait
from Susy at that age, when I came to write that book. Apart from
that, I had no formally-appointed model for Joan but her own historical self. [Yet there were several points of resemblance between the
girls: such as vivacity, enthusiasm, precocious wisdom, wit, eloquence,
penetration, nobility of character. In Joan the five latter qualities were
of a measure that has not been paralleled in any other person of like
age in history; but I comprehended them in her all the better from
comprehending them in their lesser measure in Susy.][29]

Twain's retrospective comparison of Joan and Susy—their "resemblance"
—could be understood as a father's grief and nostalgia, written as this observation was years after he had published his novel and after Susy had
died unexpectedly. It is likely, however, that it does represent what he
thought he was doing while he was actually writing Joan's life. Furthermore, in the face of Livy's frailty, and with Susy now a young woman with
literary aspirations of her own, Twain remarked that the editing practices
so long undertaken by Livy now passed to his eldest daughter.

Twain continued the habit, begun during their summers at Quarry
Farm, of entertaining his family at the end of the day with excerpts from
his writing that day. In a letter from Susy to her sister Clara, we learn
that "Papa" cried when he read one of Joan's speeches to his assembled
family, and at one point Susy held up the reading so she could go fetch
a handkerchief in anticipation of her own crying. When Twain was writing the final book of the novel, which focuses on Joan's imprisonment,
trial, and execution, the family traveled to Rouen to visit the site where
all this action took place. Susy became ill there, and instead of having
a brief visit, the family was forced to stay there a full month while she
convalesced. In retrospect, the connection in Twain's mind between his
Joan of Arc and his daughter Susy could only have been strengthened
by this coincidence. It does not, however, support the conclusion that
Susy "demanded purity, gentility, high sentiment."[30]

29. Twain on Susy at seventeen, draft of memorial to Susy, 1902, quoted in Emerson, *Authentic Mark Twain*, 200. During the time the Clemens family was in Florence
and France, Susy wrote at least thirty letters to Louise.

30. Quoted in Paine, introduction to *Personal Recollections*, xviii; on demand for gentility, see Kaplan, introduction to *Personal Recollections*, xl.

Instead, the image that emerges is of a daughter with a vexed relationship with her father. Susy wanted to be elsewhere, to regain some of the freedom that she had tasted, however briefly, at Bryn Mawr. She wanted specifically, too, to be with Louise. At the same time, she envied her sister, Clara, for being away from the family, studying in Germany, and she urged her to stay away. Most of all, she felt she was under her father's scrutiny in a way that was wholly unpleasant for her, as a letter to Clara in November 1893 revealed: "I have to go down to breakfast now, and I don't enjoy this one bit, although Papa hasn't stormed yet. Still I feel constrained and *he pierces me thru with his eyes* as if he were determined to see whether I am embarrassed or not."[31] She was no longer seventeen, no longer a moody but obedient daughter, and no longer an innocent child. She was a young woman with a life and longings of her own, with desires her father could not possibly approve of. Even though he "pierced her thru with his eyes," he could not, in fact, truly see her as she was at age twenty, sitting before him, let alone at age seventeen, given the passage of time. His "secret model" for Joan eluded him.

In 1898, two years after Susy's death, Clemens revealed that he had trouble conjuring up the detailed physical image of those closest to him; he reveals this in reference to a house that appeared to him in a recurring dream:

> When I think of that house and its belongings, I recognize what a master in taste and drawing and color and arrangement is the dream-artist who resides in us. In my waking hours, when the inferior artist in me is in command, I cannot draw even the simplest picture with a pencil, nor do anything with a brush and colors; I cannot bring before my mind's eye the detailed image of any building known to me except my own house at home. . . . I cannot bring before my mind's eye the face or figure of any human being known to me; I have seen my family at breakfast within the past two hours; I cannot bring their images before me, I do not know how they look.

---

31. Letter from Susy Clemens to Clara Clemens, November 1893, in the Mark Twain Papers.

In his Autobiographical Dictations, he confessed that he did not know the color of his children's eyes.[32]

In his 1904 essay on the historical figure of Joan of Arc, Twain complained of the way artists depicted Joan, recalling only that she was a peasant and therefore representing her "as a strapping middle-aged fishwoman, with costume to match, and in her face the spirituality of a ham." Insisting that because Joan had a beautiful character, she would have been a beautiful young woman, he continues, "The artist should paint her *spirit*—then he could not fail to paint her body aright. She would rise before us, then, a vision to win us, not repel: a lithe young slender figure, instinct with 'the unbought grace of youth,' dear and bonny and loveable, the face beautiful, and transfigured with the light of that lustrous intellect and the fires of that unquenchable spirit."[33] This is the Joan of Arc Mark Twain set out to represent, but not precisely the figure he captured in *Personal Recollections*. Instead, the image of the transgressive, cross-dressed "daughter" came through as clearly as the obedient, beautiful spirit he had hoped to give life to through his novel. If Susy exerted extraordinary influence upon Twain's depiction of Joan, it was not because of her piety or "intolerant idealism" but because her father could not fully come to terms with the reality of an independent and transgressive daughter.

In the years following Susy's unexpected death in 1896, Twain would return again and again to stories about daughters who were truly transgressive, who defied traditional notions of how a young girl should behave, or who dressed and lived their lives as men; to stories about men who passed for women; to stories in which the characters seem to be born into the "wrong" sex; and even to stories about same-sex relationships. Never again would he write a full-length novel about a transvestite character, and a number of the stories featuring transvestites or gender-transgressive figures were either never finished or never intended for publication in his lifetime. Nonetheless, he continued to play with gendered expectations in the final years of his career. Many of

32. Mark Twain, "My Platonic Sweetheart," 293; Twain, Autobiographical Dictations, *Microfilm Edition of Mark Twain's Literary Manuscripts Available in the Mark Twain Papers.*
33. Twain, "Saint Joan of Arc," 595.

the attendant themes continue to show up in these stories as well—the association of cross-dressing with death, an emphasis on the clothing one wears when cross-dressed—while other themes seem to fall away, especially Twain's exploration of cross-dressing together with racial crossing. At the same time, new themes emerge, most notably his exploration of same-sex relationships. The years 1896–1906 were rich ones in this regard and will be the focus of the final chapter in this book.

5

Transvestite Tales

Following the publication of *Pudd'nhead Wilson* and *Joan of Arc*, Mark Twain wrote at least five additional shorter pieces, only one of which was published in his lifetime, that continued the exploration of the themes of cross-dressing and gender transgression. These works, in the order of their composition, are "Wapping Alice," "Hellfire Hotchkiss," *Is He Dead?* "How Nancy Jackson Married Kate Wilson" (also known as the "Feud Story and the Girl Who Was Ostensibly a Man,"), and "A Horse's Tale." Four of these pieces have been collected by John Cooley in *How Nancy Jackson Married Kate Wilson, and Other Tales of Rebellious Girls & Daring Young Women*. The fifth selection, the previously unpublished play *Is He Dead?* was edited by Shelley Fisher Fishkin and published for the first time in 2003 by the University of California Press. All these works, with the addition of the 1870 "An Awful—Terrible Medieval Romance," have at their core male and female characters who defy social expectations regarding proper or appropriate gender behavior. Two feature young women who can best be characterized as tomboys, one features a female-to-male transvestite,

A portion of this chapter was published as "The Eloquent Silence in Mark Twain's 'Hellfire Hotchkiss,'" *Mark Twain Annual* 3 (2005): 43–51.

and two foreground male-to-female transvestitism. In at least two of the tales, Twain flirts openly with homosexual relations, while two are concerned with what Susan Gillman calls "female fatherhood," that is, female-to-male transvestites who are accused of fathering children.[1] In tone, the tales run the gamut from grim social determinism through tales that seem to have no other purpose than to celebrate gender crossings and to defy social norms, and ultimately to farce. In these tales, taken as a whole, Twain goes farther than before in exploring gender as a social construct and demonstrating the performative nature of gender. These tales are bolder and more outrageous than any of his earlier explorations of gender transgression. Nonetheless, there is still a dark side to cross-dressing and transvestitism, most notably in the continued linking of cross-dressing with the threat of death. Boundaries get crossed and recrossed, and gender gets constructed and deconstructed, all with a freedom and abandon not readily seen in the earlier published works.

The term *transvestite tales* was first applied to several of these pieces by Susan Gillman, who analyzed the stories in the context of Twain's fascination with, first, the colorful, androgynous clothing of the natives of Ceylon and Africa as articulated in *Following the Equator* (1897), and, second, with prominent criminal trials Twain was following in the press during this time. In calling them *transvestite tales*, Gillman refers to stories that express "a fascination with all that seems to unsettle sexual differentiation," with stories in which "the conceit of female fatherhood [is] on trial, an open-ended confounding of sexual categories."[2] These are tales in which for a sustained period of time a woman dresses as a man and passes as a man, or those in which a man assumes a woman's identity and passes for a woman. In every instance, the tales involve disguise, some degree of deception (although who is deceived varies considerably), and/or a central character self-consciously performing a gender. I also include in my consideration tales in which there is no transvestitism, but nonetheless a considerable degree of gender play. John Cooley characterizes such stories as featuring "rebellious girls and daring young women"; I see them more succinctly as stories

1. Gillman, *Dark Twins*, 108.
2. Ibid., 101, 107–8.

about female characters (and to some extent, male characters) who cross traditional gender boundaries not as acts of rebellion but because they cannot readily express themselves within the confines of their assigned gender categories.

Gillman has correctly pointed out that most of these stories and tales were "either unfinished, textually problematic, or 'unliterary.'"[3] To my mind, these qualities only make them more intriguing—and more revealing. Some, such as "Hellfire Hotchkiss," have a raw quality about them that makes them seem more uninhibited, and thus more revealing of Twain's concerns and preoccupations than more polished stories might be. Because they lack the constraints that Twain would have imposed upon himself were he intending to publish this work, we can see more clearly how he tried to come to terms with conventional understandings about gender as well as his more radical sense that gender was a performance as surely as it was a biological "given." In this larger sense, not only are the works themselves unfinished but so too is Twain's larger investigation into gender transgression. In the last analysis, he seemed compelled repeatedly to expose the limitations of traditional notions about gender.

While all these stories interrogate conventional understandings of gender roles, they sometimes reinscribe gender norms even as they undercut them; the more radical stories, however, do not, as we shall see.[4] As I have indicated, themes associated with cross-dressing that have been present from the beginning, such as the association of gender crossing and gender transgression with morbidity, continue in these tales, often paradoxically infused with a new sense of play. Remarkably, however, the association of cross-dressing with racial crossing so important in *Huckleberry Finn* and *Pudd'nhead Wilson* is more or less absent in these late tales. The two black characters who do appear in the tales are not themselves involved in gender crossings; instead, they are depicted primarily as comic characters. Further, Twain continues to be more interested in women than men who challenge traditional gender roles, and indeed his most "seriously" transgressive character is a female-to-male transvestite who is forced into that role by an act of revenge.

3. Ibid., 102.
4. This is a common complaint regarding contemporary gender performances as well; see Judith Halberstam, *Female Masculinity*.

For the most part, however, in these stories Twain is playful in his representations of transgressions against gendered conventions.

When writing about the transvestite tales, Gillman found it useful to divide the tales into two categories: those more or less conservative tales in which traditional gender roles are reversed, in which sexual categories are "momentarily confound[ed]," and those more radical tales in which "sexual difference turns out to be at its origin unstable and unprovable."[5] Building on Gillman's observations, I find it useful to consider the texts on a continuum. At one end I place "A Horse's Tale," whose protagonist, Cathy, is an innocent, vivacious young girl who rides her horse across the plains at great speed and who commands an army of young boys in mock Indian fights. At the other end of the continuum is the play *Is He Dead?* whose protagonist is a famous French artist who cross-dresses as his purported twin sister, and who gains the sexual attention of a man who is otherwise the villain of the piece. Between these two is a tale celebrating pure, energetic tomboyism with a substantial hint of lesbianism ("Hellfire Hotchkiss"); a story of private, personal revenge in which a young woman is forced to become a transvestite and is trapped into marrying a woman, but refuses to live with her ("How Nancy Jackson Married Kate Wilson"); and a story in which a Twain-like narrator contrives to force a marriage between a male carpenter and a female servant, only to discover after the fact that the servant is a man, not a woman as she had always represented herself to be ("Wapping Alice"). Taken together, these tales demonstrate an intensified exploration of gender on Twain's part, who repeatedly challenges essentialist and conventional notions of a stable, "natural" gender divide.

"A Horse's Tale"

Its title notwithstanding, "A Horse's Tale" is really a story about a young girl who is a classic tomboy. In fact, the extent to which she fulfills that role—the term *tomboy* was commonly understood in Twain's own time—makes this a relatively conventional portrait. There is nothing radical or really transgressive about the young protagonist, Cathy.

5. Gillman, *Dark Twins,* 111.

Still, the story is a celebration of a high-spirited girl who Twain told his publisher was unintentionally modeled on the young Susy, a fact he did not "discover" until some time later. John Cooley thought that the more likely model was Twain's "headstrong" daughter, Clara, then living in Europe, while an equally strong case could be made for seeing his youngest daughter, Jean, as the model. She was living with her father at the time, she was an accomplished horsewoman, and she loved animals as much as the story's protagonist does.[6] Perhaps Cathy is best understood as an amalgam of the Clemens daughters as their father recalled them as young girls. The story celebrates Cathy's relatively carefree childhood, but it ends abruptly and improbably in her traumatic death.

"A Horse's Tale" was written in 1905 and first published serially in *Harper's Monthly Magazine* in 1906. In 1907 it was published as a short book, by *Harper's*, with the same illustrations by Lucius Wolcott Hitchcock that graced the serialized version. According to Cooley, the story was written at the request of Minnie Maddern Fiske to expose the cruelty of bullfighting. Ironically, given the etiology of the story, bullfighting, or any mention of bullfighting, comes in only at the end of the tale and is not well integrated into the story as a whole. Nonetheless, the young protagonist, Cathy, and her beloved horse, Soldier Boy, are both killed in a bullfighting arena in Spain, far from the American West where the greater part of the story takes place. Thus a story that can properly be said to be full of good fun and good humor ends, improbably, as a tragedy. The story is set in motion when Cathy, the nine-year-old niece of General Alison, is orphaned and comes to stay with him at Fort Paxton on the western frontier. Cathy does "what the Indians were never able to do. She took the Fort" by storm.[7] Everyone finds her irresistible—the general, his black servant, Dorcas, the Indians in the fort, the historic figure Buffalo Bill, and the soldiers of the Ninth Dragoons. All succumb to her charms, and all admire her earnestness and her skill and daring as a horsewoman. The tale is told

---

6. On Susy as model, see Stoneley, *Mark Twain and the Feminine Aesthetic,* 111; see also John Cooley, "Mark Twain's Transvestite Tragedies: Role Reversals and Patriarchal Power," 42.

7. Cooley, "Transvestite Tragedies," 43; Mark Twain, "A Horse's Tale," 136 (hereinafter cited as HT).

in a series of first-person narrations that include letters from General Alison to his sister, Mercedes, and to his mother, letters from Cathy to her Aunt Mercedes (in Spain), dialogues between General Alison and his ex-slave, Dorcas, and between Buffalo Bill's horse, named Soldier Boy, and a "Genuine Mexican Plug" named Mongrel.

Under Buffalo Bill's tutelage, Cathy soon becomes the best rider among the children of the fort, especially when she is on the back of Soldier Boy, riding astride. She learns to shoot with a bow and arrow better than the others, and she is adopted by the Ninth Dragoons and given made-up titles: "Corporal-General of the Seventh Cavalry, and Flag-Lieutenant of the Ninth Dragoons, with the privilege (decreed by the men) of writing U.S.A. after her name!" (HT, 141). Good humor abounds in the tale, beginning with Soldier Boy narrating the first chapter and telling about his relationship to "him," Buffalo Bill, and how he keeps up with news at the fort through Potter, the general's dog, and Shekels, the Seventh Cavalry's dog. There is considerable wordplay throughout, with malapropisms and lines such as these, by Soldier Boy: "My mother was all American—no alkali-spider about *her*, I can tell you; she was of the best blood of Kentucky, the bluest Blue-grass aristocracy, very proud and acrimonious—or maybe it is ceremonious. I don't know which it is. But it is no matter; size is the main thing about a word, and that one's up to standard" (HT, 132).

Not only do the animals talk with each other in this text, but they are the sources for spreading most of the gossip in the story. Shekels, we learn, gets much of his gossip from the house cats, whose language he speaks. Soldier Boy also hears gossip from Potter, the general's dog, who is a Great Dane. "He is privileged, all over the post, like Shekels, the Seventh Cavalry's dog, and visits everybody's quarters and picks up everything that is going, in the way of news. Potter has no imagination, and no great deal of culture, perhaps, but he has a historical mind and a good memory, and so he is the person I depend upon mainly to post me up when I get back from a scout. That is, if Shekels is out on depredation and I can't get hold of him" (HT, 134). This kind of playfulness in the text makes it difficult to accept that in the end Twain turned the whole story into a tragedy, with Cathy moving back to Spain with her uncle and taking Soldier Boy with her. There the famous horse is stolen and treated ever more cruelly by a series of owners until he is fit only for one last ride by a picador in a bullfight. Cathy, inexplicably, is present at the bullfight and recognizes Soldier Boy as he is eviscerated by a bull; she runs to his side in the arena and is herself mortally wounded by the bull. She dies asking for someone to play "Taps."

Overall, the gender transgressions in "A Horse's Tale" are very modest. Cathy is young—preadolescent—and innocent. She is spunky and energetic, but there is little to suggest that she steps outside the bounds of acceptable behavior for a young girl, especially as her athletic abilities as a horsewoman are offset by her charming and winning ways with the older males portrayed in the story: her uncle, General Alison, and her special friend, Buffalo Bill (whom she calls B.B.). Peter Stoneley summarizes the effect of the gender disruption in these terms: "Whenever Twain pondered the idea of female figures with traditionally masculine qualities, it did not encourage him to believe that the capabilities of women generally had been underestimated, constrained or misdirected, but rather that he had discovered a special case. He could be said to reinforce traditional distinctions by drawing attention to them in this way."[8] Her military dress, made for her by the ladies of the fort, is more classically feminine than masculine: "it is all red and blue and white silks and satins and velvets: tights, trunks, sword, doublet with slashed sleeves, short cape, cap with just one feather in it; I've heard them name these things; they got them out of the book; she's dressed like a page, of old times, they say. It's the daintiest outfit that ever was—you will say so, when you see it. She's lovely in it—oh, just a dream!" (HT, 151).

The primary interest of this tale in the context of gender disruption is the ingenious explanation offered by the black servant, Dorcas, for how it is possible for Cathy to be both such a tomboy and such a clas-

---

8. Stoneley, *Mark Twain and the Feminine Aesthetic,* 113. Cooley calls attention to what he sees as a kind of sexual innuendo in the relationship between Cathy and Buffalo Bill: "In a scene of unusually suggestive eroticism for Twain, the girl side of Cathy appears to be engaged in 'innocent' sexual foreplay with Buffalo Bill. She sits in Buffalo Bill's lap and looks up lovingly into his brave eyes and rugged face. She plays with his long hair, admires his big hands, the long barrel of his dangerous carbine, and protests her love for him. Somewhat later in the story Cathy has apparently transferred her adolescent love for Buffalo Bill to a more suitable object, Bill's horse, the faithful and obedient gelding, Soldier Boy" (*How Nancy Jackson Married Kate Wilson,* 247). I do not find this analysis persuasive.

sically feminine child. Dorcas "conceived the curious idea that Cathy is *twins,* and that one of them is a boy-twin and failed to get segregated— got submerged, is the idea."

> "Look at her; she loves dolls, and girl-plays, and everything a girl loves, and she's gentle and sweet, and ain't cruel to dumb brutes— now that's the girl-twin, but she loves boy-plays, and drums and fifes and soldiering, and rough-riding, and ain't afraid of anybody or any-thing—and that's the boy-twin; 'deed you needn't tell *me* she's only *one* child; no, sir, she's twins, and one of them got shet up out of sight. Out of sight, but that don't make any difference, that boy is in there, and you can see him look out of her eyes when her temper is up."
> (HT, 143)

The comic quality of this explanation masks to some extent the fact that basic gender binaries dictating what is proper male-child behavior and female-child behavior go unchallenged in the text. Rather than desta-bilizing the fixed terms, Dorcas's explanation reinscribes them. None-theless, the tale is a celebration of a spirited young girl who enjoys a re-markable degree of physical freedom on the western frontier. In the next "tomboy" story to be considered here, Twain comes as close as he ever will in imagining, through fiction, a lesbian character. If ever a sto-ry was "Susy's story," "Hellfire Hotchkiss" is it.

"Hellfire Hotchkiss"

"Hellfire Hotchkiss," among the many stories Twain left unfinished toward the end of his career, stands out as especially enigmatic. Begun in August 1897, one year after the death of his daughter Susy and one year after the publication of *Personal Recollections of Joan of Arc,* "Hell-fire Hotchkiss" features another "Vesuvius seen through the butt-end of the telescope."[9] Rachel ("Hellfire"), with her mercurial temper, is an incurable tomboy (Twain's term) who plays only with the boys in the town. She defies to the core of her being the conventional gender role assigned her as a girl. Remarkably, Twain depicts the gender-defiant Hellfire as a fully sympathetic character and a heroine in her hometown.

---

9. Twain, "Hellfire Hotchkiss," 60 (hereinafter cited as HH).

Assuredly, the term *lesbian* is never mentioned in the text—indeed, the term was not yet in use in 1897 in the ways we understand it today. There was as yet no clear notion in the 1890s of a fixed gender identity determined by the object of one's desire. A young woman could enter into a Boston marriage, and schoolgirls and college girls could develop "smashes" on one another and have intimate romantic relationships, without such choices or activities constituting an "identity" as we have come to know it in the twenty-first century. Nonetheless, it was in the final decades of the nineteenth century that homosexuality began to have an emerging public face, and as we have seen, Twain was alert to the cultural debates taking place around him. In Twain's story "Hellfire Hotchkiss," Rachel/Hellfire is not involved in any relationship; that is not what defines her as "queer." In fact, the only character Hellfire is paired with is an effeminate male counterpart, Oscar "Thug" Carpenter.[10] Yet at least two factors invite us to "read" Hellfire as a lesbian. One centers on the challenges to gender norms embodied in the figures of both Hellfire and Oscar, and the way they are played off one another. The second is a poignant lacuna in the text—a remarkable silence that occurs at the crisis point in the story, which in our contemporary understanding "queers" the text. While in the end Hellfire is required to renounce her masculine ways and promises to reform, there is nothing convincing about her renunciation, no matter how sincere. Hellfire Hotchkiss cannot be contained either by the town's gossips or by the narrative she inhabits.

The story, set in pre–Civil War Dawson's Landing, the scene for Twain's *Pudd'nhead Wilson,* consists of just three chapters. The action begins with a chapter-long, comic dialogue between the parents of Oscar "Thug" Carpenter about their son, whom the father characterizes as "a girl in disguise." The chapter comes to an abrupt end when a boy outside the house is heard to announce, erroneously, that "Thug Carpenter got drowned." The second chapter takes up that story: the town's children were skating on the Mississippi River, the ice broke, a wide expanse of water opened up, and Thug disappeared. While a

---

10. The choice of the name "Oscar" for the effeminate counterpart to Hellfire may in fact be a reference to the most famous gay man of the times, Oscar Wilde. The nickname "Thug," by contrast, is surely ironic, given Oscar's nature.

crowd gathers, apparently helpless even to locate Thug, to the cheers of the townspeople Hellfire Hotchkiss races past them all, astride her black horse; she spots Thug, who appears as a dark speck on an ice flow on the other side of the open water. Hellfire takes off her shoes and, carrying a life preserver and a flask of whiskey, swims the one hundred to two hundred yards across the icy water to Thug. Although Thug is a poor swimmer and is deathly afraid, she persuades him to attempt to swim back with her, and they make it safely back to the firm ice.

In the third and final chapter of the story, Twain shifts his focus entirely to Hellfire—who she was, how she came to prefer the company of boys to girls, and how, now that she is sixteen years old, she has become the object of the town's gossip in what is described as an alarming new way. A well-meaning neighbor called Aunt Betsy Davis takes Hellfire aside and has a heart-to-heart talk with her, urging her to stop playing with the boys and by implication to conform to gender expectations. The conversation, as we will see, is surprisingly cryptic, but Hellfire understands what is being asked of her, and although she agrees it is "a pity," she says she will call a halt to the offending behavior, thus appearing to accede to society's wishes.

From the beginning, essentialist notions of gendered behavior are the "givens" of the story. When Rachel is only six years old, she grows weary of "girl-play." Girls, we are told, play with dolls, they cry when they receive a pin scratch, they settle arguments by calling each other names instead of fighting it out, and they are generally physically timid: "They would not jump from high places; they would not climb high trees; they were afraid of the thunder; and of the water; and of cows; and would take no perilous risks; and had no love of danger for its own sake. She tried to reform them, but it failed. So she went over to the boys" (HH, 62). Later, when she is ten, Hellfire succumbs to social pressure and again tries to play with the local girls, and again she is disappointed: "The amusements were not rugged enough; they were much too tame, not to say drowsy. Kissing parties and candy pullings in the winter, and picnics in the summer: these were good romps and lively, but they did not happen often enough, and the intermediate dissipations seemed wholly colorless to Rachel" (HH, 64). Boys' play was much more satisfactory; in the company of boys she learned to swim and skate—activities apparently forbidden to girls in Dawson's Landing:

She fished, boated, hunted, trapped, played "shinny" on the ice and ball on the land, and ran foot races. She broke horses for pastime, and for the risk there was in it. At fifteen she ranked as the strongest "boy" in the town, the smartest boxer, a willing and fearless fighter, and good to win any fight that her heart was in. The firemen conferred an honorary membership upon her, and allowed her to scale the roofs of burning houses and help handle the hose; for she liked that sort of employment, she had good judgment and coolness in danger, she was spry and active, and she attended strictly to business when on the roof. (HH, 64)

Twain's description of Hellfire's rejection of "girl-play" and her embracing of male-identified activities is remarkably similar to the sexologist Richard von Krafft-Ebing's representation of lesbian traits. According to Carroll Smith-Rosenberg, Krafft-Ebing argued that "the first symptom of *sexual* perversion . . . usually involved the rejection of conventional feminine behavior in childhood." One of his case studies includes the following description: "Even in her earliest childhood she preferred playing at soldiers and other boys' games; she was bold and tom-boyish and tried even to excel her little companions of the other sex. She never had a liking for dolls, needlework or domestic duties."[11] Oscar "Thug" Carpenter is depicted throughout as being Rachel's opposite. He is timid and indecisive, and the townspeople see him as being as mismatched with his "sex" as Rachel is with hers. As one of the town gossips observes, "'There's considerable difference betwixt them two—Thug and her. Pudd'nhead Wilson says Hellfire Hotchkiss is the only genuwyne male man in this town and Thug Carpenter's the only genuwyne female girl, if you leave out sex and just consider the business facts'" (HH, 56). Here is yet another set of "twinned" characters, as opposite in their temperaments as the famous Siamese twins of *Those Extraordinary Twins*. To the extent that Hellfire and Thug are "conjoined," there is little hope that one, Hellfire, will be dramatically reformed. Even Rachel believes that both she and Thug are somehow born into the wrong sex:

"Oh, everything seems to be made wrong, nothing seems to be the way it ought to be. Thug Carpenter is out of his sphere, I am out of

11. Smith-Rosenberg, *Disorderly Conduct,* quoting a case study from Richard von Krafft-Ebing's *Psychopathia Sexualis,* 271.

mine. Neither of us can arrive at any success in life, we shall always be hampered and fretted and kept back by our misplaced sexes, and in the end defeated by them, whereas if we could change we should stand as good a chance as any of the young people in the town. I wonder which case is the hardest. I am sorry for him, and yet I do not see that he is any more entitled to pity than I am." (HH, 68)

The story attempts to account for the "misplaced sexes" through a combination of nature and nurture. This is especially true of Rachel, in whom Twain is most interested: "Part of what she was was born to her, the rest was due to environment and to her up-bringing" (HH, 60). Rachel's mother died relatively early on, following a period of invalidism; her father is depicted as absent-minded and preoccupied. The slave woman in whose charge she was placed "petted and spoiled the child, partly out of her race's natural fondness for children of any sort or kind," and because superstition taught her that Rachel, who did not conform to her proper gender role even as a young child, was possibly possessed by the devil. As he did with Dorcas in "A Horse's Tale," Twain here attributes to a black slave or servant the only explanation offered in the story for why a young girl did not conform to the "proper" gender norms. Both explanations, one more comic than the other, rely upon superstition, and they reinforce an essentialist point of view. But by their very placement in the words of a black woman, and with their comic quality, Twain adds one more twist to his exploration of gender binaries. We have to ask if these views are meant to represent a kind of folk wisdom, reinforcing conventional social expectations, albeit in unconventional terms, or if Twain is using the logic offered by these two black women to make conventional gender expectations look foolish. No matter what conclusion we reach, both instances seem to point to Twain's deep-seated ambivalence about the fate that awaits young girls who defy gender expectations, even as he seems to celebrate their independence and freedom. But what, if any, explanation is offered for Oscar/Thug's failure to conform to proper male behavior?

The entire first chapter is in some measure an answer to this question. An extended dialogue between Oscar's mother, Sarah, and his father, James, establishes the story within a domestic frame, which in Twain is always the locus for adults' attempts to shape children's behavior. The mother, concerned about her son's future, appears to be overly indulgent but kindhearted and painfully literal minded. The father, by contrast, is highly skeptical about his son's ability to stick with anything. He is cynical, sardonic, teasing in a slightly cruel manner, and ironic. The witty interchange between them goes on for nearly ten pages without any narrative comment. The first exchange between the Carpenters sets the tone for the whole chapter:

> "But James, he is our son, and we must bear with him. If we can-
> not bear with him, how can we expect others to do it?"
> "I have not said I expected it, Sarah. I am very far from expecting
> it. He is the most trying ass that was ever born."
> "James! You forget that he is our son."
> "That does not save him from being an ass. It does not even take
> the sting out of it." (HH, 45)

Sarah, after nineteen years of marriage, has never learned how to take her husband's cynical comments, always responding to them earnestly, and James has never stopped baiting his wife. The father insists that part of Oscar's problem is that he is a person of "enthusiasms," unable to stick to anything for more than three months.[12]

The mother counters that the father has never encouraged him in anything, never praised him; the father counters that praise is all Oscar wants—that he is insatiable for praise:

> "So long as you feed him praise, he gorges, gorges, gorges, and is ob-
> scenely happy; the moment you stop he is famished—famished and
> wretched; utterly miserable, despondent, despairing. You ought to
> know all about it. You have tried to keep him fed-up, all his life, and
> you know what a job it is. I detest that word—encouragement—
> where the male sex is concerned. *The boy that needs much of it is a girl
> in disguise. He ought to put on petticoats.* Praise has a value—when it
> is earned. When it isn't earned, the male creature receiving it ought
> to despise it; and will, when there is a proper degree of manliness in
> him." (HH, 48; emphasis added)

---

12. The editors of the story as published in Mark Twain, *Huck Finn and Tom Sawyer among the Indians: And Other Unfinished Stories* attribute the characterizations of James and Sarah Carpenter to Clemens's own parents, but they readily admit that there are limitations to the parallels; the characterization of Oscar as a "person of enthusiasms" led the original editors of the story to assert that the portrait of Oscar was based on Twain's brother, Orion, who was a frequent target of Twain's criticism (287–88).

James's fixed notions about gendered behavior go unchallenged in the text, at least overtly, and an essentialist notion of how a boy should act prevails. Even so, embedded in the father's criticism is an implicit linking of gender with performance through James's notion of a needy boy being a girl in disguise—in his mind, Ocsar's putting on a "petticoat" would reveal more accurately his inner self. In nineteenth-century terms, Oscar "Thug" Carpenter is a classic "invert"—an effeminate male. As David Halperin and others have demonstrated, "effeminacy has often functioned as a marker of so-called sexual inversion in men, of transgenderism or sexual role reversal, and thus . . . of homosexual desire." Halperin goes on to insist that the precise terms of inversion are culturally specific, and thus mutable, while James Carpenter's language describing his own son, which we understand ironically, is meant to leave no room for dispute.[13] Beyond the nuclear family, the townspeoples' values, with their clearly enforced gender binaries, make themselves felt through the pressure brought to bear on both Oscar and Rachel, especially through the local gossip, as it will begin to close in on Rachel.

In the final pages of the story, Hellfire, now sixteen, rescues a male stranger in the village who is beset by the town bullies, the Stover brothers. She arrives on the scene just as Shad Stover attempts to shoot the stranger; she attacks Shad and his brother with a baseball bat, knocking the second brother "senseless," which allows the stranger to escape. It is in a conversation that follows this incident that a significant lacuna appears in the story; one has to read carefully to notice it, but ultimately it is unmistakably laced with meaning. The conversation takes place between Hellfire and Aunt Betsy Davis, who is described as "no one's aunt in particular, but just the town's," and hence the voice of the town. She begins by warning Rachel that she is being "talked about." Rachel rightly replies that she has always been talked about, but Aunt Betsy tells her that this time it is in a "new way."

---

13. David Halperin, *How to Do the History of Homosexuality*, 110. While it is unassailable that on several occasions Twain set out to capture his brother's portrait in both novelistic and dramatic form, and although Orion was a man of "enthusiasms," it is doubtful that he was more than an initial inspiration for the characterization of Oscar Carpenter. I find it unlikely that Sam Clemens would cast his brother as an invert.

"New way?"

"Yes. There is one kind of gossip that this town has never dealt in before, in the fifty-two years that I've lived in it—and has never had any occasion to. Not in one single case, if you leave out the town drunkard's girls; and even that turned out to be a lie, and was stopped."

"Aunt Betsy!" Rachel's face was crimson, and an angry light rose in her eyes. (HH, 66)

Aunt Betsy knows exactly what she is saying, and Rachel understands perfectly how to fill in the silent space about the content of the "new" gossip.

Eve Sedgwick has taught us, in *Epistemology of the Closet,* to recognize that when there is a major silence and secrecy interjected into a narrative discourse, there is a "homosexual in the text." Quoting Foucault, Sedgwick argues that "'there is no binary division to be made between what one says and what one does not say; we must try to determine the different ways of not saying such things. . . . There is not one but many silences, and they are an integral part of the strategies that underlie and permeate discourses.'" She goes on to elaborate: "Closeted-ness itself is a performance initiated as such by the speech act of a silence—not a particular silence, but a silence that accrues particularity by fits and starts, in relation to the discourse that surrounds and differentially constitutes it."[14] Applying her argument most cogently to Melville's *Billy Budd* (1891), Sedgwick insists that we know there is a homosexual in that text precisely because of the silence and secretiveness that surrounds the descriptions of Claggart, the master-at-arms aboard the *Bellipotent.* Just such a silence evokes in "Hellfire Hotchkiss" the specter of lesbianism.

Immediately following the repressed exchange, the text invests considerable interest in the implications of the gossip for Hellfire's future in the town. While earlier we learn that Hellfire "was always rousing its resentments by her wild unfeminine ways, and always winning back its forgiveness again by some act or other of an undeniably creditable sort," now, Aunt Betsy Davis insists, she has gone too far (HH, 65). "Take it all around, this is a fair town, and a just town, and has been

---

14. Eve Kosofsky Sedgwick, *Epistemology of the Closet,* 3.

good to you—very good to you, everything considered, for you *have* led it a dance, and you know it. Now ain't that so?" (HH, 67). Nothing contradicts Aunt Betsy Davis's characterization of the town in the story, but readers of *Pudd'nhead Wilson* know that Dawson's Landing, beneath its quiet exterior, is a site where deeply contested social binaries have collided. It is, after all, a town in which a stranger can be branded a fool for years because a joke of his is taken literally, in which a "white" woman can be condemned to a life of slavery "by a sarcasm of the law," where a pair of boys, one "black" and the other "white," can be switched in the cradle and their racial identities confounded for their lifetimes. It is a town, too, where gender has been shown to be mutable. Finally, it is the home of Siamese twins *(Those Extraordinary Twins)*, who are rewritten into *Pudd'nhead Wilson* as identical but temperamentally opposite. As I have indicated, Rachel and Oscar can be seen in the same light—yet one more set of twins and opposites, a set of complex, closely related binaries that need to be understood in the context of each other. In particular, this set of "twins" inhabits a set of socially constructed gender binaries that cannot contain them.

After Aunt Betsy's declaration, Hellfire asks:

> "Aunt Betsy, does anybody *believe* those reports?"
> "Believe them? Why, how you talk! Of course they don't. Our people don't believe such things about our old families so easy as all that. They don't believe it *now,* but if a thing goes on, and on, and on, being talked about, why that's another matter. The thing to do is to stop it in time, and that is what I've come to plead with you to do, child, for your own sake and your father's, and for the sake of your mother who is in her grave—a good friend to me she was, and I'm trying to be hers, now." (HH, 67–68)

At the end of the discussion, when Aunt Betsy has "closed with a trembling lip and an unsteady voice," Rachel says, with a "flush" creeping across her face, "And they are talking about me—like that!" (HH, 68). Through the elusive "such things," and "like that," the text further hints at lesbianism—the "crime" that cannot be named—that indeed had no name. But however elusive the language and expression, the gossip is real, and both Aunt Betsy and Hellfire understand it perfectly.

After Aunt Betsy leaves, Rachel determines, as she has been urged, to stop the behavior that has set the gossip in motion. Accordingly, she says "it is time to call a halt." Ironically, that determination leads immediately to her musing that "everything seems to be made wrong, nothing seems to be the way it ought to be. Thug Carpenter is out of his sphere, I am out of mine" (HH, 68). For Rachel and for Thug, gender does not line up the way it is supposed to. Yet Rachel/Hellfire is determined to try to perform the gender that she has been assigned, and "call a halt" to the behavior that has brought about the gossip. She resolves not to "train with the boys any more, nor do ungirlish things except when it is a duty and I ought to do them." She resolves not to horsewhip the Stovers "just as a pleasure; but now it will be for a higher motive," and to go to church on Sunday. "And being refreshed and contented by this wholesale purification, she went to bed" (HH, 69). With these words, the story breaks off.

John Cooley suggests that "Hellfire's independent wings appear to be clipped," and that by the end of the story she "makes her private peace with her misplaced gender." For Susan Gillman, "Hellfire Hotchkiss" is one of the tales that "momentarily confounds sexual categories, only in the end to give way to the clarification of gender and hence to proper, community sanctioned identity." Laura Skandera-Trombley sees "society closing in and crushing those who attempt to transgress rigid gender bifurcations."[15] All three critical statements seem to accept at face value the spoken words of the text, but in so doing they fall just short of the mark. In the end it is difficult to take seriously any notion that Rachel will ever perform the female gender successfully. She is too spunky to simply acquiesce to the community's wishes—twice before, she has vowed to become a more conventional girl, and both times she has failed. Moreover, the tone of even her most determined statements is suffused with an element of play: she won't do ungirlish things "except when it is a duty"; and she will in fact horsewhip the Stovers, not for pleasure but for "a higher motive." She summarizes her plan in these terms: "Withdraw from the boys. The Stovers. Church. That makes three. Three in three days. It is enough to begin with; I suppose I have never done three in three weeks before—just *as* duties" (HH, 69).

---

15. Cooley, "Transvestite Tragedies," 237; Gillman, *Dark Twins*, 111; Skandera-Trombley, "Mark Twain's Cross-Dressing Oeuvre," 92.

Finally, gender categories remain problematic in this story for at least two additional reasons. One is that Hellfire's offenses against the community standards have always been framed in the context of Thug Carpenter's equally "misplaced sex." The town understands Rachel in connection with Thug, and we are asked to do so as well. However determined Rachel might be to get out of the spotlight of the town's gossip, no change she makes will also change Thug—they are viewed as twinned opposites of each other, as mirror images in their embodied repeated challenges to essentialist notions of gendered behavior. Thug's father's inability to influence his son's behavior, let alone control it, presages the gossip's inability to change Rachel's fundamental nature. The gendered complexities on display here go much deeper than the social pressures brought to bear on the two young people with "mistaken" sexual identities.

The second reason gender categories remain problematic in this story is that Rachel's overidentification with the local boys (and young men) is only a symptom of the deeper issue, the unspoken, unnamed accusation of lesbianism. She could truly "call a halt" to her association with the boys, and do all her activities alone, as Aunt Betsy urges her to do, but that would not change her gendered nature—it would only mask the symptoms. Finally, the extent to which Rachel is asked to perform her female gender, and the extent to which her gendered performances are monitored and regulated by the community, only calls attention to the fact that the very nature of gender is itself performative and socially constructed.[16]

Instead, and in spite of the seeming conforming conclusion of the unfinished story, "Hellfire Hotchkiss" celebrates Rachel's difference, even as it remains somewhat more ambivalent about Thug's difference. In the story, Twain imagines a nonconformist, spirited "daughter" who is fully at ease with herself and who enjoys much more freedom than is allowed to any of the other daughters of the town. What concerns him, finally, is the gossip that she arouses in the townspeople, the pressures she is under because of the community's narrowly defined notion of ac-

---

16. As Judith Butler has observed, "That gender reality is created through sustained social performances means that the very notions of an essential sex and a true or abiding masculinity or femininity are also constituted as part of the strategy that conceals gender's performative character" (*Gender Trouble,* 180).

ceptable female behavior—that is, her difference. In spite of the pressures brought about through that gossip, essentialist gendered behaviors are not reinscribed in the end.

"How Nancy Jackson Married Kate Wilson"

This story, with its coy title, could be considered as another lesbian tale in that it depicts a marriage between two women, but the premise upon which the story operates would seem to preclude such categorization. The fact that one of the young women involved is forced to become a female-to-male transvestite and that the other young woman does not know her "husband" is a transvestite deprives the relationship (and the story) of any hint of lesbian desire. In contrast to the exuberance of Rachel/Hellfire Hotchkiss, the protagonist, Nancy Jackson, is a sad and despondent figure. Nonetheless, this may be the most radical story among the transvestite tales in its depiction of how a young woman is coerced into cross-dressing, is deprived of the ability to say "no" to a marriage to another young woman, and how "fatherhood" is thrust upon her. If it is not the most radical story among these tales, it is certainly the most sensational, and the most grim.

"How Nancy Jackson Married Kate Wilson" was originally assigned the title "The Feud Story and the Girl Who Was Ostensibly a Man" by Albert Bigelow Paine, who declared the story "not usable." Never published in Twain's lifetime, the story was renamed "How Nancy Jackson Married Kate Wilson" by Robert Sattelmeyer, who was its first publisher, in 1987.[17] Neither title quite does the story justice, but Sattelmeyer's title captures the more sensational aspects of the story, no doubt the very ones that caused Paine to think the story unusable, and it is the title taken up by John Cooley when he published his collection by the same name. It is likely that Paine found the story too radical and dark because it features a young woman essentially blackmailed into living as a transvestite, in the company only of strangers, to satisfy the sadomasochistic pleasure of a man who was jilted by the young woman's mother many years before. The humor of the story is grim, and all parties ultimately associated with the deception at the heart of

---

17. Quoted in Robert Sattelmeyer, "How Nancy Jackson Married Kate Wilson," 97.

the story end up miserable, except the villain of the piece, Thomas Furlong, whose sardonic laughter haunts the ending of the tale.

Like Conrad, the female-to-male transvestite in "An Awful—Terrible Medieval Romance," Nancy Jackson has her transvestitism thrust upon her; she does not chose it. And like Conrad, Nancy Jackson, renamed Robert Finlay, is caught in a prisoner's dilemma: she must either reveal her "true" gender identity, and face hanging for having accidentally killed someone, or she must spend the rest of her life as a man and marry a woman who falsely accuses her of being the father of her illegitimate child. Unlike "A Medieval Romance," the story follows the hero into his loveless marriage, in which he fulfills the letter of the law but refuses to live in the same house as his bride. Because there are so many overtones to the story, those relatively few critics who have addressed it emphasize different strands. Sattelmeyer finds the story "most striking for its frank depiction of a seducer seduced," referring not to Robert but to the woman he marries, who had broken many a heart but had been herself jilted by the "real" father of her child. John Cooley directly associates the story with "Susy Clemens' love relationship with Louise Brownell" and sees in the story "a lesbian subtext beneath what is for Twain a fairly commonplace plot of switched identities." As he does with "Hellfire Hotchkiss," Cooley reads the story as a corrective to transgressive behavior: "Nancy's physical and Kate's sexual assertiveness counterbalance each other, resulting in a possible double warning to transgressive women that they will become unmarriageable, at least heterosexually, because of their violations of acceptable behavior." Laura Skandera-Trombley categorizes Robert as a "gender-trickster," which he certainly is, but he fulfills his transvestite role so unwillingly that he does not have any of the energy and guile ordinarily associated with a trickster.[18] Gillman, then Skandera-Trombley, note that the story was an attempt on Twain's part to rewrite "A Medieval Romance," here drawing the story to a close instead of walking away from the dilemma he has once again created for his cross-dressed heroine.

The story begins when Nancy Jackson, who has apparently killed a

---

18. Sattelmeyer, "How Nancy Jackson," 98; John Cooley, "Mark Twain, Rebellious Girls, and Daring Young Women," 241; Skandera-Trombley, "Mark Twain's Cross-Dressing Oeuvre," 92.

man in self-defense and is being pursued by a lynch mob, takes refuge in the house of Thomas Furlong, who hates the Jackson family, especially Jackson's mother, who had rejected him years before. Furlong was a witness to the killing and could prove Jackson's innocence, but instead he withholds that information from Jackson and offers to help her escape only if she agrees to live many miles away, to never return to the community or to her mother, and to live solely as a man. Nancy Jackson believes she has no choice but to comply with his demands or be lynched. Furlong takes a fiendish pleasure in punishing Jackson by making her into a transvestite: "'I'll trim your head and make a young fellow of you. Every day you'll practice, and I'll help you; and by and by when you're letter perfect and can walk and act like a male person and the lynch-fever has blown over, I'll take you out of this region some night and see you safe over the border and on your way. You will call yourself Robert Finlay.'" Then the narration describes Furlong's vengeful satisfaction: "He was very happy, and smiled the smile of a contented fiend."[19] Finlay does become a credible male and sets out to live a new life. He is befriended by a family named Wilson and takes up residence in a cabin on their farm. The Wilsons' daughter, Kate, age eighteen, has a two-year history of being an irrepressible flirt, causing "the young fellows of the farmsteads and the village" to come court her; she soon tires of them and throws them over. Then a stranger with "fine manners and eastern ways" enters the village, "and Kate rejoiced, and straightway she set a trap for him" (NJ, 113). She appears to be successful—they become engaged, but then he mysteriously disappears. Kate then turns her attention to Robert Finlay, who is perfectly civil to her but does not respond to any of her flirtatious overtures. This humiliates Kate. The narrator states that she devises a plan to avenge herself for Robert's lack of response, but Twain does not reveal what that plan is. Soon Mrs. Wilson spreads the word in the village that Robert and Kate are engaged, and two weeks later they are married.

Only after the wedding does it become clear what her plan has been: she is pregnant, by the stranger, but lays the blame on Robert. Trapped in his transvestite role, he is forced by the senior Wilsons to marry their

---

19. Mark Twain, "How Nancy Jackson Married Kate Wilson," 112 (hereinafter cited as NJ).

daughter: "'You commanded, mother Wilson; I have obeyed. Against my will. I obeyed because I could not help myself; I obeyed because there was no possible way out, and I had to do it; if there had been a way out, I never would have obeyed'" (NJ, 119). She rebukes him by saying that although he denied the charge, his obedience is tantamount to a confession. Their discussion ends with Robert vowing that Kate will never be his wife except in name: "'I will never live with her—not even so much as a single day'" (NJ, 120).

Meanwhile, Furlong, who intercepts all Robert's letters to his mother, learns of the marriage. His response reveals what a thoroughgoing villain he is. It is also one of Twain's most elaborate descriptions of bone-shaking, grotesque, physical laughter:

> Furlong put down pipe and letter and threw back his head and delivered himself of crash after crash, gust after gust of delighted laughter; then, middle-aged man as he was, got up, mopping the happy tears from his leathery cheeks, and expended the remaining remnant of his strength in a breakdown of scandalous violence, and finally sank into his chair, heaving and panting, limp and exhausted, and said with what wind he had left—
> "Lord, it's just good to be alive!" (NJ, 121)

The story concludes by returning once again to the Wilson farm, with the neighbors dropping by "to spy out the conditions," and everyone concluding that something is radically wrong. Finally one of Kate's friends asks why things are as they are, and Kate replies, "'How would it do to say it is none of their business?' At last the child was born—a boy" (NJ, 122, 123).

"How Nancy Jackson Married Kate Wilson" is one of the darkest of all Mark Twain's gender-bending tales. As a transvestite, committed to keeping his "true" identity a secret, Robert Finlay agrees to perform the male gender, successfully, but only to a point. As the central cross-gendered figure, he in fact *plays* with gender not at all. The story itself does, however, and here I must differ with Cooley's speculation that in the story Twain is "struggling to imagine a lesbian partnership." It is heterosexuality, not implied homosexuality, that has gone wrong in the story. For instance, Thomas Furlong's sadistic manipulation of the future of Jackson/Wilson comes about because he is deeply bitter about being rejected by Nancy Jackson's mother some twenty years earlier. The worst punishment he can imagine for Jackson is to make her become, for all intents and purposes, a man. Like Huck, Jackson has to practice performing the opposite gender, but there is no fun in it for him/her, and none surrounding it in the text. It is also heterosexuality gone awry in the story that traps Finlay in his disastrous marriage. In the first instance, Kate not only lets herself be seduced by a stranger, with the promise of marriage, but also is impregnated by him. He, in turn, we learn only in passing, has been set up by Thomas Furlong to seek out Kate and seduce her, then disappear.[20] The mild-mannered "waif," Robert Finlay, is chosen by Kate to bear the brunt of the "revenge for the insult which had been put upon her" (NJ, 114). She turns all her charms on Robert:

> When Sunday came around she happened by his cabin and took him for a walk through the sweet solitudes of the wooded hills, and talked sentiment and romance and poetry to him; she allowed her elbow to touch his, but could not discover that it communicated a thrill; she gave a little scream at an imaginary snake, and put her hand upon his arm, and forgot it and left it there a while; then took it away with inviting reluctance and slowly, but he did not try to retain it. . . .
>
> Her pouting lips were near to his; languidly she whispered, "Kiss me, Robert," and closed her eyes.
>
> She waited. Nothing happened. She unclosed her eyes; they were spouting anger. He began to explain humbly that she had misunderstood him; that he *liked* her—liked her ever so much, but—
>
> "I hate you!" she burst out, and gathered up her skirts and strode away without looking backward. (NJ, 117–18)

Throughout all this heterosexist drama, Robert is impassive—wholly impervious to Kate's coy ways. It is not even clear from the text that he recognizes her moves as seductive until she asks him to kiss her. There are clear limitations to his successful performance as a man. Robert Finley's connection to the Wilson family comes primarily

---

20. Cooley, "Mark Twain, Rebellious Girls," 241; on the mysterious seducer, Twain unmistakably borrows from his earlier story, "An Awful—Terrible Medieval Romance," which also includes a mysterious lover who impregnates a young woman at someone else's behest.

through Mrs. Wilson: "He was very gentle, and very winning in his ways, but inclined to sadness. Mrs. Wilson pitied him, mothered him, loved him, and the gratefulness that shone in his kind eyes and fell caressingly from his tongue was her sufficient reward" (NJ, 115). Robert, in fact, goes into raptures of gratitude to Mrs. Wilson, which Mr. Wilson finds disconcerting—like James Carpenter, no doubt finding such behavior unmanly:

> The only fault papa Wilson could find in him was these outbursts. He was a plain man and destitute of "gush," and these things discomforted him. He kept his thought to himself for a time, but at last, with caution—feeling that the ice was thin—he took a risk and privately suggested to his wife that the young fellow protested too much. It fired a mine! He did not make that venture a second time. He continued to hold his opinion, but he did not air it any more. (NJ, 116)

This passage is one of the few in the story where there is much playfulness at all, and it is in passing reference to the dynamic between a man and wife—the husband's wariness of setting off his wife's anger by expressing his opinion. The other places where the narrative is lighter centers around the way gossip functions in the story. Mother Wilson understands perfectly how gossip circulates in her small farm community, and she uses it, whenever possible, to her advantage. First, the mother uses the gossip circuit to announce that Kate is engaged to the attractive stranger who has come into the community. When he disappears, and when it becomes clear that he is not coming back, she makes a trip into town to create gossip to the effect that Kate has thrown him over. Then she spreads the gossip in the village that Kate and Robert are engaged, a story that the village accepts, then adds their own interpretation to the matter: "and as soon as her back was turned the friends discussed the matter and pitied the bridegroom." Some say that it isn't over yet, that she could still back out—"There was wisdom in this remark, and it sensibly cooled the general joy produced by the prospect of the exasperating flirt's early retirement from her professional industries" (NJ, 118). Once Kate and Robert are married, the local gossips function almost like a Greek chorus, commenting on the funereal tone of the wedding, at the obvious trouble brewing at the Wilson farm. They all notice that Papa Wilson will not look at his son-in-law, that he was "grave and austere" (NJ, 119). They come around in the months following the wedding "to spy out the conditions. On these occasions efforts were made by all the family to seem friendly and content, but those made by papa Wilson were so lame and poor that they spoiled the game and no visitor went away deceived" (NJ, 122).

In the end, however, they all are deceived, for no one ever imagines that the major problem with the marriage is that Robert is really Nancy, a young woman forced to play a man's role against her will. Kate Wilson gets both more and much less than she bargained for in trapping Robert into marrying her. Robert, in turn, is paying the price for his mother rebuffing Thomas Furlong, the mastermind, the "author" of the whole story. Robert Sattelmeyer describes it as a "story of sexual betrayal." "Who," he asks, is "the ultimate villain, who the ultimate victim?"[21] It is far easier to answer the first part of the question than the last—Thomas Furlong is the villain, determined to wreak havoc on innocent people for his own pleasure—but who indeed is "the ultimate victim"? Two mothers play a terrible price for Furlong's revenge—one deprived for life of her daughter's companionship, the other doomed to bear witness to her daughter's misery. Robert Finlay is the character who earns our greatest sympathy, but it is Nancy Jackson who ultimately is lost. If only she had the spunk of Hellfire Hotchkiss, she might find her way through the tangle Twain and Furlong construct for her. It is precisely Twain's *denial* of "an imagined lesbian subtext" that creates the darkness in this story and that likely rendered it "unusable" to Paine.

"Wapping Alice"

The story known as "Wapping Alice" is without doubt the most complicated of the transvestite tales, involving as it does at least three different iterations over a three decade span. Like "How Nancy Jackson Married Kate Wilson," it depicts a forced same-sex marriage, this time between two men, one of them a male-to-female transvestite. It has none of the grim seriousness of its counterpart; instead, it is farcical. The homosexuality of the tale is not submerged but instead is em-

---

21. Sattelmeyer, "How Nancy Jackson," 97.

phasized both by the name of the lead character, and of the story, with "Wapping" evoking the notion of "thumping," as Hamlin Hill has pointed out, and Alice's partner being given the middle name Bjuggerson, clearly associating him with "buggery."[22] Most remarkably, in writing a fictionalized version of a strange episode that actually took place in the Clemens household, Twain changed a clandestine heterosexual relationship into a homosexual one.

The story now known as "Wapping Alice" had a fairly long and complicated history, beginning with three letters from Sam Clemens to his wife, Livy, all written on one day, July 17, 1877. The letters offer a running account of an intrigue then unfolding in the Clemenses' Hartford house, beginning with a burglar alarm that kept going off in the servant's quarters in the house, and continuing with Clemens's discovery of a scandalous relationship between one of his serving women, Lizzie, and a workman named Willie, which ended with a forced marriage of the two that very day, engineered by Sam Clemens. In his letters, Clemens takes great pride in his detective skills, even comparing himself to one of his own characters, detective Simon Wheeler. He sets up an elaborate scheme of interrogating Lizzie, then brings in a minister and a policeman, and he forces Willie to marry Lizzie. According to Hamlin Hill, Twain's first written version of the story (in contrast with the version conveyed in his letters to Livy) was entitled "The McWilliamses and the Burglar Alarm." As its title suggests, the story features a burglar alarm system and an extended comedy of errors arising because of its idiosyncrasies, not on the ensuing scandal in the household. Published in *Harper's* during the Christmas of 1882, this version of the story will not be the focus of our attention.[23] It is the

22. Hamlin Hill, afterword to *Wapping Alice*, 78. The spelling of the Swede's name varies in the Hill text. In this "Keepsake Issue by the Friends of the Bancroft Library for Its Members," Hill untangles the history of the story, its relationship to the Clemens family, and Twain's revisions of the story. Hill offers the most thorough critical and biographical account yet available of "Wapping Alice" in his introduction and afterword.

23. As Hill observes, McWilliams served as a stand-in for Samuel Clemens in several stories, although he was always a more inept and bumbling version of the author. In two out of three published McWilliams stories, McWilliams narrates his tales to a frame narrator identified as Mr. Twain. In this particular story, McWilliams has an elaborate alarm system installed in his large house, which seems to be the continual target of burglars. When he discovers a burglar entering a second-floor window one night, he adds alarms to that floor; when they enter on the third floor, he adds yet more alarms, each one at-

second written version of this story ("Wapping Alice," ca. 1897–1898), never published in Twain's lifetime, that is of paramount interest. In this version, Twain narrates a tale of scandal and seduction parallel to the one relayed in his letters to Livy, but transforming the Clemenses' maid Lizzie into Wapping Alice, a highly successful male-to-female transvestite whose "secret" no one discovers until after the forced marriage, engineered by the narrator of the story; Twain also changes the workman Willie into a Swede named Bjurnsen Bjuggerson Bjorgensen. Despite several attempts to get this story published, Twain was never successful. According to Hill, Twain subsequently revisited the story again a decade later, in 1907, in his Autobiographical Dictations, this time laying out how he wished to turn Alice back into a woman. Thus the span of the story and Twain's interest in it covers three decades— even so, Hill says, Twain never settled on a concluding line for the story that satisfied him. In its various incarnations, "Wapping Alice" is a story of sexual intrigue, gender performance, deceit, masquerade, false accusations of paternity, and overt male homosexuality. It is also a story about the failure of the patriarch to keep control over his own household, and about his inability to read correctly the sexual intrigues taking place within his home. Finally, it is a story suffused with good-natured humor and all manner of gender play.

"Wapping Alice," as edited by Hamlin Hill and published for the first time in 1981, is set up as a traditional frame tale. The external narrator, called Mark Twain, strikes up a friendship with a man named "Jackson" on board a ship somewhere in the Indian Ocean. Jackson is the core narrator—it is his house, his servant, his story that he tells to Twain. But it is the Clemenses' story (more or less) that Jackson ultimately narrates, and his voice resembles Twain's own to a remarkable degree. The story is told in two parts. The first half sets up an elaborately detailed domestic framework for the unfolding scandal, which then occupies the entire second half of the story; instead of an exchange

---

tached to an "annunciator" that rings a bell so loud it throws McWilliams out of his bed. Eventually the burglars steal the burglar alarm system itself, right down to the miles of copper wire. The McWilliamses have it all installed again, this time with an automatic clock mechanism that continues to fail, turning the system off during the night and on during the day. In the end, McWilliams has the whole system torn out and gets a dog instead. Then he shoots the dog.

between Clemens and Livy, however, as in the original letters, the domestic space is occupied by Jackson and his black servant, George. The relationship between them is at once familial and faintly absurd, with Jackson all but admitting that George, not he, is in charge of the family home: "Consider this further light: my grandfather owned George's grand-father, my father owned George's father, and George owned *me*—at any rate that is what the family said."[24]

Jackson's family has been away for the summer, but Jackson comes home, unannounced, and is told before he reaches the house that his home has been burglarized. He finds the door unlocked and all the servants absent. George returns three hours later and calmly announces that they have all been "down the river on the excursion boat." In the extended dialogue between the two men, George reveals, with no concern, that he has taken all manner of liberties while his "master" and his family have been away. When Jackson admonishes him about the unlocked door (but not about being off on a boat), George runs upstairs in a panic. Jackson imagines he has dashed upstairs to be sure all the family's belongings are safe but learns that George was afraid the fifteen hundred dollars he had won at the races and hidden between his mattresses had been stolen. He also admits that he and the other servants had been on other excursions. When they came home from one, they entered through the ground-floor bedroom window "because it was handier than the annex" (WA, 90). While sitting in the library, the servants saw a strange man go by in the dining room; that stranger then set off the front-door alarm by exiting the house. George gave chase, and the man ran away. George's story becomes increasingly preposterous. He tells Jackson he suspects Wapping Alice "ain't what she ought to be," and then pieces together—as a detective might—a case against Alice. This includes earlier incidents of the alarm on the laundry door going off mysteriously, then not going off again once George explains to Alice what an alarm system is. He says he later entered her room and found a suit of men's clothing; Alice explained that she was repairing the seat of the pants for the young carpenter, Bjorgensen, who was

---

24. Mark Twain, "Wapping Alice," 86 (hereinafter the edition reprinted in *How Nancy Jackson Married Kate Wilson* [University of Nebraska Press, 2001] will be cited as WA).

working on the house. George concludes that Alice has been cross-dressing as a man so she can go out drinking at night, and that she was the strange man discovered by the servants in the dining room. At that point, George and Jackson go off together to examine the laundry-room door alarm and realize that the pin has been filed down so it will no longer set off the alarm.

George's detective work in the first part is matched, flaw for flaw, by the detective work Jackson himself undertakes in the second half of the story. Confronted with the information that the "laundry door has been tampered with for a purpose," Jackson surmises that Alice has been "harboring" a thief. Jackson decides to hold court in his own household to corner Alice into confessing that she had a role in the burglaries. He calls a number of witnesses, last of all Wapping Alice. He then weaves a narrative of all the other servants' stories, trapping Alice into making "a clean breast" of it. Alice admits that because she felt sorry for Bjorgensen, she has allowed him to sleep in the main cellar, entering and exiting by the laundry-room door and thus initially setting off the alarm. But, she assures him, Bjorgensen is not a thief; he has taken nothing. Jackson accepts Alice's story at face value, and while he is relieved, he expresses disappointment that there is not more drama in the story. Then Alice drops a bombshell:

> "Oh, sir, he—he"—Through the breaks in her sobs words escaped which conveyed a paralyzing revelation.
> "What!"
> "Oh, dear-dear, it is too true, sir—and now he won't marry me! And I a poor friendless girl in a strange land." (WA, 97)

Jackson becomes enraged and hatches an elaborate plan to force Bjorgensen to marry Alice. He calls upon his friend, Rev. Thomas X, to get a marriage license, and he arranges for a plainclothes officer to come to the house at 7:30 that evening. Rev. Tom is shut up in the bathroom, the policeman is shut up in the library, and at 8:00 Bjorgensen is brought into Jackson's presence. "My native appetite for doing things in a theatrical way feasted itself with a relish on this spectacular program" (WA, 99). Jackson springs his trap, accusing Bjorgensen of robbing Alice of her purity. Bjorgensen rages away at the accusation, saying that he'd "see her hanged a hundred times, first, and *then* I wouldn't [marry her]" (WA, 100). He tells Jackson that it is all an elaborate game to make him marry "that lying baggage," and Jackson readily admits it is. But he holds firm to his purpose, giving Bjorgensen the choice of marrying Alice at 10:00 that night or going to prison, and he has the minister and the policeman on hand to carry out either threat. Bjorgensen finally agrees, and all the household comes forth to witness the wedding. Rev. Tom, we are told, is melted down to half his size from sitting shut up for three hours in "that little blistering bathroom," but he performs the wedding service nonetheless.

> In my time I have seen millions of astonished carpenters, but not all of them put together were as astonished as our bridegroom. It knocked him groggy; and he was a married man before he knew what he was about. At the preacher's suggestion he kissed the bride—it didn't seem to taste over-good to him—and said to me, with a sigh—
> "It's your game, sir. What a hand you held!"
> Then they all cleared for the dining room below and the refreshments, and Tom and I sat down, I to smoke and he to fan; and we talked the whole grand thing over, and were very, very happy and content. And he put his hand in blessing on my head, and said, with tears in his voice—
> "Jackson, dear boy, you will be forgiven many a sin for the good deed you have done this night."
> I was touched, myself. Just then George staggered in, looking stunned and weak, and said—
> "That Wapping Alice—blame her skin, she's a *man!*" (WA, 104)

The performative nature of gender, and the confusion of gender categories, are never more explicit in Twain's work than in "Wapping Alice":

> It is very creditable to his ingenuity that he was able to masquerade as a girl seven months and a half under all our eyes and never awake in us doubt or suspicion. It must not be charged that a part of the credit is due to our dulness; for no one can say that our friends and neighbors were dull people, and they were deceived as completely as we were. They knew Alice almost as well as we knew him, yet no suspicion of the fraud he was playing ever crossed their minds. He

must have had years of apprenticeship in his part, or he could not have
been so competent in it. Why he unsexed himself was his own affair.
In the excitement of the grand climax in August the matter was over-
looked and he was not questioned about it.

For conveience [*sic*], now, I will stop calling him "he." Indeed, with
that fair and modest and comely young creature in blossomy hat and
fluttering ribbons and flowing gown framed before me now in the
mirror of my memory, it is awkward and unhandy to call it anything
but "she." (WA, 84)

This passage is full of gender play. The narrator's seriousness makes his
juxtaposition of "Alice" and "him" seem both silly and somehow right.
What, after all, is the correct pronoun under the circumstances? Given
the efficacy of Alice's gender performance as it is "framed before me
now in the mirror of my memory," to the narrator Alice was both man
and woman. In the closing paragraph of the story, Alice explains not
why she is a man passing as a woman—no one asks—but only why she
chose to make "that dire charge against poor Bjorgensen": It was to
satisfy Jackson's desire that the episode be "theatrical enough." "Well,
her effort wasn't bad—you see it, yourself. I keep calling her *she*—I
can't help it; I mean *he*" (WA, 104).

Remarkably, Twain claimed in his Autobiographical Dictations that
he had changed the Lizzie/Alice character into a male to allow the story's publication "without risk of overshocking the magazine's readers,"
but at the time of his dictations (in 1906) he was wishing to change her
back. He explains:

There is one considerable detail [in the story] which is fictitious, but
it is a non-essential. In that instance I diverged from fact to fiction
merely because I wanted to publish the thing in a magazine present-
ly, and for delicacy's sake I was obliged to make the change [of Lizzie
into a man]. But this Autobiography of mine can stand plainnesses
of statement which might make a magazine shiver; it has stood a
good many already, and will have to stand a good many more before
I get through. For my own pleasure, I wish to remove that fictive detail now, and replace it with the fact. This considerable but not essential fact was this, to wit: Wapping Alice was a *woman,* not a man.
This truth does not relieve or modify by even a shade the splendid
ridiculousness of the situation, *but the temporary transformation of
Alice into a man does soften the little drama sufficiently to enable me*

to exploit it in a magazine without risk of overshocking the magazine's readers.[25]

Lest there be any misunderstanding here, what Twain was claiming in his Autobiographical Dictations, having intended to insert the entire 1897 "Wapping Alice" story into the manuscript, was that for "delicacy's sake" he had changed Lizzie into a man in order to get the piece published—that magazines would have "shivered" over the "real" story of heterosexual misconduct. Hamlin Hill remarks,

> However ingenuous that sounds to us, Mark Twain may have honestly believed that the *Harper's* audience was naïve enough to prefer an "innocent" all-male relationship to a consummated heterosexual one. . . . His public telling and retelling of "Wapping Alice" to mixed groups supports the notion that he did not expect his audience (or at least some of it) to impute a consummated all-male affair to Alice's relationship.
>
> But it is equally certain that the homosexual possibilities of the story as he transformed it were clear to Mark Twain.[26]

In Twain's Autobiographical Dictations, he also added information about the original episode that actually took place in 1877, the episode he reported to Livy. At that time he acted as private detective, judge, and jury, cornering Willie into marrying Lizzie on the basis of her accusations of paternity. According to Twain, three years after the event (and well before he wrote "Wapping Alice"), he encountered the original heterosexual Willie and Lizzie driving a fashionable carriage; he stopped to greet them and was told the following story by Willie:

> "Mr. Clemens, when you made me marry Alice that time three years ago I could have killed you, but I want to thank you now! It was the greatest favor anybody ever did me. I hadn't a cent; I hadn't any work; I hadn't a friend, and I couldn't see anything in front of me but the poorhouse. Well, Alice is the girl that has changed all that; she saved me, and I thank you again. She got work for me, all I could do, from

---

25. Twain, Autobiographical Dictations, April 10, 1907, quoted in Hill, *Wapping Alice*, 71, final emphasis added.
26. Hill, afterword to *Wapping Alice*, 78.

Garvie and Hills, the contractors who built your house; she started a little restaurant down in Main Street, and got Mr. Bunce and Mr. Robinson and Gen. Hawley and Mr. George Warner, and all your other influential friends who had known her in your house, to come and try her bill of fare. They liked it, and brought everybody else, and pretty soon she had all the custom she could attend to, and was making money like a mint, and it's still going on yet. She took me out of wage-work and made a contractor and builder out of me, and that is what I am now, and prospering. This is our turnout; these are our clothes, and they are paid for. We owe it all to you, Mr. Clemens, and your arbitrary and mistaken notions of justice, for if you hadn't forced me to marry Alice or pack up and go to the penitentiary it never would have happened." He paused; then he added, without any bitterness in his tone, "But as to that child, it hasn't ever arrived, and there wasn't the damndest least prospect of it the time that she told you that fairy-tale—and never *had* been!"

Then he laughed, and Alice laughed, and, naturally, I did the same. Then we parted.[27]

Once Twain had been assured that there been no extramarital sex taking place in his household, at least between Lizzie and Willie, he would have had no reason to cover over the scandalous heterosexual activity with what he apparently thought was the less provocative homosexual union that takes place in "Wapping Alice." What in fact Twain knew full well at the time he originally composed the story, in 1897, was that Lizzie had put one over on him. In response, he created a greater sexual illusion than the one perpetrated by Lizzie. One way or another, Twain was going to have the last word in this story, even if it meant turning Lizzie into a transvestite. As he had in the narration cited above from his Autobiographical Dictations, Twain had the last laugh. In so doing, however, he opened up the space of homosexuality and located that space, imaginatively, in the Clemens household. No wonder the burglar alarm went off.

Is He Dead?

The final work under consideration is the comedy *Is He Dead?* It continues issues present in other transvestite tales, especially emphasiz-

27. Quoted in ibid., 73–74.

ing the performative and constructed nature of gender, and the strong association of cross-dressing with death, as even the play's title suggests. Yet it is dissimilar in fundamental ways as well. The play differs from the other works first and foremost because it was written as a drama to be staged, with Twain making serious efforts to have the play produced shortly after he wrote it in 1897.[28] Because it is a play, not a story or tale, there is no narrative perspective to guide us (or misguide us), and it features, by name, a historical character of considerable renown, the French artist Jean-François Millet, whose masterpieces included *The Angelus* and *The Sower*, both highlighted in the play. In spite of its grounding in historical fact, the humor and comedy of the play is much more exaggerated than even the most lighthearted and playful of the stories we have examined thus far. It is a farce that takes great freedom in its representation of a man who appears for much of the play destined to live out his life as a woman. The death that hovers over the play, far from being the serious matter that faces previous transvestite characters such as Joan of Arc or Nancy Jackson, is also represented in a farcical manner.

These differences notwithstanding, the play is similar enough to the other works to warrant being the anchor piece in this chapter on gender play and transvestitism. It is in many ways, in fact, the most performative of all the pieces under consideration, not simply because it is a play, but because it features a male-to-female cross-dresser who for fully half the length of the play plays two roles simultaneously: himself and also his own fictive twin sister. Further, it is unabashed in embracing cross-dressing, of male-to-female transvestitism, and it openly depicts the romantic seduction of a man by another man cross-dressed as a woman. At the end of her afterword to the edition of the play, Shelley Fisher Fishkin asks what it means that "one of the most interesting female characters Twain created is really a man." She asks, "What are we supposed to make of Millet's gender-bending masquerade?"[29] This is the question I intend to answer.

28. Shelley Fisher Fishkin documents Twain's attempts to have his play produced in England by his friend Bram Stoker; when that failed, he asked Henry Huttleston Rogers and C. C. Rice "to help him try to place the play in the United States." Rice, in turn, tried to enlist the help of Alf Hayman, also to no avail (afterword to *Is He Dead?* 198).
29. Ibid., 203.

Because the play is relatively unfamiliar, having been published only in 2003, and the plot complicated, it is necessary to examine in some detail the play's cast of characters, the shape of its plot, the problems raised by the play, and the resolution to those problems. We need to pay particular attention to the specific transvestite tradition from which the play evolves, and to the remarkable range of gendered performances embodied in the figure of the cross-dressed Millet.

The main characters in the three-act play, set in Paris in about 1848, are Jean-François Millet, a young artist yet to receive much public acclaim; his sweetheart, Marie Leroux; a creditor, Bastien André; the Widow Daisy Tillou, who is Millet's fictive twin sister (played by Millet); and a host of young artists who surround Millet, the most notable of whom are "Dutchy" and "Chicago." A number of other characters crowd the stage from time to time, but these are the most important. At the beginning of the play, André, a classic villain—unscrupulous, greedy, and heartless—threatens to call in the debts owed him by both Marie's father and by Millet if Marie will not agree to marry him. She refuses because she is in love with Millet. Hoping to raise enough money to pay off André, Millet's friends hold a sale of his paintings, but André and his friends circulate among the would-be buyers, convincing them that the paintings are worthless. Millet and his friends despair and attempt to commit suicide by building a charcoal fire inside his studio. They nearly succeed. Fortunately, Chicago arrives in time to wake them all out of their stupors and to announce his plan to save them from financial ruin: they will send Millet away, claiming that he is terminally ill, and have him turn out paintings as rapidly as possible for another three months. They then will declare him dead, greatly enhancing the market value of his paintings.[30]

As act 2 opens, the friends have put their plan into action, spreading the word that Millet has gone to some unknown place to die. As Chicago and his friends expect, the press descends upon them, none willing to admit he had never heard of Millet before, and reporting in their papers that Millet's only living relative, a twin sister, refuses to sell any

30. Mark Twain, *Is He Dead? A Comedy in Three Acts*, 46 (hereinafter cited as *IHD*). On the number of characters in the play, see Mark Davidziak's review of *Is He Dead?* for the Mark Twain Forum: "conservatively, you would need at least fifty actors to effectively stage the play as Twain has written it."

of his paintings except four. Meanwhile, for the duration of the play, whenever Millet appears he is cross-dressed as his sister, called "the Widow," who "comes mincing out of the bedroom, smoking a corn-cob or briarwood pipe" (*IHD*, 62). Millet chafes against the circumstances—painting pictures for three months in the bedroom wearing "awkward clothes" he says he "can't endure" (*IHD*, 63). But buyers soon descend upon the studio and start a bidding war among themselves for the four paintings, including *The Sower*, which fetches sixty thousand francs. This bidding and counterbidding, which at times sounds like the betting around a poker table, occupies fully ten pages of text, suggesting that Twain had more than a casual interest in the whole issue of the value of artistic production and the vicissitudes of the marketplace. When Millet hears that his paintings have brought ninety thousand francs, he collapses. This portion of the play ends with the friends bestowing upon the Widow a first name, Daisy, so she can open a bank account; then they help her practice writing her signature.

The scene that follows this one is particularly instructive, for it imagines an adult transvestite figure still in the process of becoming the gender she is performing. Huck, who needed to "practice" being a girl and did so under the amused but watchful eye of Jim, "soon got the hang of it" and went on his way. In contrast, the Widow knows she does not know how to perform her sex, and she is afraid she will accidentally reveal herself to a group of old women who were friends of Millet: "I haven't got the hang of these clothes yet. They'll see that I'm not a woman. . . . You see I'm femininely ignorant. I could make fatal mistakes in talking" (*IHD*, 82). To protect her, Chicago tells the friends that the Widow's mind has been "a little touched" by the sudden illness of her brother. "She's a little bit stiff in one leg, yet—please don't notice it" (*IHD*, 84).[31] The eccentricity Chicago promises is more than provided by the Widow, whose conversation is completely bizarre. After the women comment on how much her voice, her face, her hands resemble her brother's, the Widow explains that she is her brother's twin, although "considerably younger than he"—by a full six days. She quickly adds that she cannot remember things anymore: "I used to, but

31. This enigmatic reference is never clarified; if it was a familiar turn of phrase to express someone who is still not herself after an emotional blow, I'm unable to confirm it.

I don't now. Years and years ago I got hit here—just about here. (Touching top of head.) And it injured my memory; and so, since then I can't remember it at all, I only remember that I *used* to remember it" (*IHD*, 86). What follows then is one of the several instances in the play when Twain incorporates bits of a story that he has used before. As Davidziak noted in his review, Twain "borrowed" from his previous works at least five times in the play. This is one, with the Widow claiming to have been hit in the head by an Irishman falling off the roof; her being there was "the hand of Providence. . . . If I hadn't been there that Irishman would have been killed" (*IHD*, 87).

The conversation becomes even more exaggerated, descending into true farce. The Widow claims to have had "slathers" of children, though she is only twenty-five years old; as Mother Leroux says, she "talks just as a rabbit might" (*IHD*, 89). She claims to have seven children in two years, "some in the spring, some in the fall, others along here and there." All nine of the children died, she reports, and when asked if it were seven or nine, she weeps and says, "I speak of another vintage" (*IHD*, 90). The conversation becomes even more farcical:

> Mother Leroux: Were they—
> Widow: Boys and girls? Some of them—yes.
> Mother Leroux: *Some* of them? Weren't they all?
> Widow: Many thought so.
> Madame Audrienne: What did *you* think?
> Widow: At this late date I could not be certain, of course. Still, I
> think there was considerable variety. (*IHD*, 91)

The act ends with a visit from André, who presses to have the debt paid but is then surprised when the Widow writes a check to pay off Millet's debt as well as Leroux's. André tears up Millet's check, vowing to have Millet's paintings instead. The addle-headed Widow suddenly becomes fierce as she upbraids André for his villainous ways:

> You found my brother and his poor young artist-friends struggling honestly and manfully for their bread against hunger and misery, and you have traded upon their poverty. . . . You have bought their pictures for francs, and sold them for Louis d'or, you have hidden their

talents, such as they were, from the world, . . . you have beguiled
them into debt and robbed them in a hundred mean and pitiful ways;
and yonder, stretched upon his bed lies that blameless old man whom
your deceptions, your inhumanities, your pitiless brutalities have
brought there— . . .

. . . I am a lady, and I know the limitations that are upon me, but
this I *will* say—that from head to heel, from heart to marrow, from
pallet to midriff you are a mean, cowardly, contemptible, base-begotten
damned scoundrel! (*IHD*, 98–99)

Fishkin characterizes the Widow as "a ditzy nonsense-spewing ec-
centric old lady and a woman who rises to heights of eloquence usually reserved, on the Victorian stage, for men. What other woman in
nineteenth-century theatre had a speech as searing as that with which
the Widow Tillou excoriates André at the close of the second act?
Even the most outspoken woman on the Victorian stage did not get to
call the villain a "contemptible, base-begotten damned scoundrel!"[32]
Madame Caron (one of the old ladies visiting the Widow) is more succinct: "Mind's as sound as a nut" (*IHD*, 99).

After witnessing such a thoroughgoing denounciation of André by
the Widow, our credulity is once again stretched when the final act
opens, three months later, and the Widow reveals that André has been
"making love" to her for weeks:

After all these weeks Monsieur André's love-making begins to tire me
a little. But it has been a mine of satisfaction to the boys, and a body
can't refuse them anything. They want me actually to marry him—
but I draw the line there——I wonder how it would do to—to—Of
course I must get that forged contract out of him somehow or other,
or he will seize and hold the 3 million francs, and we can't very well
afford that—certainly can't afford to let *him* get rich out of us—oh
no!——Nobody but I can prove the document a forgery, and I can't
do it without exposing our game and who I am.—He's due now, and
I'm not ready.——Suppose I *promise* to marry him on condition that
he— (*IHD*, 103)

32. Fishkin, afterword to *Is He Dead?* 203.

Once again we see a transvestite caught in a dilemma that requires him either to go along with something fraudulent, in this case a forged contract supposedly entered into between André and Millet, or set the record straight and thereby expose his identity as a transvestite. In the previous stories, "An Awful—Terrible Medieval Romance" and "How Nancy Jackson Married Kate Wilson," the issue at stake is paternity, whereas here it is the question of another sort of creative issue—artistic production. The Widow, unlike Conrad or Robert, takes control over the situation by plotting a way out of her dilemma and by making love to the one who has wronged Millet. André's arrival interrupts her musing, and a truly remarkable scene follows:

> André: (Kissing Widow's forehead.)
> My precious!
> (Aside.)
> Phew! She's been smoking.
> Widow: (Tapping him with her fan.)
> Naughty boy! I suppose I ought to scold you.
> André: (Puts his arm around her—she does not resist.)
> Dearest if you would always be like this.
> Widow: I will. Dear Bastien you have conquered me.
> André: At last! O, this *is* bliss.
> (Kisses her passionately several times.)
> Widow: O, you frighten me! But—
> André: But what, sweetest?
> Widow: (Slyly.)
> I like it.
> André: You darling!
> (Kiss.)
> O, I could eat you!
> (Kiss.)
> Widow: Do you really love me, Bastien? Really and truly? (*IHD*,
> 104–5)

André offers to tear up the (fake) contract if the Widow will marry him, but she stalls for more time to think through the dilemma, reminding André that this is the day of her brother's funeral and she cannot betroth herself at such a time. André exits, and Marie enters, "in deep mourning" (*IHD*, 108).

At this point the play makes a fairly dramatic shift, with the Widow consoling Marie and assuring her that Millet is better off than before.

> Marie: It is so consoling to think it. You *do* believe he is better off, *don't* you, Daisy?
> Widow: O, I know it.
> (Pressing Marie close.)
> Kiss me for his sake, dear.
> (Kiss.) (*IHD*, 109)

Marie then admits that she loves to have Daisy kiss her: "It's just the way he used to do it his own self" (*IHD*, 110). Millet also hugged her the same way, she says, and notes that she has his voice, his walk, and even swears like him. Their lovemaking, for so it is, is interrupted by the actual (but fraudulent) funeral procession for Millet that fills the Champs-Elysées—"the nobbiest funeral Paris has seen in fifty years, bar Napoleon's" (*IHD*, 116). Chicago expresses surprise that the Widow is not going to the funeral, which occasions one more of the self-referential jokes in the text: "No I'm not. The idea of a man attending his own funeral. I never heard of such a thing" (*IHD*, 117). The Widow and Marie continue to interact, after a slight interruption, with the Widow secretly coming up with a plan whereby Millet would not "have to disappear from the world at all—shan't even have to leave Paris!" (*IHD*, 130). Once again she comforts Marie, asking her to imagine with her that everything going on is an illusion—that Millet is not really dead, that he appears before her in disguise—calling himself Placide Duval—and asks her to marry him; Marie readily assents, then begins to cry because she believes Millet to be dead instead. They both leave the stage, and André enters, still scheming to marry the Widow. Then, in the most improbable and bizarre scene in the play, the Widow re-enters accompanied by these stage directions: "She is entirely bald, black patch over one eye, has a slovenly old peignoir on, which conceals her dress; face is yellow; has a hand mirror; walks on crutches" (*IHD*, 134). Acting as though she does not know André is just out of sight, she proceeds to make herself "supremely beautiful for him." She asks a page to bring her her new teeth, then a fresh glass eye, which first gets stuck and then turns "gilded side to the front." She puts on a new com-

plexion, and tells the page to fetch her her artificial legs.[33] As a ploy to
alienate André, it works perfectly, for he sneaks out declaring that "I
wouldn't marry that debris if she was worth a billion. I'm going to get
out or die" (*IHD*, 139). From this point on, the play draws to a rapid
close. The old ladies, Marie, Chicago, and Dutchy all join the Widow
in their collective mourning. The Widow announces she is going to go
back to her country home, and that

> To-morrow a rich stranger will occupy this grand house—with his
> young wife—a good man and kind, but a recluse—a man with a se-
> cret sorrow gnawing at his heart—he thought he was born to fame,
> but knows he must die unknown. You will know him. Be good to him.
> He goes disguised—pretend not to notice it.
>   (Marie looks up wistfully.)
> He bears a fictitious name—Placide Duval—
>   (Marie rises, gazing.)
> —Keep his secret. And so, good-bye dear friends. And let me, also
> leave you with a secret. Swear to keep it thirty days—after that, tell it
> if you choose—nobody will believe you. (*IHD*, 142–43)

The Widow embraces Marie, music plays, and the curtain falls.

There is more transvestitism in this play than in any of the other stories, and for that matter than in any of the other works by Twain with
the exception of *Personal Recollections of Joan of Arc*. The tone here,
however, could not possibly be further from the tone of *Joan of Arc;*
instead of reverence, here we encounter farce and sexual liberties.
Fishkin places the transvestitism of *Is He Dead?* squarely within the tradition of male cross-dressing in the American theater. She points out
that *Charley's Aunt,* which was arguably the biggest theater success of
the 1890s, was a comedy based on cross-dressing. She further invokes
the longer theatrical history of the "dame," as exemplified by the per-
former Neil Burgess as the Widow Bedott, as Josiah Allen's Wife (later called "Vim"), and as Abigail Prue in his *Country Fair.* All these representations, which in turn had their origins in vaudeville, according to
Fishkin, are like the Widow in *Is He Dead?*—"Unlike the 'prima don-
na' character who aspires to a complete, unbroken illusion of being fe-

33. All these grotesque details are familiar; they reach far across the span of Twain's
career, back to *Roughing It.*

male, the 'dame's' underlying maleness is never completely hidden from the audience's awareness." Yet Twain's "dame"—for that is what she is—goes beyond anything Burgess performed on the American stage. All the parts Burgess played, indeed made famous, featured older women—women well into their middle ages, who were presented as wholly comic characters, as mildly absurd figures, as the objects of laughter.[34] But Twain's Widow is twenty-five years old, and far from being beyond the marriage plot, she/he is entertaining a marriage relationship with two different characters in the play—one male, one female. While it is true that the purported audience of *Is He Dead?* would always know that "she" was really a "he," for they are in on the cross-dressing from the beginning, key characters in the play are entirely taken in by Millet as a female figure, most notably the two suitors, André and Marie.

In the course of the play, Millet performs a remarkable range of gendered characters. He begins, of course, as a healthy but impoverished young artist, a man's man, surrounded by a coterie of other male artists and students. Midway through the play, in his first appearance as his twin sister, the Widow Tillou, he appears as a transvestite in transition; one could argue that his was a high camp performance at this point, with the Widow in female dress but smoking a pipe. Next we see the Millet as the Widow-seductress, entrapping André with her charms and her passionate kisses. Moments later, he is a dear friend to Marie, sharing intimacies and consoling Marie for the loss of her lover; their kissing and caressing is ostensibly same-sex kissing, which both characters seem to enjoy. The fifth incarnation is rather more difficult to characterize. The Widow appears as a repulsive old woman, a regular wreck of a human being, or, as André says, "that debris." Her final appearance is once again transitional, in that Millet still speaks in his sister's voice and persona, but is letting enough of himself come through that Marie suddenly understands that the Widow is her lover in disguise. This all happens as the Widow prepares to leave her new friends, but

---

34. On *Charley's Aunt*, see Fishkin, afterword to *Is He Dead?* 194; on the dame, 192–93; on the dame's masculinity, 193; on Burgess playing older women, see the chapter "Women in Sheep's Clothing" in Morris, *Women Vernacular Humorists*. See also Linda A. Morris, *Women's Humor in the Age of Gentility: The Life and Works of Frances Miriam Whitcher*.

announces that a newcomer, Placide Duval, and his wife will soon come to live in Millet's apartment. The "natural" order would seem to be restored. But when Millet does come back, an action that will take place after the curtain has dropped, he will come back not as himself but as another man in disguise.

In its continuum of cross-dressed illusion, *Is He Dead?* literally stages gender more completely than does any other work by Twain. Even wrapped in farce, the male-to-female transvestitism represents a public commitment on Twain's part to the notion that gender is a performance—nothing more and nothing less. Thus the answer to Fishkin's question—what are we supposed to make of Millet's gender-bending masquerade?—is that ironically behind Millet's masquerade, Twain is revealing himself, and his career-long fascination with gender play, more fully than ever. For Twain, the mask is off. Long before social scientists and literary theorists articulated any notion that gender is a social construction, Mark Twain had made sense (and supreme nonsense) of that notion.

Works Cited

Anderson, Fredrick. Introduction to *Pudd'nhead Wilson and Those Extraordinary Twins,* by Mark Twain, vii–xxxii. San Francisco: Chandler, 1968.

Bakhtin, Mikhail. *Problems of Dostoevsky's Poetics.* Trans. Caryl Emerson. Minneapolis: University of Minnesota Press, 1984.

———. *Rabelais and His World.* Trans. Helene Iswolsky. Bloomington: Indiana University Press, 1984.

Beaver, Harold. "Run, Nigger, Run." In *The Critical Response to Mark Twain's Huckleberry Finn,* ed. Laurie Champion, 187–94. New York: Greenwood Press, 1991.

Bird, John. "Killing Half a Dog, Half a Novel: The Trouble with *The Tragedy of Pudd'nhead Wilson* and *The Comedy of Those Extraordinary Twins.*" In *A Companion to Mark Twain,* ed. Peter Messent and Louis J. Budd, 441–48. Oxford: Blackwell Publishing, 2005.

Blair, Walter. *Mark Twain and Huckleberry Finn.* Berkeley and Los Angeles: University of California Press, 1960.

Budd, Louis J., ed. *Mark Twain: Collected Tales, Sketches, Speeches, and Essays, 1852–1890.* New York: Library of America, 1992.

———. *Mark Twain: Collected Tales, Sketches, Speeches, and Essays, 1891–1910.* New York: Library of America, 1992.

Bullough, Vern L., and Bonnie Bullough. *Cross Dressing, Sex, and Gender.* Philadelphia: University of Pennsylvania Press, 1993.

Butler, Judith. *Gender Trouble: Feminism and the Subversion of Identity.* New York: Routledge, 1999.

———. "Imitation and Gender Insubordination." In *The Lesbian and Gay Studies Reader,* ed. Henry Abelove, Michele Aina Barale, and David M. Halperin, 307–20. New York: Routledge, 1993.

————. *Undoing Gender.* New York: Routledge, 2004.

Camfield, Gregg. *The Oxford Companion to Mark Twain.* Oxford: Oxford University Press, 2003.

Chabannes, Armand de. *La Vierge Lorraine: Jeanne d'Arc.* Paris: E. Plons, 1890.

Clemens, Clara. *My Father, Mark Twain.* New York: Harper and Brothers, 1931.

Clemens, Olivia Susan. Letters of Olivia Susan Clemens to Louise Brownell. In Saunders Family Papers, Hamilton College Library, Clinton, New York.

Cooley, John. "Mark Twain, Rebellious Girls, and Daring Young Women." In *How Nancy Jackson Married Kate Wilson and Other Tales of Rebellious Girls & Daring Young Women,* ed. John Cooley, 229–49. Lincoln: University of Nebraska Press, 2001.

————. "Mark Twain's Transvestite Tragedies: Role Reversals and Patriarchal Power." *OVERhere* 15 (1995): 34–48.

Cooley, John, ed. *How Nancy Jackson Married Kate Wilson and Other Tales of Rebellious Girls & Daring Young Women.* Lincoln: University of Nebraska Press, 2001.

Cox, James. "A Hard Book to Take." In *The Critical Response to Mark Twain's Huckleberry Finn,* ed. Laurie Champion, 171–86. Westport, Conn.: Greenwood Press, 1991.

————. *Mark Twain: The Fate of Humor.* 1966. Reprint, Columbia: University of Missouri Press, 2002.

————. "Remarks on the Sad Initiation of Huck Finn." In *Huck Finn among the Critics: A Centennial Selection,* ed. M. Thomas Inge, 141–55. Frederick, Md.: University Publications of America, 1985.

Davidziak, Mark. Review of *Is He Dead? Mark Twain Forum* (2003), http://www/twainweb.net/reviews/IsHeDead.html.

D'Emilio, John, and Estelle B. Freedman. *Intimate Matters: A History of Sexuality in America.* New York: Harper and Row, 1988.

De Voto, Bernard. "Mark Twain's Presentation of Slavery." In *Pudd'nhead Wilson and Those Extraordinary Twins,* 2d ed., ed. Sidney Berger, 247–48. New York: Norton, 2005.

Dolgin, Ellen Ecker. "So Well-Suited: The Evolution of Joan of Arc as a Dramatic Image." PhD diss., New York University, 1995.

Duggan, Lisa. *Sapphic Slashers: Sex, Violence, and American Modernity.* Durham: Duke University Press, 2000.

———. "The Trials of Alice Mitchell: Sensationalism, Sexology, and the Lesbian Subject in Turn-of-the-Century America." *Signs* 18 (1993): 791–814.

Ellis, James. "The Bawdy Humor of 'The King's Camelopard' or 'The Royal Nonesuch.'" *American Literature,* December 1991, 729–35.

Emerson, Everett. *The Authentic Mark Twain: A Literary Biography of Samuel L. Clemens.* Philadelphia: University of Pennsylvania Press, 1984.

Engle, Gary D. *This Grotesque Essence: Plays from the American Minstrel Stage.* Baton Rouge: Louisiana State University Press, 1978.

Faderman, Lillian. *Odd Girls and Twilight Lovers: A History of Lesbian Life in Twentieth-Century America.* New York: Columbia University Press, 1991.

Ferris, Lesley, ed. *Crossing the Stage: Controversies on Cross-Dressing.* London: Routledge, 1993.

Fiedler, Leslie. *Love and Death in the American Novel.* New York: Stein and Day, 1966.

Fishkin, Shelley Fisher. Afterword to *Is He Dead? A Comedy in Three Acts,* by Mark Twain, 147–232. Berkeley and Los Angeles: University of California Press, 2005.

———. "Mark Twain and Women." In *The Cambridge Companion to Mark Twain,* ed. Forrest G. Robinson, 52–73. Cambridge: Cambridge University Press, 1995.

———. "Race and Culture at the Century's End: A Social Context for *Pudd'nhead Wilson.*" *Essays in Arts and Sciences* 19 (1990): 1–27.

Fryer, Jonathan. *Wilde.* London: Haus Publishing, 2005.

Garber, Marjorie. *Vested Interests: Cross-Dressing and Cultural Anxiety.* New York: Routledge, 1992.

Gillman, Susan. *Dark Twins: Imposture and Identity in Mark Twain's America.* Chicago: University of Chicago Press, 1989.

Graff, Gerald, and James Phelan. "Controversy over the Ending: Did Mark Twain Sell Jim Down the River?" In *Adventures of Huckleberry Finn: A Case Study in Critical Controversy,* ed. Gerald Graff and James Phelan, 279–84. Boston: St. Martin's Press, 1985.

Greenblatt, Stephen. *Renaissance Self-Fashioning: From Moore to Shakespeare.* Chicago: University of Chicago Press, 1980.

Halberstam, Judith. *Female Masculinity.* Durham: Duke University Press, 1998.

Halperin, David. *How to Do the History of Homosexuality.* Chicago: University of Chicago Press, 2002.

Harris, Susan K. "Afterword." In *Personal Recollections of Joan of Arc,* by Mark Twain, 1–11. Oxford: Oxford University Press, 1996.

———. "The Dream of Domesticity." In *The Oxford Companion to Mark Twain,* ed. Gregg Camfield, 170–80. Oxford: Oxford University Press, 2003.

———. "Mark Twain and Gender." In *A Historical Guide to Mark Twain,* ed. Shelley Fisher Fishkin, 163–93. New York: Oxford University Press, 2002.

———. "Mark Twain's Bad Women." *Studies in American Fiction* 13 (1985): 157–68.

Henrickson, Gary P. "Biographers' Twain, Critics' Twain: Which of the Twains Wrote the 'Evasion'?" *Southern Literary Journal* (1993): 14–29.

Hill, Hamlin. Afterword to *Wapping Alice,* by Mark Twain, 75–79. Berkeley: Friends of the Bancroft Library, University of California, Berkeley, 1981.

Hoffman, Andrew. *Inventing Mark Twain: The Lives of Samuel Langhorne Clemens.* New York: Morrow, 1997.

Horowitz, Helen. *Alma Mater: Design and Experience in the Women's Colleges from Their Nineteenth-Century Beginnings to the 1930s.* Amherst: University of Massachusetts Press, 1984.

Howard, Jean E. "Crossdressing, the Theatre, and Gender Struggle in Early Modern England." *Shakespeare Quarterly* 39 (1988): 418–40.

Jehlen, Myra. "Reading Gender in *Adventures of Huckleberry Finn.*" In *Adventures of Huckleberry Finn: A Case Study in Critical Controversy,* ed. Gerald Graff and James Phelan, 505–18. Boston: St. Martin's Press, 1995.

———. "The Ties That Bind: Race and Sex in *Pudd'nhead Wilson.*" In *Pudd'nhead Wilson and Those Extraordinary Twins,* 2d ed., ed. Sidney Berger, 411–26. New York: Norton, 2005.

Kaplan, Justin. Introduction to *Personal Recollections of Joan of Arc*, by Mark Twain, xxxi–xlii. Oxford: Oxford University Press, 1996.

———. *Mark Twain and Samuel Clemens*. New York: Simon and Schuster, 1970.

Knoper, Randall. *Acting Naturally: Mark Twain in the Culture of Performance*. Berkeley and Los Angeles: University of California Press, 1995.

Kole, W. "Joan of Arc's Armor." *San Francisco Chronicle*, June 29, 1996.

Krauth, Leland. *Mark Twain and Company: Six Literary Relations*. Athens: University of Georgia Press, 2003.

Lott, Eric. *Love and Theft: Blackface Minstrelsy and the American Working Class*. New York: Oxford University Press, 1993.

———. "Mr. Clemens and Jim Crow: Twain, Race, and Blackface." In *The Cambridge Companion to Mark Twain*, ed. Forrest G. Robinson, 129–52. Cambridge: Cambridge University Press, 1995.

Lynn, Kenneth. *Mark Twain and Southwestern Humor*. Boston: Little, Brown, 1959.

Margolis, Nadia. "Trial by Passion: Philology, Film, and Ideology in the Portrayal of Joan of Arc." *Journal of Medieval and Early Modern Studies* 27, no. 3 (1997): 445–93.

Messent, Peter. *New Readings of the American Novel: Narrative Theory and Its Application*. London: Macmillan, 1990.

———. *The Short Works of Mark Twain: A Critical Study*. Philadelphia: University of Pennsylvania Press, 2001.

Michelet, J. *Jeanne d'Arc, 1412–1432*. 3d ed. Paris: Librairie Hachette et Cie, 1873.

Moers, Ellen. "A Note on Mark Twain and Harriet Beecher Stowe." In *Harriet Beecher Stowe and American Literature*, 39–47. Hartford: Stowe-Day Foundation, 1978.

Morris, Linda A. "Beneath the Veil: Clothing, Race, and Gender in Mark Twain's *Pudd'nhead Wilson*." *Studies in American Fiction* 27, no. 1 (1999): 37–52.

———. "The Eloquent Silence in Mark Twain's 'Hellfire Hotchkiss.'" *Mark Twain Annual* 3 (2005): 43–51.

———. *Women's Humor in the Age of Gentility: The Life and Works of Frances Miriam Whitcher*. Syracuse: Syracuse University Press, 1992.

————. *Women Vernacular Humorists in Nineteenth-Century America: Ann Stephens, Frances Whitcher, and Marietta Holley.* New York: Garland Press, 1988.

Morrison, Toni. *Playing in the Dark: Whiteness and the Literary Imagination.* New York: Vintage, 1993.

Neider, Charles. Introduction to *Papa: An Intimate Biography of Mark Twain, by His Daughter, Susy Clemens.* Garden City, N.Y.: Doubleday, 1985.

Newlyn, Andrea K. "Form and Ideology in Transracial Narratives: *Pudd'nhead Wilson* and *A Romance of the Republic.*" *Narrative* 8, no. 1 (2000): 43–65.

Newman, Judie. "Was Tom White? Stowe's *Dred* and Twain's *Pudd'nhead Wilson.*" In *Soft Canons: American Women Writers and Masculine Tradition,* ed. Karen L. Kilcup, 67–81. Iowa City: University of Iowa Press, 1999.

Odell, George C. D. *Annals of the New York Stage.* Vol. 11. New York: Columbia University Press, 1939.

Paine, Albert Bigelow. Introduction to *Personal Recollections of Joan of Arc,* by Mark Twain, xv–xxiv. New York: Gabriel Wells, 1923.

————. *Mark Twain, a Biography: The Personal and Literary Life of Samuel Langhorne Clemens.* 3 vols. New York: Harper and Brothers, 1912.

Pettit, Arthur. "The Black and White Curse: *Pudd'nhead Wilson* and Miscegenation." In *Pudd'nhead Wilson and Those Extraordinary Twins,* 2d ed., ed. Sidney Berger, 322–36. New York: Norton, 2005.

Porter, Carolyn. "Roxana's Plot." In *Mark Twain's Pudd'nhead Wilson: Race, Conflict, and Culture,* ed. Susan Gillman and Forrest G. Robinson, 121–36. Durham: Duke University Press, 1990.

Powers, Ron. *Mark Twain: A Life.* New York: Free Press, 2005.

Rogers, Franklin R., ed. *Mark Twain's Satires and Burlesques.* Berkeley and Los Angeles: University of California Press, 1967.

Sahli, Nancy. "Smashing: Women's Relationships before the Fall." *Chrysalis* 8 (1979): 17–27.

Sattelmeyer, Robert. "How Nancy Jackson Married Kate Wilson." *Missouri Review* 10 (1987): 97–98.

Sedgwick, Eve Kosofsky. *Epistemology of the Closet.* Berkeley and Los Angeles: University of California Press, 1990.

Senelick, Laurence. "Boys and Girls Together: Subcultural Origins of Glamour Drag and Male Impersonation in the Nineteenth-Century Stage." In *Crossing the Stage: Controversies on Cross Dressing,* ed. Lesley Ferris, 80–95. London: Routledge, 1993.

Sepet, Marius. *Jeanne d'Arc.* Tours: A. Meme et Fils, 1869.

Skandera-Trombley, Laura. *Mark Twain in the Company of Women.* Philadelphia: University of Pennsylvania Press, 1994.

———. "Mark Twain's Cross-Dressing Oeuvre." *College Literature* 24, no. 2 (1997): 82–96.

Smith, Henry Nash. *Mark Twain: The Development of a Writer.* Cambridge: Harvard University Press, 1962.

———. "*Pudd'nhead Wilson* as Criticism of the Dominant Culture." In *Pudd'nhead Wilson and Those Extraordinary Twins,* 2d ed., ed. Sidney Berger, 271–78. New York: Norton, 2005.

Smith-Rosenberg, Carroll. *Disorderly Conduct: Visions of Gender in Victorian America.* New York: Oxford University Press, 1985.

———. "The Female World of Love and Ritual." *Signs* 1, no. 1 (1975): 1–29.

Somerville, Siobhan. *Queering the Color Line: Race and the Invention of Homosexuality in American Culture.* Durham: Duke University Press, 2003.

———. "Scientific Racism and the Invention of the Homosexual Body." In *The Gender/Sexuality Reader: Culture, History, Political Economy,* ed. Roger N. Lancaster and Micaela de Leonardo, 37–52. New York: Routledge, 1997.

Stone, Albert. "Introduction to *Personal Recollections of Joan of Arc.*" Unpublished manuscript. Mark Twain Papers, University of California, Berkeley, n.d.

Stoneley, Peter. *Mark Twain and the Feminine Aesthetic.* Cambridge: Cambridge University Press, 1992.

Sundquist, Eric J. "Mark Twain and Homer Plessy." In *Mark Twain's Pudd'nhead Wilson: Race, Conflict, and Culture,* ed. Susan Gillman and Forrest G. Robinson, 46–72. Durham: Duke University Press, 1990.

Toll, Robert. *Blacking Up: The Minstrel Show in Nineteenth-Century America.* New York: Oxford University Press, 1974.

The Trials of Jeanne d'Arc: A Complete Translation of the Text of the Original Documents. Trans. W. P. Barrett. London: Routledge, 1931.

Trilling, Lionel. Introduction to *Adventures of Huckleberry Finn,* by Mark Twain, v–xviii. New York, Rinehart, 1948.

Tuckey, Janet. *Joan of Arc: "The Maid."* London: Marcus Ward, 1880.

Turner, Patricia. *Ceramic Uncles and Celluloid Mammies: Black Images and Their Influence on Culture.* Charlottesville: University of Virginia Press, 2002.

Turner, Victor. *From Ritual to Theatre: The Human Seriousness of Play.* New York: Performing Arts Journal Publications, 1982.

Twain, Mark. *Adventures of Huckleberry Finn.* Berkeley and Los Angeles: University of California Press, 2001.

———. *Adventures of Huckleberry Finn.* In *The Works of Mark Twain,* vol. 8. Berkeley and Los Angeles: University of California Press, 2003.

———. "An Awful—Terrible Medieval Romance." In *Mark Twain: Collected Tales, Sketches, Speeches, and Essays, 1852–1890,* ed. Louis J. Budd, 332–39. New York: Library of America, 1992.

———. *A Connecticut Yankee in King Arthur's Court.* Berkeley and Los Angeles: University of California Press, 1979.

———. *Following the Equator: A Journey around the World* and *Anti-Imperialist Essays.* New York: Oxford University Press, 1996.

———. "Hellfire Hotchkiss." In *How Nancy Jackson Married Kate Wilson and Other Tales of Rebellious Girls & Daring Young Women,* ed. John Cooley, 43–69. Lincoln: University of Nebraska Press, 2001.

———. "A Horse's Tale." In *How Nancy Jackson Married Kate Wilson and Other Tales of Rebellious Girls & Daring Young Women,* ed. John Cooley, 125–79. Lincoln: University of Nebraska Press, 2001.

———. "How Nancy Jackson Married Kate Wilson." In *How Nancy Jackson Married Kate Wilson and Other Tales of Rebellious Girls & Daring Young Women,* ed. John Cooley, 105–23. Lincoln: University of Nebraska Press, 2001.

———. *Huck Finn and Tom Sawyer among the Indians: And Other Unfinished Stories.* Berkeley and Los Angeles: University of California Press, 1989.

———. *Is He Dead? A Comedy in Three Acts.* Ed. Shelley Fisher Fishkin. Berkeley and Los Angeles: University of California, 2003.

———. Joan of Arc Manuscript. In *Microfilm Edition of Mark Twain's Literary Manuscripts Available in the Mark Twain Papers.* Box 36A. Berkeley: Bancroft Library, University of California, Berkeley. 2001.

———. "My Platonic Sweetheart." In *Mark Twain: Collected Tales, Sketches, Speeches, and Essays, 1891–1910,* ed. Louis J. Budd, 284–96. New York: Library of America, 1992.

———. "Notebook 32." In *Microfilm Edition of Mark Twain's Literary Manuscripts Available in the Mark Twain Papers.* Berkeley: Bancroft Library, University of California, Berkeley, 2001.

———. "1002nd Arabian Night." In *Mark Twain's Satires and Burlesques,* ed. Franklin R. Rogers, 88–133. Berkeley and Los Angeles: University of California Press, 1967.

———. *Personal Recollections of Joan of Arc.* New York: Oxford University Press, 1996.

———. *Pudd'nhead Wilson and Those Extraordinary Twins.* 1st ed., ed. Sidney Berger. New York: Norton, 1980.

———. *Pudd'nhead Wilson and Those Extraordinary Twins.* 2d ed., ed. Sidney Berger. New York: Norton, 2005.

———. "Saint Joan of Arc." In *Mark Twain: Collected Tales, Sketches, Speeches, and Essays, 1891–1910,* ed. Louis J. Budd, 584–96. New York: Library of America, 1992.

———. "Wapping Alice." In *Wapping Alice,* ed. Hamlin Hill, 41–67. Berkeley: Friends of the Bancroft Library, 1981.

———. "Wapping Alice." In *How Nancy Jackson Married Kate Wilson and Other Tales of Rebellious Girls & Daring Young Women,* ed. John Cooley, 81–104. Lincoln: University of Nebraska Press, 2001.

Walker, Nancy. "Reformers and Young Maidens: Women and Virtue in *Adventures of Huckleberry Finn.*" In *Mark Twain's Adventures of Huckleberry Finn: A Case Study in Critical Controversy,* ed. Gerald Graff and James Phelan, 485–504. Boston: St. Martin's Press, 1985.

Warner, Marina. *Joan of Arc: The Image of Female Heroism.* New York: Knopf, 1981.

Weeks, Jeffrey. *Making Sexual History.* Cambridge, U.K.: Polity Press, 2000.

Wiggins, Robert. "The Flawed Structure of *Pudd'nhead Wilson.*" In *Pudd'nhead Wilson and Those Extraordinary Twins,* 1st ed., ed. Sidney Berger, 255–59. New York: Norton, 1980.

Winsor, Elizabeth. Letters from Elizabeth Winsor to Louise Brownell. In Saunders Family Papers, Hamilton College Library, Clinton, New York.

Zwarg, Christina. "Women as Force in Mark Twain's *Joan of Arc:* The Unworkable Fascination." *Criticism* 27, no. 1 (1985): 57–72.

Index

Adventures of Huckleberry Finn, 1–2, 26, 28–29, 31, 34–58, 86–87, 89, 90, 91, 126, 159; edited scenes, 48–53; "Evasion," 54–58; Huck cross-dresses, 34–44, 54–57; homoeroticism in, 51–53; Huck and death, 39–42; Huck and Jim (exchange of subject-object position), 34, 37–38, 42; Jim and Aunt Sally, 56–57; Jim and death, 41–42, 46–48; Jim cross-dresses, 46–48, 56; Jim's "ghost story," 48, 51–53; Judith Loftus and gender tests, 36, 38, 39, 42, 44, 55, 86–87; Tom Sawyer cross-dresses, 56
Alden, Henry, 90*n2*
Anderson, Frederick, 68
Androgyny, 3, 108*n23*, 114, 125. *See also* Gender
Autobiographical Dictations (Twain), 150, 154–56
"Awful—Terrible Medieval Romance, An," 26, 27–28, 29–31, 124, 143, 162; cross-dressing and death in, 31; female paternity, 30; forced transvestitism, 29; language play in, 30

Bakhtin, Mikhail, 24–26, 40–41, 77, 112
Beard, Dan, 7, 108*n23*
Beaver, Harold, 48
Bernhardt, Sarah, 6–7, 9, 108*n23*
Betsey Bobbet: A Drama, 5
Bird, John, 91

Blackface, 2, 4, 44–45, 69, 80, 82–83. *See also* Minstrelsy and minstrel theater
Blair, Walter, 49
Brownell, Louise, 4, 11–20, 119–21, 143. *See also* Clemens, Olivia Susan
Bryn Mawr, 12, 14–15, 119, 121
Bullough, Vern L., and Bonnie Bullough, 5*n3*, 6*n4*, 7*n6*
Burgess, Neil, 5–6, 164–65. *See also* Vaudeville
Burlesque, 6, 30, 31, 44–45, 76. *See also* Minstrelsy and minstrel theater; Vaudeville
Butler, Judith, 23–24, 35*n8*, 77*n16*, 141*n16*

Camfield, Gregg, 5*n3*, 110*n24*
Carnivalesque, 24–25, 40–41, 51, 77, 112
Category crisis, 41, 47, 80, 100
Chabannes, Armand de, 91
Clemens, Clara, 11, 12, 16, 97*n11*, 119, 120, 121, 128
Clemens, Jean, 128
Clemens, Olivia (Livy), 15, 16, 119, 120, 149–51, 155
Clemens, Olivia Susan (Susy), 4, 119–22, 128, 131; at Bryn Mawr, 12–16, 119; death of, 121–22, 128, 131; and "Hellfire Hotchkiss," 131; meets Oscar Wilde, 18, 19; meets Vernon Lee, 18–19; as model for *Joan of Arc*, 20, 91–92, 93, 119–20; "Papa," 11–12, 15*n19*; relationship with Louise

Brownell, 4, 11–20, 119, 120*n29*, 143

Clemens, Samuel. *See* Twain, Mark

Clothing, 1, 2, 32, 38–39, 41, 43–44, 46–48, 54, 60, 64, 71–76, 86–87, 90–91, 101–3, 104–9, 113–15, 123, 125. *See also* Cross-dressing; Gender

Connecticut Yankee in King Arthur's Court, A, 7, 107, 118

Cooley, John, 30–31*n3*, 124, 125, 128, 140, 142, 143, 145–46

County Fair, The, 5, 164

Cox, James, 34*n7*, 40, 87–88, 93–94

Craft, Ellen, 42*n18*, 69

Cross-dressing: and biological sex, 29, 32, 33, 42, 126, 137; as disguise, 53, 69, 78–84, 89, 125, 136–37, 157–66; drag, 23; female impersonators, 5, 35; and (female) paternity, 27, 28, 31, 125, 142, 143, 144, 150, 155, 162; as gender disruption, 3, 20–22, 25, 40, 48, 60–61, 89–90, 116–18; historical contexts of, 4, 20–22; male impersonators, 6; and (male) maternity, 28, 32–33; and minstrel theater, 4–7; and race, 4–7, 21–22, 26, 28, 42*n18*, 48, 59, 69, 77, 84, 89–90; theatrical, 4, 6*n4*, 41; as transgression, 1, 2, 4, 19, 25, 26, 40, 48, 87–88, 89–90, 94, 98, 100–102, 122, 124–27, 143; and transvestitism, 2, 19, 21–22, 26, 28, 31, 47, 65–66, 80, 83, 89–90, 94, 98, 100, 105, 113–18, 122, 124–27, 142–45, 148, 150, 151–54, 156–66. *See also* Gender; and individual works

Davidziak, Mark, 158*n30*, 160

Death, 28, 73–74, 121–22, 128; associated with cross-dressing, 24–25, 27, 31, 39–42, 47–48, 51–53, 83, 86, 90, 113–14, 123, 125, 126, 131, 148, 157–66; and rebirth, 40–41. *See also* Bakhtin, Mikhail

D'Emilio, John, and Estelle Freedman, 11*n12*

DeVoto, Bernard, 64–65

Dolgin, Ellen Ecker, 97*n11*

Domesticity, 1, 135, 149–56

Du Bois, W. E. B., 83

Duggan, Lisa, 7, 8*n8*, 9

Du Mond, F. V., 101–4

Ellis, Havelock, 7, 10–11

Ellis, James, 49

Eltinge, Julian, 6

Emerson, Everett, 90*n2*, 93–94, 120*n29*

Engle, Gary, 44

Essentialism. *See* Gender, essentialism

Faderman, Lillian, 14*n17*

Ferris, Leslie, 21, 41

Fiedler, Leslie, 40, 65, 67

Fishkin, Shelley Fisher, 5, 6, 57*n30*, 59*n1*, 84, 124, 157, 161, 164–65

Following the Equator, 3, 125

Fryer, Jonathan, 9*n11*

Garber, Marjorie, 2, 6*n4*, 20–22, 28, 46*n21*, 65–66, 74*n15*, 80, 83–84

Gender: authenticity, 1, 31, 34, 55; boundaries, 30, 39, 40, 55, 56–58, 85, 87, 125, 130–31, 139; categories of, 4, 20–21, 22–23, 27, 28–29, 41, 74*n15*, 83, 87, 89–90, 100, 126, 127, 140, 141, 153; essentialism, 1, 20, 32, 36, 39, 127, 132, 133, 135, 136–37, 141–42; and fixed norms, conventions, and roles, 1, 19, 20, 23–24, 33, 37–38, 41, 90, 93–94, 114, 122, 124, 126, 132–37; identity, 38–40, 54, 57, 78, 80, 83, 84, 125, 139, 143, 145; and marriage, 66, 127, 142, 143, 144, 149–56, 162, 165; and performativity, 20, 23, 35, 37, 39, 40, 77, 79, 85, 86–87, 125, 126, 137, 140–42, 145–48, 150, 153–54, 157–59, 165–66; and play, 1, 4, 7, 20, 22, 34, 41, 46, 60, 86,

125, 126, 140, 145, 146, 150, 154, 157, 165; and race, 2, 21–22, 28, 37–38, 44, 48, 56–58, 71–77, 79, 80; and sexual differentiation (biological sex; "misplaced sex"), 3, 30, 32, 33, 125, 126, 127, 134–35, 140, 141; and sexuality, 48*n23, 77n16;* social construction of, 4, 23–25, 36, 84, 141, 165; and transgression, 19–26, 53, 87–90, 101–2, 125–27, 130, 143. *See also* Cross-dressing
Gillis, Jim, 48–49
Gillman, Susan, 3, 21*n25,* 30, 72, 125–26, 127, 140, 143
Girardot, Etienne, 6
Gossip, 129, 137–42, 147–48
Graff, Gerald, 54*n28*
Greenblatt, Stephen, 6*n4*

Halberstam, Judith, 126*n4*
Halperin, David, 137
Harris, Susan K., 27, 33, 48*n23,* 64*n5,* 65, 107*n22*
"Hellfire Hotchkiss," 4, 21*n25,* 124, 126, 127, 131–42, 148; gender essentialism in, 133, 136–37; gossip in, 138, 139, 142; lesbianism in, 131, 132, 134, 141; and "misplaced sex," 135, 141; silence in, 138; and Susy Clemens, 131; tomboyism in, 131; twinning in, 134, 139, 141
Henrickson, Gary P., 54
Heterosexual misconduct, 145–48, 149, 155–56. *See also* Sexuality
Hill, Hamlin, 149, 150, 155
Hindel, Annie, 6, 7*n6*
Hitchcock, Lucius Wolcott, 128
Hoffman, Andrew, 16
Holley, Marietta, 6*n4*
Homoeroticism, 51–53
Homosexuality, 132, 137, 145, 148–49, 150, 156, 163; and silence, 138–39. *See also* Homoeroticism; Same-sex relationships
Homosociality, 22
Horowitz, Helen, 14–16
"Horse's Tale, A," 124, 127–31;

Cathy as tomboy, 130–31; clothing in, 130; language play in, 129; twinning in, 130–31
Howells, William Dean, 33, 92–93
"How Nancy Jackson Married Kate Wilson" (a.k.a. "The Feud Story and the Girl Who Was Ostensibly a Man"), 124, 127, 142–48, 157, 162; and "An Awful—Terrible Medieval Romance," 143; failed heterosexuality in, 145–46; female-to-male transvestitism, 142; gossip in, 147–48; laughter in, 145; and Susy Clemens, 143
"How to Tell a Story," 110
Humor, 24, 34, 59, 92, 112, 142, 150
Hutton, Laurence, 92

Is He Dead? 124, 127, 156–66; clothing in, 159; cross-dressing and death in, 157; and gender performativity, 159–66; homosexuality, 157, 161; and male cross-dressing in theater, 164–65; male-to-female cross-dressing, 157; transvestitism, 164

Jacobs, Harriet, 42*n18*
Jehlen, Myra, 39, 76–77, 85–86*n22*
Joan of Arc, 2, 3, 19–20, 26, 60–61, 87–88, 157; as historical figure, 90–91, 94–101. *See also Personal Recollections of Joan of Arc*

Kaplan, Justin, 93–94, 120*n30*
Kemble, E. M., 35, 38, 55
Knoper, Randall, 100
Krafft-Ebing, Richard von, 10, 134
Krauth, Leland, 71

Language, 31, 57, 129; and black vernacular, 45, 72; gender and pronoun use, 27, 28, 33, 74*n15,* 154, 165; and silence, 138–39
Laughter, 25, 111–12, 142–43, 144, 165
Lee, Vernon, 18–19

Lenepveu, J. E., 104
Leon, Francis, 5. *See also* Minstrelsy and minstrel theater
Lesbianism, 127, 131, 132, 134, 138–39, 141, 142, 143, 145, 148. *See also* Same-sex relationships
Liminality, 87, 89, 99–102
Lott, Eric, 5$n3$, 58, 76–77, 84$n20$, 86
Lynn, Kenneth, 64–65, 67–68, 70–71

Margolis, Nadia, 97$n11$
Masquerade, 37, 42, 54, 57, 77, 79, 150, 153–54, 157, 166. *See also* Cross-dressing, as disguise
Michelet, Jules, 95, 115–16
Millet, Jean François, 157–66. *See also Is He Dead?*
Minstrelsy and minstrel theater, 4–7, 44–47, 58, 75, 82; and Shakespeare, 45–46
Mitchell, Alice, and Freda Ward, 7–9, 10
Moers, Ellen, 70$n11$
Morris, Linda A., 6$n4$, 165$n34$
Morrison, Toni, 53, 66$n6$

Neidler, Charles, 15$n19$
Newlyn, Andrea, 86
Newman, Judie, 70$n11$

Odell, George C., 5
"1002nd Arabian Night," 26, 27–28, 31–33, 74$n15$; gender essentialism in, 32; language play in, 33; male maternity, 32–33; twinning in, 32

Paine, Albert Bigelow, 94, 117, 120$n30$, 142, 148
Personal Recollections of Joan of Arc, 2, 3, 20, 26, 59–64, 87–88, 89–123, 124, 131, 164; characterization of Joan, 89, 93–94, 106–8; clothing in, 90, 101–3, 104–9, 113–15; compared to Roxana, 89; composition of, 92; criticism of, 91, 92–94, 103$n17$; cross-dressing and death in, 90, 113–14, 117–18, 121–22; De Conte as narrator of, 91, 106–12; historical contexts of, 90–91, 94–101, 105–6, 113, 122; and iconicity, 92, 98, 101, 103; illustrations in, 101–4, 114–15; Joan's "male attire"/transvestitism, 90–91, 96, 98, 100, 101–7, 113–17; King Charles's dress, 107–8; laughter in, 111–12; and the Paladin, 108–10; patriotism and, 118; piety and sexual purity in, 93, 101, 114–16; and Susy Clemens, 91–92, 119–22; and the women's suffrage movement, 98, 101
Pettit, Arthur, 65
Phelan, James, 54$n28$
Porter, Carolyn, 65, 79$n17$
Powers, Ron, 12$n14$
Prince and the Pauper, The, 3–4, 28, 36$n9$, 71–72, 118
Pudd'nhead Wilson, 2, 3, 4, 26, 28, 59–88, 89–90, 91, 124, 126, 132, 137; black vernacular in, 72, 85; characterization of Roxana, 64–65, 66, 67–68, 69–71; clothing in, 71–76; and Harriet Beecher Stowe, 69–71; "Motive," 62–64; sexuality in, 61, 65, 66–68; slavery in, 59, 65–66, 68–69, 84–85, 86; relationship between Tom and Chambers, 75–76; Roxana compared with Joan of Arc, 59–61, 87–88; Roxana's cross-dressing, 80–82, 84; Tom's clothing, manners, and cross-dressing, 76–80, 82–83; veiling in, 83–84

Quicherat, Jules, 97
Quirk, Tom, 29, 30

Race, 22, 26, 28, 49–51, 53, 54, 55, 56–58, 130–31, 151; boundaries and categories of, 69, 71–72, 74$n15$, 75, 83, 84–85, 86–87, 89–90; clothing as a marker of,

71–77; and identity, 47, 73, 75, 80, 83, 84, 85, 86, 139; and passing, 68, 76–77, 83, 86; and racial mixing, 4, 26, 61, 62*n4*, 64, 65, 66–68, 70, 72–73; and racial stereotypes, 65; and representation, 38. *See also* Cross-dressing, and race; gender, and race; Minstrelsy and minstrel theater

Same-sex relationships, 2, 7–11, 12–14, 22, 30, 119–21, 122, 123, 125, 132, 142–48, 157. *See also* Homoeroticism; Homosexuality; Lesbianism; Sexuality
Sattelmeyer, Robert, 142, 143, 148
Schiller, Friedrich, 97
Sedgwick, Eve, 138
Senelick, Laurence, 7*n6*
Sepet, Marius, 91
Sexology, 7, 9, 10–11, 134
Sexual innuendo, 1, 48–53
Sexuality, 4, 6, 10, 22, 23, 48–53, 61, 65, 66–67, 77*n16*, 87–88, 108, 116, 119, 125, 127, 134, 137, 141, 143, 145–48, 150; and the "New Sexuality," 7–11. *See also* Gender; Homoeroticism; Homosexuality; Lesbianism; Same-sex relationships
Shaw, George Bernard, 93
Skandera-Trombley, Laura, 37, 38, 42*n18*, 98*n12*, 140, 143
Slavery, 46–48, 57–58, 59–60, 65, 73–74, 84–85, 134, 139; and slave narratives, 69, 81–82
"Smash" (infatuation), 12–14, 132
Smith, Henry Nash, 39, 64–65
Smith-Rosenberg, Carroll, 7–8, 9, 14*n16*, 134
Somerville, Siobhan, 7*n7*, 85*n22*
Southey, Robert, 97
Stone, Albert, 97*n11*
Stoneley, Peter, 11, 12*n14*, 93–94, 128*n6*
Stowe, Harriet Beecher, 69–71
Sundquist, Eric, 84

Thomas, Brandon *(Charley's Aunt)*, 6
Thomas, M. Carey, Mamie Gwinn, and Mary Garrett, 14
Those Extraordinary Twins, 28, 60, 61, 62*n3*, 134, 139
Toll, Robert, 5*n3*
Tomboyism, 2, 124–25, 127, 129, 130–31, 134
Tuckey, Janet, 95, 104–5*n19*, 114–15
Transgression, 19–20. *See also* Cross-dressing, as transgression; Gender, as transgression
Transgressive figures, 3, 19–20
Transvestitism. *See* Cross-dressing, and transvestitism
"Transvestite tales" (as term), 124–27, 148, 156–57
Trilling, Lionel, 54
Turner, Patricia, 38*n11*, 73*n14*
Turner, Victor, 87
Twain, Mark: and Clara Clemens, 119, 120, 128; in Europe, 15–16, 60, 119, 120*n29*; and family life, 4, 12, 13 *illus.,* 90, 97*n11*, 119, 136*n12*, 137*n13*, 149–51; formal and compositional concerns, 30, 38, 48–49, 50–51, 52–54, 60, 61–64, 91–92, 109–10, 126; and gender transgression, 20–26, 135; and Harriet Beecher Stowe, 69–71; and Livy Clemens, 15, 119, 120, 149–51, 155; and Susy Clemens, 4, 13 *illus.,* 15–16, 19–20, 91–92, 93, 119–22, 128; travels of, 3, 119. *See also* individual works
Twins, 127, 130–31, 134, 139, 141, 157–66

Vaudeville, 4, 5–6, 164
Victorian society, 1, 4, 7, 10, 12–14, 19
Vim, 5

Walker, Nancy, 57*n30*
"Wapping Alice," 124, 127, 148–56; forced marriage in, 152–53; gender performativity in, 153–54;

homosexuality in, 148–49, 156; language in, 154; laughter in, 156; male-to-female transvestitism, 148, 150, 156
Warner, Marina, 97*n11*
Weeks, Jeffrey, 10–11
Whitcher, Frances M., 6*n4*

Widow and the Elder, The, 5
Wiggins, Robert, 68
Wilde, Oscar, 7, 9–11, 18, 19, 132*n10*
Winsor, Elizabeth, 16

Zwarg, Christina, 100

About the Author

Linda A. Morris is Professor Emeritus of English at the University of California–Davis and lives in Berkeley. She is the author of *Women's Humor in the Age of Gentility: The Life and Works of Frances Miriam Whitcher* and, most recently, editor of *American Women Humorists: Critical Essays.*

Photo by Janie Guhin